Critical Essays *in*

SPORT MANAGEMENT

EXPLORING AND ACHIEVING A PARADIGM SHIFT

EDITED BY

Andy Gillentine
UNIVERSITY OF SOUTH CAROLINA

Robert E. Baker
GEORGE MASON UNIVERSITY

Jacquelyn Cuneen
BOWLING GREEN STATE UNIVERSITY

lcomb Hathaway, Publishers
Scottsdale, Arizona

Library of Congress Cataloging-in-Publication Data

Critical essays in sport management : exploring and achieving a paradigm
shift / edited by Andy Gillentine, Robert E. Baker, Jacquelyn Cuneen.
    p. cm.
  ISBN 978-1-934432-26-6 (print edition) — ISBN 978-1-934432-27-3 (ebook
edition) 1. Sports--Management. 2. Sports administration. I. Gillentine,
Andy. II. Baker, Robert E. III. Cuneen, Jacquelyn.
  GV713.C75 2012
  796.068—dc23
                                                            2011042873

Dedication

This collection of essays is dedicated to those who initiated the movement to formalize the study of sport management, to those who currently work diligently at making sport management a valuable member of the academy, and to those future leaders who will take the field of sport management to new levels of inquiry and accomplishment.

Consulting Editor: Packianathan Chelladurai

Holcomb Hathaway, Publishers, Inc.
8700 E. Via de Ventura Blvd., Suite 265
Scottsdale, Arizona 85258
480-991-7881
www.hh-pub.com

10 9 8 7 6 5 4 3 2 1

ISBN PRINT: 978-1-934432-26-6
ISBN EBOOK: 978-1-934432-27-3

Printed in the United States of America.

contents

foreword

Packianathan Chelladurai

THE OHIO STATE UNIVERSITY

Kuhn's (1970) conception of a paradigm as the assumptions, theories, and frameworks on which research in science and other fields of inquiry is based is significant for this text. In *The Structure of Scientific Revolutions,* Kuhn contends that progress in science results not from a continuous accumulation of knowledge but from revolutions that produce a paradigm shift. When such shifts occur in a discipline, they provide a new direction for research in that discipline in the form of new questions to ask and new methods to employ in answering those questions and interpreting the results. As a young discipline, sport management has relied on the paradigms in mainstream management and in established sport disciplines such as sport sociology, sport psychology, and sport history. Any discipline, established or not, has to come to grips with this question: does the existing paradigm(s) fully and unambiguously explain to the discipline the observed phenomena of interest in a study? If not, does the existing paradigm constrain scholars from pursuing different models and approaches to the study?

I applaud Andy Gillentine, Robert E. Baker, and Jacquelyn Cuneen, the editors of this book, for alerting scholars, practitioners, and students in the field regarding the need to evaluate the existing paradigm(s) that shapes our thinking in the research, teaching, and practice of sport and sport management. It is timely that both scholars and practitioners take a second look at the traditional perspectives of sport that have guided us in our operations and examine the feasibility and utility of using different lenses (perspectives) to view the issues we face as well as the ways in which we have been managing them.

Following Gillentine's call for new thinking in how we research, teach, and practice in the field (see Essay 1), the other contributors advance glimpses of paradigm change. The issues tackled by these authors are critical and varied, and each one of them offers new perspectives on how to solve the challenges they explore. I am pleased to be associated with this excellent work by these renowned authors.

As noted, a *paradigm* refers to what is being observed, the basic assumptions about the observed phenomenon, the kinds of questions to be asked about it, what methodology(ies) is used to answer those questions, and how the results are interpreted. From this perspective and in the spirit of this text, let me begin this book with the question of "what" is observed, and our assumptions and the practices that result.

MANIFESTATIONS OF SPORT

While the broad and all-inclusive definitions and descriptions of the sport industry and/or sport management do indicate the breadth of the field, they also mask sharp distinctions among the segments of the sport industry as they are practiced. At one level, we treat the term *sport industry* as referring to a single unified entity. At another level, we think of the industry as composed of professional sports, intercollegiate sport, youth sport, recreational sport, mass sport, elite sport, and so on. While these classifications are popular, they are not based on clear-cut criteria. In the absence of such criteria, I contend that clear managerial guidelines cannot be developed. For example, youth sport refers to sports participation by the youth (i.e., persons younger than a given age). But we have youth participating in sport for the fun of it, and we also have youth who participate in sport with a view to excel in that activity. The differences in the purposes of the enterprises indicate that the structural and procedural elements of the two enterprises should be differentiated for effective management of them.

RETHINKING THE SEGMENTS OF THE SPORT INDUSTRY

Given the differences in the manifestations of sport, I suggest that the sport industry is composed of three segments: egalitarian sport, elite sport, and entertainment sport, as shown in Exhibit I.1 (Chelladurai, in press; Chelladurai, 2010).

Egalitarian sport. I chose the label *egalitarian* as it means a free, classless, equal, open, and unrestricted domain of activity. Originally, sport referred to a pleasurable activity that was a diversion from daily grinding routine (Keating, 1964). In egalitarian sport, any group of people of any age and any background can come together to engage in some physical activity to enjoy the kinesthetic sensations of the activity. In general, there will not be much planning and preparation for such an activity. While the contestant may strive hard to win the contest, in the end, it does not matter who wins because the ultimate aim in this form of sport is the enjoyment of the activity by both parties. This model of sport is duly followed and enjoyed by the numerous pick-up games and intramural teams at our universities and in some manifestations of youth sport.

Elite sport. The purpose of elite sport is the pursuit of excellence in a sporting activity. Excellence means being superior in performance to others in comparable

EXHIBIT I.1

Rethinking the segments of sport.

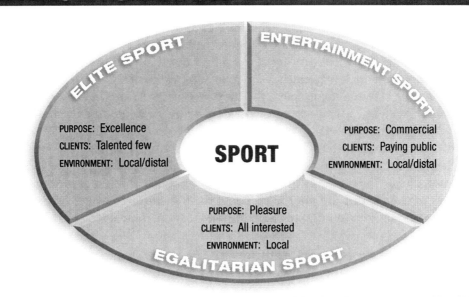

ELITE SPORT

PURPOSE: Excellence
CLIENTS: Talented few
ENVIRONMENT: Local/distal

ENTERTAINMENT SPORT

PURPOSE: Commercial
CLIENTS: Paying public
ENVIRONMENT: Local/distal

SPORT

PURPOSE: Pleasure
CLIENTS: All interested
ENVIRONMENT: Local

EGALITARIAN SPORT

groups (e.g., high school track and field, women's basketball, under-20 soccer), and excellence is established through victories against others who also vie for excellence. Thus, winning is important in elite sports. It is also characterized by dedication, planned and prolonged practice, and great expense in terms of money and personal sacrifices. For example, Ericsson, Krampe, and Tesch-Römer (1993) suggest that it requires 10,000 hours of deliberate practice to excel in an activity. We must note that the term *athletics* refers to pursuit of excellence (Keating, 1964) and is derived from the words *athlos* (i.e., a contest), *athlon* (i.e., a prize), and *athlein* (i.e., to contend for a prize).

Entertainment sport. Entertainment sport refers to the segment wherein excellence in sport is purveyed as entertainment in the form of organized competitions by a sport governing body (e.g., FIFA World Cup) or a league (e.g., Major League Soccer). While sport governing bodies typically engage in identifying the talent and developing the talented individuals into world class athletes, professional sport leagues most often are engaged in purchasing excellence produced elsewhere by others and exhibiting such excellences as entertainment. While the professional leagues with multiple franchises in each is the dominant model in entertainment sport, we also have individual athletes competing on their own in competitions organized by specific organizations. The more notable examples are PGA golf tournaments and tennis tournaments such as the U.S. Open and Wimbledon Championships.

Clients of sport segments. The differences in purposes of the three segments help us define the differences in the clients of these segments. They are the general public in egalitarian sport, meaning that anybody can participate in it without reference to their abilities. In contrast, the clients of elite sport are the few talented and dedicated individuals in elite sport. It follows then that egalitarian sport is inclusive in nature whereas elite sport is exclusionary because those who do not have the ability are excluded from the process. Conventionally, we think of a try-out as the process of selecting a team, but in essence, it is a process of eliminating the less talented.

As for entertainment sport, the most important clients are the fans of the sport, the clubs, and athletes in individual sports (e.g., golf and tennis). Commercial enterprises outside of sport may also become interested in and involved with entertainment sport because the fan base of a sport represents a market for their products that can be easily reached through sponsorship of the sport, the team, and/or the tournament. We must also recognize that the professional athletes in team sports are not the clients of the franchise. They are the employees (i.e., the human resources) of the professional sport franchises.

Environments of sport segments. The three segments are also distinguished on the basis of the environment they interact with and the opportunities and threats therein. For egalitarian sport, the environment is localized, consisting of the community, local government(s), social clubs, the educational institutions, and local media if any. While elite sports is still dependent on the local environment to support its existence, it also relies on more distal environmental elements such as the regional and national governments; regional, national, and international sport governing bodies; and other competing units in the pursuit of excellence. A unit in entertainment sport (i.e., a professional sport franchise) is dependent on both the local and distal environments. For the most part, the paying public hails from the local community. That is, the immediate vicinity constitutes the market. The local governments sanction and to some extent sustain the professional franchise. However, its environment extends to national and international sponsors, media, and other agencies that promote the franchise. Further, the other franchises in the league and the league that controls the local franchise are also significant elements in its environment.

RETHINKING THE RELATIVE EMPHASES ON SPORT SEGMENTS IN OUR RESEARCH

Once we have begun to reconceptualize the sport industry segments as egalitarian, elite, and entertainment sport, we can use this way of thinking as a new paradigm to guide our research. In considering the research carried out in sport management, it is apparent that much of the research relates to entertainment sport. And that focus has been legitimate because that segment of sport captures the imagination of society, the media, and would-be sponsors. We are also fascinated with individual athletes and their exploits, and the remuneration they receive.

I would suggest, however, that we consider placing greater emphases on egalitarian sport than has been the practice so far. First, as entertainment sport constitutes only about 40 percent of the entire sport industry (Milano & Chelladurai, 2011), both elite and egalitarian sport merit more attention from scholars and practitioners. While the economic impact is one factor, there is an even more compelling reason why we should focus on egalitarian sport to a greater degree than at present: It is widely known and accepted that participation in physical activity reduces the health risks of the population at large and thereby decreases health care costs. We in sport management should join the government's efforts to promote physical activity participation among the masses. Our contributions would be in designing appropriate sport programs for all age groups, making sure that such programs emphasize and facilitate the *pleasure* of participation, and managing those programs efficiently and effectively. We can also contribute by bringing the principles of social marketing to bear upon the promotion of sport participation and an active lifestyle. From this perspective, our greater engagement with egalitarian sport is our social responsibility. I invite you to consider this and the other perspectives offered in this book's essays for meeting the challenges we face in the sport management field.

REFERENCES

Chelladurai, P. (2010). Human Resource Management in the Sport Industry. Opening Keynote Address at the 6th Congress of the Asian Association for Sport Management. Kuala Lumpur, Malaysia. October 2010.

Chelladurai, P. (in press). Leadership and manifestations of sport. In S. Murphy (Ed.). *The Handbook of Sport and Performance Psychology.* New York: Oxford University Press.

Ericsson, K. A., Krampe, R. T., & Tesch-Römer, C. (1993). The role of deliberate practice in the acquisition of expert performance. *Psychological Review, 103,* 363–406.

Kuhn, T. S. (1970). *The Structure of Scientific Revolutions.* Chicago: University of Chicago Press.

Milano, M., & Chelladurai, P. (2011). Gross domestic sport product: The size of the sport industry in the United States. *Journal of Sport Management, 25*(1), 24–35.

preface

The historical academic model on which sport management programs were founded developed as a result of programs borrowing ideas and concepts from or collaborating with a variety of related disciplines. While this method of development is beneficial to new academic programs, it presents problems as the discipline matures. From the discipline's earliest inception, the academic preparation model for the sport industry professional has transformed continually, along with the proliferation of programs. The need for essential discipline-specific expertise has grown as the sport industry itself has evolved in the marketplace.

As a "new" academic field of study becomes sufficiently distinct, the discipline must develop specific models that become the rule rather than the exception. Boyer (1990) encouraged scholars to synthesize and to look for new relationships between parts and the whole, to relate the past and future to the present, and to discern patterns of meaning not readily seen through traditional and disciplinary foci. Programmatic decisions should be based on industry as well as academic needs, and information should be widely and clearly shared through multiple forums and platforms (e.g., NASSM, SMA, SRLA, EASM, NASSS), mediums (e.g., Internet, newsletters), and journals (e.g., *JSM, SMEJ, SMQ, JLAS, ESMQ, SSJ*). Yet all too often, the hardiest and most challenging issues facing our discipline go unanswered. These emotionally charged topics frequently are relegated to informal discussions and seldom receive the formal vetting that they demand. Thus, sport management today stands at an academic crossroads, faced with numerous questions that have emerged about our discipline.

This anthology offers a collection of essays written by experienced, respected sport management educators and scholars to shed light on a plethora of challenges and issues facing sport management academic programs. Our goal is to begin a professional and scholarly dialogue to identify the best, or at least most logical, paths for our future. These essays address specific interrelated issues critical to sport management and its fit within the academy. Contributors were invited to participate based on their recognized areas of expertise and were asked to address specific topics using their own unique voices and writing styles. They also had the option of inviting others to join them in composing their essays. Here is a brief summary of the essays:

- Andy Gillentine begins by outlining views related to sport management's need to consider paradigm shift.

- Janet Fink and Carol Barr outline the prevailing issues regarding the academic home of sport management and its logical fit within appropriate units.

- Jay Gladden and Jo Williams explain the principles and cornerstones of sport management accreditation and examine the argument for the importance of accreditation for sport management programs.

- Daniel Mahony, Anita Moorman, Timothy DeSchriver, and Marion Hambrick tackle the controversial topic of identifying criteria that might be useful in sport management program rankings.

- Dianna Gray and Linda Sharp examine the issue of sport management as a unique discipline as well as best practices in teaching and learning.

- David Stotlar and Lori Braa confront the issues regarding the applied versus theoretical emphasis in sport management's preparation programs and the relationship of those programs to the sport industry.

- John Miller summarizes the many controversial and divisive issues surrounding the "publish or perish" viewpoint associated with many institutions' tenure, promotion, and merit policies.

- Robert Baker analyzes concerns regarding external funding and the expenses and outcomes, both monetarily and programmatic, accompanying grants and contracts.

- William Sutton describes his personal journey as an academician collaborating with the sport industry and as an industry professional collaborating with the sport management academy.

- Joy DeSensi addresses the various cultural, historical, and social contexts that are crucial to applying ethical principles to the new challenges in sport management.

- Mary Hums and Meg Hancock deliberate the purposes of sport management as an academic discipline as it relates to the broader aims and greater purposes of a society in which sport holds a high status.

- Karen Danylchuk shares her expertise on the crucial emerging issue of sport management on the global stage, and speaks to the importance of internationalizing our academicians and students through curricula, research, and service.

- William Stier catalogs the key principles and elements of effective sport management practicum and internship experiences, and addresses the free labor dilemma often associated with students' field experiences.

- James Weese charts the status of sport management doctoral programs as they prepare our future faculty and scholars, and identifies several issues that impact best practices in doctoral education.

- Jacquelyn Cuneen and Heather Lawrence describe possible changes in academe that may result from the pending influx of millennial-era faculty.

It is the hope of the editors and publisher that this collection of essays will generate discussion among (a) the sport management professoriate; (b) those industry professionals who serve as adjunct faculty, participate on sport management program advisory boards, and/or otherwise harbor a continued interest in academic preparation; (c) doctoral students who intend to teach in sport management programs; and (d) others who explore and critique higher education in general. We and the outstanding authors who contributed to this exchange of ideas invite your comments. To contribute, visit the discussion forums at **www.hhpcommunities.com/sportmanagement**. See page xiv for more information.

Andy Gillentine
Robert E. Baker
Jacquelyn Cuneen

To Contribute to This Book's Discussion Forums

To contribute ideas and respond to the questions generated by this book's essays, visit the discussion forums on the HHP Sport Management Community site, www.hhpcommunities.com/sportmanagement. (In this book, the forum topics are underlined.) On the site, you will find the forum topics organized by essay under the "Paradigm Shift" tab in the top menu. You may also access each topic using the PowerPoint presentation provided; see the download link on the "Paradigm Shift" tab.

Beyond this book's discussion forums, the Sport Management Community site highlights the connections among the various subject areas in the sport management curriculum and is a convenient resource for sport management educators and scholars. On the site, participants can interact and share sport management information and news and read author commentaries across disciplines.

About the Ebook

This book is available as an ebook. The ebook version can be purchased on our website, **www.hh-pub.com**. The electronic version of the book offers a colorful layout and matches the print book page for page. In addition, those reading the ebook will find the following interactive features:

- Active links to forum questions being discussed, allowing readers to learn more about the topics and see what others have to say.
- Direct links to the author introduction videos.
- Instant access to cross-reference links between essays.
- Digital note-taking and unlimited bookmarking.

To Access Author Introduction Videos

Visit www.hhpcommunities.com/sportmanagement and click on the "Paradigm Shift" tab. Links to the author videos appear with the essay segments.

Moving Mountains

ENCOURAGING A PARADIGM SHIFT IN SPORT MANAGEMENT

"Sometimes we are lucky enough to know that our lives have been changed, to discard the old, embrace the new, and run headlong down an immutable course."

JACQUES COUSTEAU

The author introduces the book and his essay
(see page xiv for video URLs)

Andy Gillentine UNIVERSITY OF SOUTH CAROLINA

Andy Gillentine, Ph.D., currently serves as Professor and Chair of the Sport and Entertainment Department at the University of South Carolina. Prior to this appointment, he held positions as the Associate Dean, Associate Professor, and Director of the Sport Administration Programs at the University of Miami, and as Graduate Program Director at Mississippi State University. In April of 2009, he received the Sport Management Outstanding Achievement Award from the National Association for Sport and Physical Education (NASPE). Additionally, he served as a founding Commissioner of the Council of Sport Management Accreditation (COSMA). Prior to this appointment, Gillentine served as Chair of a joint task force of NASPE/NASSM charged with formalizing the curricular standards required for accreditation. In 2007, he was appointed to serve as a board member of the Miami Dade Sports Commission, which is charged with developing and expanding the presence of the sport industry in Miami Dade County and South Florida. Previously, he served on the Sport Management Program Review Council Executive Board and as Chair of the National Sport Management Council. Gillentine has conducted research projects for numerous sport organizations that have resulted in over 50 publications and over 100 national and international presentations. In 2007, he was appointed as a Research

Fellow of the Research Consortium of American Alliance of Health, Physical Education, Recreation, and Dance. Gillentine earned his bachelor's degree in History from Oklahoma State University, his master's degree in Educational Administration from Northeastern Oklahoma State University, and his Ph.D. from the University of Southern Mississippi.

Introduction

Twenty years ago, Trevor Slack forewarned sport management academicians that "like scholars in any emerging academic discipline, those of us in sport management face a number of challenges as we look toward the future" (Slack, 1991, p. 95). Slack's words should still serve as a charge for professionals today as the academic study of sport management must continue to evolve and respond to the ever changing and expanding sport industry as well as to the increasing demands in higher education. It is important that sport management scholars acknowledge that new challenges will consistently emerge in our profession, and it is imperative that we position our academic profession to accept those challenges and move the profession, as well as the sport industry, forward. Yet, unless there is "a state of acknowledged crisis" (Birnbaum, 1988, p. 205), academia has been slow to respond to change. According to Lueddke (1999), "Generally speaking, fundamental changes in teaching and learning are rare in higher education. Although it is not uncommon to find a few early adopters or enthusiasts (some estimate that there are about 10–15% in each department) who initiate most cycles of innovation, their 'track record' for embedding serious educational reforms remains rather weak" (p. 240).

In sport management, scholars need to acknowledge that new challenges in balancing the needs of higher education and the sport and entertainment industry will consistently emerge in our profession. While sport organizations ceased collecting gate receipts in cigar boxes decades ago, the "cigar box mentality" still seems to permeate both the industry and the academy. Cigar box mentality refers to the belief that "we have always done it this way and therefore we should continue to do so." This mentality also implies a level of simplicity that is at the same time reassuring and comforting to some within the discipline. Reasons for the continued predominance of the cigar box mentality are at best naiveté and at worse complacency on behalf of sport industry and academy. At a minimum, the impact of this philosophical choice is a slow adaptation to change and the development of an environment that impedes adjustment to new and perhaps innovative methodologies. Today's sport management academicians must closely examine all aspects of business and academic methodologies to ensure that they are being conducted in the most effective and efficient manner. Moreover, we must position our academic profession to accept those challenges to move the profession as well as the sport industry forward. As Chelladurai (1992) stated, "our game is management, but we need to demonstrate that we play it better than others" (p. 217).

To "play it better than others," today's sport management academicians must closely examine all aspects of professional sport and the entertainment industry and academic methodologies to ensure that they are operating within an effective and efficient paradigm. *Paradigm* is a term originally derived from the Greek word *paradeigma* and refers to a model, perception, assumption, or a frame of reference. It is also often considered "as the complete view of reality or way of seeing, as relating to the social organization of science in terms of different schools of thought, and as relating to the specific use of instruments in the process of scientific puzzle solving" (Arndt, 1985, p. 15). As the number of supporters of a specific paradigm grows, the transformation from advocacy group to discipline or profession occurs (Pajares, 2003). All industries and fields of academic study have a paradigm from which they operate. It allows for consistency within all functions of the profession or discipline and should clearly identify the relationship between each component within the paradigm. However, as with any entity, problems and issues will arise for which the existing paradigm can no longer provide optimal or even adequate answers. When methods are identified as being ineffective, inefficient, or are simply archaic, the sport management scholar is obliged to be an agent of change and to seek out a better paradigm from which to operate (Anderson, 1983). This metamorphosis, which is the fundamental building block of developing an effective and efficient model, is referred to as *paradigm shift.*

DEFINING AND UNDERSTANDING PARADIGM SHIFT

The term *paradigm shift* was introduced by Thomas Kuhn (1962) in his groundbreaking work, *The Structure of Scientific Revolutions.* Kuhn proposed that nearly every significant breakthrough is first a break with traditional methodologies, old ways of thinking, old paradigms (Covey, 1989). These contentions should prompt sport management educators seeking breakthroughs to re-examine the current position of sport management education to search for the best model for operation. Further support for examination of existing paradigms is evident in Patton's description of the potential philosophical shortcomings of failing to do so, "Paradigms are deeply embedded in the socialization of adherents and practitioners: paradigms tell them what is important, legitimate, and reasonable. Paradigms are normative, telling the practitioner what to do without the necessity of long existential or epistemological considerations" (1990, p. 37). Promoting a paradigm shift in sport academia will involve the modification of existing policies, practices, procedures, and strategies to which faculty and administrators have become accustomed. Each of these modifications will require a successful paradigm shift to be well planned and implemented. Sport management educators must not be surprised if the announcement of organizational change is initially met with little support and tremendous resistance.

Change is not always an easy process, but it is an inevitable part of the evolution of any academic program. If a profession fails to adapt and grow, it chooses a path of extinction. Resistance to a paradigm shift occurs for a variety of reasons. For example, individuals affiliated with sport management often are resistant to change because of (1) job insecurity; (2) fear of lost income; (3) uncertainty; (4) loss of status and/or power; and (5) personal inconvenience. While many of these reasons should not be a source of fear for sport management educators or practitioners, they do nonetheless serve as potential barriers to change. Although these barriers cannot be totally eliminated, steps can be taken to minimize them.

In order to minimize resistance to an organizational paradigm shift, an effective strategy should incorporate: (1) empathy; (2) open channels of communication; (3) open participation; (4) trust; (5) an explanation of the implementation schedule for proposed changes; and (6) an emphasis on benefits. Each of these steps can help ensure that the paradigm shift will proceed with minimal resistance. Remember that most people are resistant to change if it means an upset in the status quo. But change does impact the status quo, so proponents of a paradigm shift in sport management should adhere to the Boy Scouts motto "Be Prepared." Leaders of change must clearly identify the stakeholders involved and what their roles will be both during and after the change process. This will require involving them in the planning process and allowing their input. If recommended changes are simply delivered and others ordered to comply, you risk maximum resistance and potential failure. Those trying to build consensus for a paradigm shift must be creative and innovative in their approaches to developing solutions and recommendations.

Despite the documented growth of sport management academia and the sport industry, the overall paradigm has been slow to shift. The challenge to develop innovative responses to the issues that have evolved in the discipline would seem apparent. However, sport management programs frequently fall back on "tried and true" solutions from other disciplines that may not be an exact fit for sport management. <u>Should our ever-expanding and successful discipline continue to mimic and model other disciplines and perpetuate their successful strategies—as well as their shortcomings—or do we determine our own path and thus our own contemporary, specific model for academic success? If we continue to model ourselves on other programs, will we eventually become that which we mimic? Will our identity as a distinct discipline be at risk?</u> As Chelladurai (1992) indicated:

> There is the danger that the other fields may usurp that knowledge and claim it as their own. It is happening with the other disciplinary areas such as exercise physiology, sport psychology, and sport sociology. For example, several of the courses developed in these fields are now being taught in their respective mother disciplines. (p. 216)

Sport, by itself, holds a high status as a cultural phenomenon in the United States as well as globally (see Essay 12). Coakley (2007) recognized the sports industry as one of the most influential in the United States, eclipsing real estate, health care, banking, and transportation. According to Higgs and McKinley (2009), sport in the United States parallels what is occurring in the rest of society. They contend that if extraterrestrials viewed a sports event for the first time, they might associate the sport with world happenings due to how it appears in the stadium or on the television. The perception may very well be that sport represents a microcosm of the American culture (Higgs & McKinley, 2009). As such, the popularity of sport, as a national and global phenomenon, may make the discipline of sport management so alluring that other academic disciplines may attempt to overtake the program and integrate it into their curriculum.

The rapid growth and expansion of the sport management academic discipline can most certainly be viewed as one of the many challenges that Slack warned sport management educators about 20 years ago. However, the future depends as much on what has already occurred as on what is being planned. To facilitate discussion examining the evolution of sport management academic programs, the following developmental eras are suggested.

ERAS OF SPORT MANAGEMENT

Meeting new challenges requires a change of paradigm. The challenges created by the growth of the sport management discipline may be best explored by categorizing the overall growth into five eras. Such categorization will provide scholars with reference points from which to examine causes of existing challenges as well as to identify possible opportunities to solve them and understand the need for a future paradigm shift.

The Era of Incubation (1957–1966)

This era reflects the period of time between the composition of a letter in 1957 from Walter O'Malley, of the Brooklyn Dodgers, to James Mason, a promising young educator, and the establishment of the first graduate program (Mason, Higgins, & Owen, 1981). In his letter O'Malley speculated on the need for individuals specifically educated to work in the sport industry. This initial query resulted in the formation of what is widely recognized as the first graduate program in sport management at Ohio University, nine years later in 1966 (Mason, Higgins, & Owen, 1981). There is some evidence that an initial independent attempt to establish a sport management–based program, referred to as the Baseball Administration School curriculum, occurred in 1949 at Florida Southern College (Issacs, 1964). While this information is noteworthy, it did not have the impact that the collaboration of O'Malley and Mason fostered.

During this era, Mason and other scholars refined the concepts of what should be included in a sport management academic education. The seeds planted in this period have grown. Evidence of such growth appears in the continual process of refining a potential sport management curriculum (Gillentine, Crow, & Harris, 2009). The nine-year period that it took for sport management to become an accepted academic discipline may reflect the reluctance of academia to react to requests to develop new programs or modify existing programs. The period also marks the beginning of cooperation between the sport industry and academia and clearly defines the roots of the discipline.

The Era of Maturation (1967–1987)

During this period additional institutions of higher education and athletic organizations recognized the potential for sport management academic programs. Programs expanded and academic leaders emerged within this timeframe. One pioneer, Guy Lewis, is recognized for his role in the development of sport management programs at the University of Massachusetts and the University of South Carolina (Masteralexis, Barr, & Hums, 2009; Roach, 2010). Lewis developed one of the first degree-granting sport administration programs in 1971 at the University of Massachusetts (Parkhouse & Pitts, 2005). After a number of years at the University of Massachusetts, he collaborated with other progressively minded sport management professionals to establish the Department of Sport & Entertainment Management (formerly the Department of Sports Administration) at the University of South Carolina (Roach, 2010). This program was significant in that it was an independent sport management department unaffiliated with an education, recreation, or physical education department or college (Baugus, 2008).

It was during this time that the initial meetings for the premier organization for sport management academics, the North American Society for Sport Management (NASSM) took place. Founded in 1985, the NASSM's purpose is to "promote, stimulate, and encourage study, research, scholarly writing, and professional development in the area of sport management—both theoretical and applied aspects" (NASSM, n.d.). This was the first scholarly organization dedicated to fulfilling the scientific and professional interests of individuals in academic sport management (NASSM, n.d.). The period also serves as an example of the struggle for self-identity and belonging within the academy (see Essay 5). Sport management programs were housed in a variety of colleges or schools (see Essay 2), which may not have been the most appropriate fit but were deemed as such by university preferences (NASPE–NASSM, 1993). The lack of coordination among the growing number of programs led to the early fragmentation between programs and sport management professionals (Gillentine, 1998).

The Era of Rapid Growth (1988–2000)

This era marks the period of the greatest and most rapid expansion of sport management programs. As a result of the growing need for well-trained and qualified personnel, sport management programs flourished, resulting in over 200 U.S. programs by 2000 (Parkhouse & Pitts, 2001). A little more than a decade later, we have 327 programs in the United States (College Programs, 2010), 9 in Canada, approximately 10 in Europe, and 14 in Australia and New Zealand. During this period institutions recognized the demand and popularity of the sport management discipline and quickly implemented programs. The expansion of programs was not only found in the United States but was also prevalent on campuses around the world. Three distinct areas of concern within the profession became apparent during this era: (1) lack of qualified instructors; (2) inadequate textbooks; and (3) non-standardized curriculum (Bridges & Roquemore, 1992).

The discipline responded to this rapid growth by forming the Sport Management Program Review Council (SMPRC) through a joint project between the National Association for Sport and Physical Education (NASPE) and NASSM (Gillentine, Crow, & Harris, 2009). The group helped ensure sport management program quality (see Essay 3).

The Era of Dualism (2001–2007)

This era witnessed both the good and bad consequences of the previous period of unbridled expansion. Sport management research became firmly established and legitimized during this era. The expansion of programs generated academic positions in many universities globally. They were filled with outstanding researchers who established a solid base of discipline-specific research upon which others could build. Academic journals were developed, giving rise to new lines of research in sport management. Additional outlets for this research arose from organized professional meetings and conferences worldwide. These forums promoted scholarly sport management research throughout the globe.

Ironically, this period is also representative of the negative impact of unmonitored growth. Continued expansion of sport organizations and event offerings at all levels taxed existing methodologies and operating procedures. The demand for well-educated employees with specific skill sets produced an explosion in the number of institutions offering specialized degrees in sport management, which they recognized as an impressive source of revenue. As such, some institutions formed sport management programs with little or no regard to the guidelines suggested by the academy or SMPRC. This disregard caused a negative side effect in that some sport management programs were viewed as nothing more than cash cows. They represented dollars generated through student credit hours instead of a viable academic discipline.

Institutions contributed to such a perception in several ways. One tactic some universities used was to offer large mega-classes with seemingly no concern for the quality of instruction. For example, many of these charlatan programs hired instructors who lacked discipline-specific education, training, and/or experience. A second tactic employed by some universities was the use of unqualified instructors to meet the increasing demands for sport management courses. Instructors from a variety of disciplines and backgrounds were thrust into sport management classrooms. Internship courses also reflected this nonchalant attitude toward instruction. Often students enrolled in these courses received no on-site supervision and/or evaluation from on-campus personnel or representatives due to university restrictions and the absence of funding for supervision. Moreover, instructors responsible for internships were expected to oversee large numbers of students without being paid for the task. As a result, the institution realized an increased profit margin generated by these popular courses. Also evident was the rise of private companies claiming to be able to teach students how to become everything from general managers of sport teams to athlete representatives (agents). These programs took advantage of uninformed students' desires to enter the sport industry through the promise of insider information and contacts.

The Era of Reflection, Assessment, and Refinement (2008–present)

This era describes the current period in which many sport management professionals from both academia and industry are evaluating the status of sport management academic preparation. Sport management has also entered the first stages of program assessment through the implementation of a formal program accreditation process (see Essay 3). In the previous era, sport management programs were viewed as ever-expanding academic programs; however they have recently been experiencing signs of contraction. Many institutions are re-evaluating their commitment to offering quality sport management programs because of the costs associated with them. As a result all of the parties concerned, including academia, the industry, and students, are becoming more aware of the necessary components of a quality sport management program.

Perhaps the sport management academic discipline is following in the footsteps of Mississippi blues legend Robert Johnson and is at its developmental crossroads. The crossroads Johnson faced was a literal one—the intersection of U.S. Highways 61 and 49, which run through the north Mississippi Delta—where Johnson allegedly sold his soul to the devil in exchange for becoming an innovative musical genius (King, 2004). The decision facing sport management will be similar to the choices that Johnson faced: (1) stay the same and thus become no better; (2) sell your soul for fame and fortune and ultimately pay the steepest of payments; or (3) boldly challenge the status quo and not be afraid to chart a new course of action.

Additional support for the consideration of change can be found in the formula E + R = O. In this formula, E = events, R = response, and O = outcome. Simply stated, this formula indicates that events happen with or without our input; R indicates what we do or don't do in reaction to E; O, the outcome, is going to occur whether we choose to respond or not. The question for sport management educators is, where do you have control? This leads us to the answer that the only way the sport management discipline can have any input in what happens is in how it responds to an event or issue. An emphasis, therefore, is placed upon the sport management academy to evaluate the need for change and decide how to react accordingly. Above all else, the discipline must respond, otherwise problems will best be summarized by a statement from the comic strip *Pogo,* "We have met the enemy, and it is us!" (Kelly, 1987).

PREPARING FOR A PARADIGM SHIFT

n order to determine an effective and efficient response to the issues presented in sport management education and bring in a new era of paradigm shift, the academy must first undergo an intense self-examination. Answering the question, "Who are we really?" will provide an excellent starting point for this exercise. The sport management discipline often finds itself divided in responding to this question. One segment of our constituency might respond, "We are researchers." Another may respond, "We are educators." Yet another might respond, "We are the professional development vehicle for the sport industry." Perhaps the most appropriate response might be, "We are all of the above." Each of these responses has its supporters and detractors.

To avoid conflict, sport management educators often segregate themselves based on their idea of what sport management really is. Parks remarked: "We freely acknowledge that we share commonalities with other areas within the academy, but we also insist that we have our own unique characteristics and contributions that set us apart from them" (1992, p. 221). This separation, however, may generate problems when gathering responses from each vantage point. By segregating itself and developing fragmented positions, the professorate actually impedes progress that could move the sport management profession forward. To move forward, I recommend several preparatory steps, including thinking outside the box, focusing on sport management for the greater good, establishing the right direction for change, and the inclusion of all in the process.

Thinking Outside the Box

"Different is not always better, but if you want to go different, better make sure it's better, not just different."

MIKE LEACH, FORMER TEXAS TECH FOOTBALL COACH

One overused phrase is to "think outside the box." This is an attempt to encourage decision-makers to take an innovative approach to finding solutions. The development of a new paradigm for sport management education will require all parties to develop and consider a variety of innovative strategies and ideas. Moreover, these decisions must be made as efficiently and quickly as possible. Having said that, if sport management educators are not cautious about how they undertake their quest for outside-the-box thinking, they could render themselves ineffective decision-makers and find themselves in a quagmire.

While thinking outside the box seems to be a healthy approach to identifying new and innovative solutions, it can add to the sometimes agonizing duty of problem solving. By continually searching for new and innovative answers to problems, sport management educators may cause decision-making delays and reduce their efficiency. Before venturing outside the box, sport management educators need to identify frequently occurring problems. A series of simple questions helps determine where to look for solutions:

- Has this happened before?
- How was it solved?
- How effective was the previous solution?
- Has this happened to other organizations?
- Was their solution more effective than ours?
- Would other organizations' solutions fit our situation?
- Will this problem continue to occur?

If the answers to these questions are yes, then this problem can be considered a reoccurring or resident problem. By looking outside the box too quickly, an obvious solution may be missed. Often these types of problems can best be solved with a programmed decision. Programmed decisions are the most effective and efficient way to deal with reoccurring problems. These are solutions that are often found inside the box and that will relieve the sport educator of having to develop a new solution to a familiar problem. It must also be noted that reoccurring problems may be evidence of an operational model that is no longer able to function optimally. It is important not to readily accept this as just part of doing business but to examine the cause of the problem and determine if it can be corrected. This may encourage outside-the-box thinking as a means of identifying a solution to the root of the reoccurring problem.

Outside-the-box thinking can be most effectively and efficiently utilized if sport management professionals are selective regarding when they seek to implement it. Outside-the-box thinking produces the best results when current ideas and solutions no longer offer the desired or optimal outcome and, thus, new and innovative methods are needed to sustain viability of the response(s), solution(s) and/or outcome(s). As mentioned above, outside-the-box thinking requires sufficient time for the exploratory and creative process to unfold. It is very much like solving a crossword puzzle. For any given problem, a number of possibilities and clues exist to lead managers to the best solutions.

In order to solve many of the challenges facing sport management education, it will be important for all involved to identify all possible solutions whether they are inside or outside of the current sport management box. In order for outside-the-box thinking to be effectively utilized, it is imperative that the individuals and/or the organization involved be receptive to new and different ways of conducting and evaluating solutions and operations. The effectiveness of outside-the-box thinking is also enhanced when ideas are well thought out and when evidence supports the potential effectiveness of the proposed change. The clarity with which a new idea or method is communicated to all stakeholders will also impact how quickly it is accepted overall.

Focusing on Sport Management for the Greater Good

The sport management academy must seek answers that can serve the greater good. Utilitarian philosopher John Stuart Mill encouraged decisions to be made in accordance to his Greatest Happiness Principle, which states that "actions are right in proportion as they tend to promote happiness, wrong as they tend to produce the reverse of happiness" (Keele, 2008). While it is not the intent of this essay to encourage a simplistic response to the issues faced by sport management education, we can gain insight to guide us in our paradigm shift by examining them from Mill's standpoint.

Mill maintained that any given action was right, depending on the level of happiness it brought to all of the people involved, and wrong, depending on the number of people it made unhappy. Mill claimed that one person's personal level of happiness could count no more than anyone else's. Thus, the best action is that which brings happiness to the largest number of individuals possible, making that action ethically justified. While there have been many philosophical arguments surrounding this approach, it can provide sport management educators with a starting point for deliberation. If we focus on what is best for sport management education as a whole, perhaps within this and other philosophical debates we will be able to find broad based solutions and mechanisms for bettering the profession (Downward, 2005).

Establishing the Right Direction for Change

In his book *The Principle of the Path,* Andy Stanley (2009) brought to light a simple yet important concept regarding determining the outcome of any undertaking if the initial direction is not thoroughly examined. Stanley stated that "direction—not intention—determines our destination" (p. 13). This is an important lesson to consider as we take actions to move our profession forward. Simply stated, if we are not following the appropriate path or direction, we will never get there, no matter how badly we may want to determine specific goals and objectives. If we follow the directions or paths of other professions, for example, we must carefully consider all of the consequences of following that direction. Stanley's dictum again points out the need for serious introspection, consideration, and discussion regarding what our goals and desired outcomes (destination) for sport management really are. The academy and the industry cannot allow the path to our destination to become littered with the desires of an influential few. Rather, the selected path should be determined by what is best for all parties involved. We cannot expect to follow the paths blazed by other professions and disciplines and expect the outcome to be any different. However, we can incorporate the positive attributes of other disciplines and professions, but only in such a manner that it allows us to determine our own path.

At times it seems as if we have taken too literally the concept of "management by wandering around" as a means for addressing issues facing sport management education and the sport industry. Too often discussions related to issues and problems have been relegated to the hallways and the water coolers and not tackled head-on. In these informal settings when topics or issues make individuals uncomfortable, they may simply wander off rather than engage in the discussion. By allowing discussions of important topics to be bantered about casually rather than through directed debate and/or philosophical inquiry, we only exacerbate the problem and leave ourselves vulnerable to the influence of a few, or at worst by forces from outside of the sport management profession. In order to determine the path sport management should follow, it is vital to involve all concerned individuals and groups in identifying the areas of concern and bringing them to the forefront of academic discussion.

Inclusion of All

The eclectic nature of sport management demands that discussions be as inclusive as possible. Members of academia, industry, and students should be solicited on how to best identify and prioritize these areas of concern. Such solicitation is key, because each group may respond differently. For example, academics may wish to explore how to improve appropriate research designs and methodologies. Those in the professional sport industry may wish to identify specific research needs and concerns that can be applied in the industry. Both groups may wish to begin a discourse regarding the funding of such research and ways to place value upon the researcher's undertaking as well as the potential return on investment (ROI) for the industry (see Essay 9). Sport management students may wish to open a dialogue regarding the make-up of the sport management curriculum and its impact on their employment qualifications and opportunities.

By employing an inclusive approach, these groups may reach a consensus about a number of similar issues that need to be addressed. Some of these issues may include the sport industry's growing dependence on student interns (paid and unpaid); identifying the best way to manage the internship experience (see Essay 13); and adapting to new technologies in the classroom and the workplace. Each of the essays in this collection identifies areas of concern and challenges for parties entering discussions regarding improvements that need to be made in each area.

THE TIME FOR A PARADIGM SHIFT IS *NOW!*

"The significant problems we face cannot be solved at the same level of thinking we were at when we created them."

ALBERT EINSTEIN

Wandersman (2010) stated that all organizations need to establish a formal means for continuous quality improvement (CQI) in order to reach desired outcomes. Before sport management can proceed much further, we must determine, as a discipline, our desired outcomes. We must then identify the best paths to follow in order to achieve these outcomes and how to monitor our progress and success.

To fully shift the paradigm of sport management will require making sure that it will be responsive to the changing environment in which we operate. Sport management education must reflect demands for greater accountability in a number of areas. It is important to evaluate our tracking systems to accurately inform interested parties about the graduate placement rate. This information would include an accurate description of the type of jobs industry partners are offering graduates as well as the long-term implications for our majors at all levels. In order to establish this level of accountability, all groups involved in sport management education, including academics, students, and sport and entertainment industry partners, need to record and report such information. Accountability involving all stakeholders will demonstrate a willingness to shoulder responsibility by making sport management education transparent.

The discipline of sport management education must establish an efficient and effective system of verifying not only what is happening to the graduates of our programs but also whether we are delivering the educational components desired by sport industry organizations. Our sport industry partners will then need to systematically provide feedback to academia regarding the content and development of appropriate courses that will enhance the workforce and make sport management graduates qualified for the workforce (see Essay 6). Additionally, we should examine what we are doing to encourage the best and the brightest students to enter the professional sport industry and eliminate barriers that may be driving them away. Issues such as unpaid internships, low-level entry pay, and lack of specific work or degree requirements for entry-level positions all represent issues that our field must address.

Open and honest communication among sport industry participants is the first step in gathering the information necessary to formulate a paradigm shift. If we continue to collect tuition dollars, then it is our responsibility to ensure that the material and methods being taught to students meet current workforce needs.

Sport industry organizations must share their concerns about their educational and research needs with sport management educators in order to address those needs. Developing such a collective mechanism will require high levels of cooperation and participation from all interested parties. A project of this magnitude may require the services of an independent sport management group, such as an accreditation group (see Essay 3).

The changing sport management paradigm will also impact the scope, focus, and methodologies of sport management research. It could be suggested that lines of research focus on specific professional sport industry needs, as identified through a collaborative forum, rather than on individual projects. This requires that researchers clearly define the need area(s) their research addresses. While some researchers already adhere to a similar model, perhaps this will offer a model for all participants in sport management education to consider. Such a research consortium could well provide future direction(s) for sport management education, research, and industry advancement. Examples of potential new research areas include (1) sustainability, (2) diversity, (3) innovation, and (4) philanthropy. Each of these can be broadly interpreted, allowing for as much inclusion as possible. Establishing these research needs will encourage innovative thought and research methodologies. Additionally, areas identified may also prove invaluable in directing student dissertations and research (see Essay 14). Sport management researchers can evaluate their lines of inquiry to determine where and how they contribute to each of these areas. While these are merely suggested focus areas, the concept of determining specific needs areas as a group could well provide a unique operating paradigm for many years.

CONCLUDING THOUGHTS

John F. Kennedy once said, "Change is the law of life and those who look only to the past or the present are certain to miss the future." We need to consider, discuss, and implement new paradigms for the continued growth of sport management as an academic discipline. In order to plan for the future of sport management, a paradigm shift is needed now!

REFERENCES

Anderson, P. (1983, Fall). Marketing, scientific progress, and scientific method. *Journal of Marketing, 47,* 18–31.

Arndt, J. (1985, Summer). On making marketing science more scientific: Role of orientations, paradigms, metaphors, and problem solving. *Journal of Marketing, 49*(summer), 11–23.

Baugus, R. V. (2008, June/July). The pro's prof. *Facility Manager,* 43–48.

Birnbaum, R. (1988). How colleges work: The cybernetics of academic organization and leadership. San Francisco: Jossey-Bass.

Bridges, F., & Roquemore, L. (1992). Management of athletic/sport administration: Theory and practice. Decatur, GA: ESM Books.

Chelladurai, P. (1992). Sport management: Opportunities and obstacles. *Journal of Sport Management, 6,* 215–129.

Coakley, J. (2007). *Sport in society: Issues and controversies* (9th ed.). New York: McGraw Hill.

College programs in sport business. (2010, December 6–12). *Street and Smith's SportsBusiness Journal, 13*(32), 41–50.

Covey, S. R. (1989). *The seven habits of highly effective people.* New York: Simon & Schuster.

Downward, P. (2005). Critical (realist) reflections on policy and management research in sport, tourism and sports tourism. *European Sport Management Quarterly, 5*(3), 303–320.

Gillentine, A. (1998). The evolution of sport administration/management graduate programs. *MAHPERD Journal, 4*(1), 7–10.

Gillentine, A., Crow, B., & Harris, J. (2009). Introduction to the sport industry. In A. Gillentine and B. Crowe (Eds.), *Foundations of sport management* (2nd ed.), pp. 1–14. Morgantown, WV: Fitness Information Technology.

Higgs, C., & McKinley, B. (2009). Why sports matter. In A. Gillentine & B. Crowe (Eds.), *Foundations of sport management* (2nd ed.), pp. 15–28. Morgantown, WV: Fitness Information Technology.

Isaacs, S. (1964). *Careers and opportunities in sports.* New York: Dutton.

Keele, L. (2008). The utilitarianism of John Stuart Mill: Ethics and the greatest happiness principle. Retrieved May 22, 2011 from www.suite101.com/content/the-utilitarianism-of-john-stuart-mill-a63950.

Kelly, W. (1987). *Pogo: We have met the enemy and he is us!* New York: Simon & Schuster.

King, S. A. (2004). Blues tourism in the Mississippi Delta: The functions of blues festivals. *Popular Music & Society, 27*(4), 455–475.

Kuhn, T. (1962). *The structure of scientific revolutions* (3rd ed.). Chicago: University of Chicago Press.

Lueddke, G. (1999). Toward a constructivist framework for guiding change and innovation in higher education. *The Journal of Higher Education, 70*(3), 235–260.

Mason, J. G., Higgins, C., & Owen, J. (1981). Sport administration education 15 years later. *Athletic Purchasing and Facilities,* 44–45.

Masteralexis, L. P., Barr, C. A., & Hums, M. A. (2005). *Principles and practice of sport management* (2nd ed.). Sudbury, MA: Jones & Bartlett.

NASPE–NASSM Joint Task Force on Sport Management Curriculum and Accreditation. (1993). Standards for curriculum and voluntary accreditation of sport management education programs. *Journal of Sport Management, 7*(2), 159–170.

NASSM, n.d. Retrieved May 12, 2011 from http://www.nassm.com/InfoAbout/NASSM/History.

Pajares, F. (2003). A synopsis of The Structure of Scientific Revolutions. Retrieved May 12, 2011 from http://des.emory.edu/mfp/kuhnsyn.html.

Parks, J. B. (1992). Scholarship: The "other" bottom line in sport management. *Journal of Sport Management, 6,* 220–229.

Patton, M. (1990). *Qualitative evaluation and research methods.* Newbury Park, CA: Sage.

Roach, F. (2010, August/September). Reality vs. Jerry Maguire. *Facility Manager,* 30–35.

Slack, T. (1991). Sport management: Some thoughts on future directions. *Journal of Sport Management, 5,* 95–99.

Stanley, A. (2009). *The principle of the path: How to get from where you are to where you want to be.* Nashville, TN: Thomas Nelson.

Wandersman, A. (2010, February 10). Promoting real use of evidence-based approaches: New ways to bridge research and practice. Paper presented at the Research Colloquium, University of Miami.

SUGGESTED READINGS

Bernacki, E. (2002). Exactly what is thinking outside the box? *Canada One Magazine* (April).

Boucher, R. L. (1998). Toward achieving a focal point for sport management: A binocular view. *Journal of Sport Management, 12,* 76–85.

Brassie, P. S. (1989). A student buyer's guide to sport management programs. *Journal of Physical Education, Recreation, & Dance, 60*(9), 25–28.

Brown, M., Rascher, D., Nagle, M., & McEvoy, C. (2010). *Financial management in the sport industry.* Scottsdale, AZ: Holcomb Hathaway.

Carrol, R. (2002). Occam's razor—the skeptics dictionary. Retrieved from www.skepdic.com.

Cuneen, J., & Sidwell, J. (1998). Evaluating and selecting sport management undergraduate programs. *Journal of College Admissions* (winter), 6–13.

Danylchuk, K. L., & Judd, M. (1996). Journal of Sport Management: Readership survey. *Journal of Sport Management, 10,* 188–196.

Hardy, S. (1987). Graduate curriculums in sport management: The need for a business orientation. *Quest, 39,* 207–216.

Heylighen, F. (1996).The growth and structural and functional complexity during evolution. In F. Heylighen & D. Aerts (Eds.), *The evolution of complexity.* Retrieved May 22, 2011 from http://pespmc1.vub.ac.be/papers/complexitygrowth.html.

Kriegel, R., & Brandt, D. (1997). *Sacred cows make the best burgers: Developing change ready people and organizations.* New York: Warner Books.

Mahony, D., Mondello, M., Hums, M., & Judd, M. (2004). Are sport management doctoral programs meeting the needs of the faculty job market? Observations for today and the future. *Journal of Sport Management, 18,* 91–110.

Mullin, B. J. (1987). Sport management: The nature and utility of the concept. *Arena Review, 4*(3), 1–11.

Olafson, G. A. (1995). Sport management research: Ordered change. *Journal of Sport Management, 9,* 338–345.

Pitts, B. (2001). Sport management at the millennium: A defining moment. *Journal of Sport Management, 15*(1), 1–9.

Pitts, B. G., Fielding, L. W., & Miller, L. K. (1994). Industry segmentation theory and the sport industry. *Sport Marketing Quarterly, 3*(1), 15–24.

Pransky, G. (2002). Thinking outside the box: What is the box and how did it get here? Retrieved from www.sdlcg.com/sdlsite/Articles/outsidebox.com.

Ross, P. (2003). Outside the box. Retrieved from www.business-specialties.com.

Sawyer, T. H. (1993). Sport management: Where should it be housed? *Journal of Physical Education, Recreation & Dance, 64*(9), 4–5.

Slack, T. (1996). From the locker room to the boardroom: Changing the domain of sport management. *Journal of Sport Management, 10,* 97–105.

Stier, W. (2001). The current status of sport management and athletic (sport) administration programs in the 21st century. *International Journal of Sport Management, 2*(1), 66–79.

Stier, W. (1993). Alternate career paths in physical education: Sport management. Washington, DC: ERIC Digest. Retrieved from http://www.eric.ed.gov:80/PDFS/ED362505.pdf.

Weese, W. J. (1995). If we're not serving practitioners, then we're not serving sport management. *Journal of Sport Management, 9,* 237–243.

Weese, W. J. (2002). Opportunities and headaches: Dichotomous perspectives on the current and future hiring realities in the sport management academy. *Journal of Sport Management, 16,* 1–17.

Yohalem, K. (1997). *Thinking outside the box: How to market your company into the future.* New York: John Wiley & Sons.

Zakrajsek, D. B. (1993). Sport Management: Random thoughts of one administrator. *Journal of Sport Management, 7,* 1–6.

Where Is the *essay* Best "Home" for Sport Management?

2

As our discipline grows, certainly tensions will increase.
Rather than allowing them to cause fragmentation,
we must focus on our commonalties.

Janet S. Fink UNIVERSITY OF CONNECTICUT

Janet Fink received her Ph.D. from The Ohio State University in 1997 and currently is an associate professor at the University of Connecticut. Her research interests include diversity issues in sport, sport media and the female athlete, and sport fan behavior. Fink was inducted as a NASSM Research Fellow in 2006, and in 2007 was awarded The Ohio State University's Award for Distinguished Teaching. She serves as the 2011–2012 President of NASSM and is an associate editor for the *Journal of Sport Management*.

Carol A. Barr UNIVERSITY OF MASSACHUSETTS, AMHERST

Carol Barr currently serves as Vice Provost of Undergraduate and Continuing Education in the Isenberg School of Management at the University of Massachusetts Amherst. She holds a B.S. in Athletic Administration from the University of Iowa, and an M.S. and Ph.D. in Sport Management from the University of Massachusetts Amherst. Barr served on the Executive Council of NASSM, and as NASSM President in 2006–2007. She has also served on the Editorial Board of the *Journal of Sport Management*.

Authors' Note: The authors would like to acknowledge Hyong Il Yim, previously a doctoral student at the University of Connecticut, for compiling the information and constructing the tables for this chapter.

Introduction

As discussed in Essay 1, sport management has long suffered from an identity crisis, or perhaps more aptly stated, crises. Are we sport or sports management; sport or sports administration; practitioners, scholars, or all of the above (Parkhouse, 2001; Parks, 1992)? Are we a distinctive discipline or, by nature, a discipline destined to always be a specialty within a broader context (Chalip, 2006; Chelladurai, 1992)? Have we become too little about sport, and too much about business (Boucher, 1998)? Do we need an even greater foundation in the management literature to become more viable (Slack, 1996)? As Chalip (2006) noted, "There has been substantial malaise among sport management scholars about the field's status, direction, and future" (p. 1). Given such dissatisfaction and differing opinions about how to resolve these issues, it is no wonder there might be some disagreement about the best place for sport management to be housed within academia. Because our sport management programs are located in different units at our respective universities, we have been asked to provide our opinions on this matter. The sport management program at the University of Connecticut is located in the Department of Kinesiology in the Neag School of Education, while the sport management program at the University of Massachusetts Amherst is a stand-alone department located in the Isenberg School of Management. Thus, we bring our personal perspectives relative to the advantages and disadvantages of being situated in these different academic units. However, we want to be clear that this chapter represents just that—our own personal opinions, shaped by our experiences and our interpretations of those experiences. Others in similarly situated units may have varying experiences and opinions, while still others may have different thoughts based on the uniqueness of where their sport management unit is housed (e.g., the sport management department at the University of Massachusetts Amherst was first located in the School of Physical Education and then joined the College of Food and Natural Resources prior to joining the business school). Further, because we both reside within institutions in the United States, our perspectives may be different from those of our Canadian counterparts or other sport management faculty outside of the United States.

EVOLUTION OF THE ACADEMIC HOMES FOR SPORT MANAGEMENT

As Essay 1 discusses, the academic field of sport management grew quickly, especially after 1980. In 1980, only 20 institutions offered sport management programs in the United States; by 2000 there were over 200 (Parkhouse, 2001). The majority of these programs were housed in physical education or kinesiology units as they evolved from traditional physical education programs (Boucher, 1998). This is attributed largely to the physical education faculty who, when faced with declining enrollments in coaching and teaching, modified traditional physical education curricular offerings to attract students interested in more marketable areas (Parkhouse, 2001). Over time and with the growth in sport management, the curriculum within these programs evolved as did where the initial course offerings or programs were housed. According to information provided by NASSM, 295 institutions currently provide sport management programs in the United States (NASSM, 2010; also see Appendix A). The *SportsBusiness Journal* ("College Programs," 2010) tallies over 325 sport management programs in the United States. Additionally, sport management programs have been developed in other countries (including approximately 19 in Europe, 14 in Australia and New Zealand, 2 in India, 4 in Africa, and 3 in Asia). In contrast, the number of programs in Canada, approximately 9, has remained relatively steady since 2000. In 2009, roughly 24,000 U.S. students were majoring in sport management; 6,000 students were in graduate programs for sport management; and 8,000 students graduated with a bachelor's or graduate degree considered "sport focused" (King, 2009). Appendix A illustrates that the number of institutions offering sport management programs outside of a physical education/kinesiology derivative has increased substantially. In the United States, 64 sport management programs have home units in business, while 74 have home units in a physical education/kinesiology derivative. An additional 29 programs are housed in liberal arts schools. The rest are either online or housed in what Mahony (2008) refers to as the "schools of misfit toys—i.e., units that combine a number of unrelated programs that all have no other good home in the university" (p. 6). In Canada, three of the programs are housed in business, while about one-fourth of programs in other countries have business as their home unit (see Appendix B).

Thus, currently the two most common home units for sport management programs are business and kinesiology/education. Where is the "best" place for sport management? We recognize that there are certain advantages and disadvantages to each. We will offer our insights and invite you to decide.

As faculty members, we are often asked by parents and students about the difference between a sport management program housed within a business school and one housed in kinesiology/education. Given that course requirements are fairly similar across programs, conceivably there is little difference. While some may vary in their course requirements (e.g., those in business schools may require more core business courses, while those in kinesiology may require more core kinesiology classes), sport management's accreditation body, the Commission on Sport Management Accreditation (COSMA), suggests a "common professional component" of topics that all sport management programs should have in common. Obviously, though, course requirements are only a small part of the picture. Where we are housed can provide certain advantages and disadvantages for faculty and students alike.

ADVANTAGES AND DISADVANTAGES
OF KINESIOLOGY AS A HOME UNIT

Being housed in kinesiology allows the primary focus of the program to be on *sport,* without apology. As Chalip (2006) notes, "if sport management is to be anything more than the mere application of general management principles to the sport context, then there must be something about sport that renders distinctive concerns, foci, or procedures when sport is managed. If that is not the case, then there is little reason for sport management to exist as a separately identified field of study" (p. 3).

Our colleagues in exercise science, sport sociology, athletic training, etc. may not be overly concerned with the management aspects of sport, but they are typically interested in sport/physical activity. Therefore, most do not have to be convinced of the importance and distinctiveness of the sport context relative to the study of management processes. However, faculty in different units of the university may not hold such perceptions. As Chalip, Schwab, and Dustin (2010) argue, "In the popular imagination, play is the stuff of childhood, and when practiced by adults, it is perceived as mere escape from the importance and business of daily life" (p. 3).

Indeed, sport management is often a low priority in institutions (Mahony, 2008), but within kinesiology there is typically a shared understanding that sport is a unique and worthwhile context for teaching, research, and service efforts. The importance of sport in our culture and the understanding that sport can be a powerful platform for change are beliefs common among most of our faculty. We do not have to justify the study of sport as a serious, worthwhile endeavor.

Because faculty within kinesiology share sport/physical activity as a context, there should be more opportunities for collaboration than in other units. However, such collaborations typically focus on what Chelladurai (1992) terms the "provision of human services in sport versus the provision of entertainment services through sport" (p. 218). That is, we should be able to use the knowledge derived from sport management to collaborate with our kinesiology colleagues using a sport underpinning to eradicate numerous social ills (e.g., childhood obesity, racial inequities) and work toward positive social change. Subsequently, sport management programs and faculty with a focus beyond "sport as entertainment" (Chalip et al., 2010) might feel greater connections and support for such activities in a kinesiology unit than a business unit. Similarly, students in sport management programs in kinesiology may be exposed to more sport-centered coursework—classes that highlight the uniqueness and nuances of the sport context relative to management strategies. As Boucher (1998) states, "Regrettably, we may have shifted our balance off center to the degree that we have a preoccupation with the structural and organizational aspects of sport at the expense of experiential, social, and philosophical discourses that have been part of our earliest connections with sport" (p. 79).

He notes that an emphasis on sport should be the "first pillar" for the sport management profession (Boucher, 1998). Obviously, sport *is* big business. However, as argued previously, it is quite distinct from other business enterprises. Thus, exposure to these distinctions through a wide variety of sport-centered classes is necessary in preparing effective sport managers.

Unfortunately, being housed in a kinesiology unit can also pose some disadvantages. Kinesiology units are typically comprised of faculty with physical *and* social science backgrounds, and in many of these units those with physical science backgrounds outnumber the social scientists. These vastly different backgrounds can lead to intense specializations within the kinesiology discipline, a situation that fragments the unit (Andrews, 2008). Even worse is the hierarchy that arises within these fragmented units. "With a few exceptions, the pecking order is clear and we (sport management) are often at or near the bottom" (Mahony, 2008, p. 6). Andrews (2008) argues that this stems from an "epistemological hierarchy that privileges positivist over postpositivist, quantitative over qualitative, and predictive over interpretive ways of knowing" (p. 45). Such an epistemological hierarchy appears to exist in many kinesiology units, but even sport management researchers with more positivist, quantitative, and predictive inclinations experience this low status in some kinesiology units. Thus, even though sport management often has the largest enrollments among kinesiology units, its lower status often results in less financial support (e.g., fewer faculty lines, less funding for graduate students).

Mahony (2008) argues this low status stems from and is exacerbated by the fact that there is little grant money available for sport management research. This poses another disadvantage for sport management researchers in kinesiology units: pressure to obtain grant funding because our colleagues obtain it, despite the fact that available research funds are miniscule at best. As a result, sport management faculty often must focus their research efforts in areas that are more "fundable" (e.g., obesity, exercise adherence), but perhaps less intrinsically interesting from a scholarly standpoint. Sport management faculty in kinesiology units experience this pressure even if their research endeavors can be carried out without grant funding—that is, our colleagues' research efforts often require expensive equipment and extensive personnel, making grants a necessity. However, that is not necessarily true for a great deal of sport management research. Still, as long as grant funding is important to kinesiology ranking systems and departments/schools continue to rely further on the funds received as part of grant pay-outs, all faculty within these units will be expected to acquire funding. And, if grant funding is a large part of the merit/tenure system, sport management faculty are at an intense disadvantage.

ADVANTAGES AND DISADVANTAGES OF BUSINESS AS A HOME UNIT

We are often reminded through various press outlets that the sport industry is big business. The U.S. Department of Commerce (2008) estimated the combined gross economic output of the sport, recreation, entertainment, and arts categories in the United States to be about $221 billion in 2008. Many would agree that sport management academic programs should be housed in business schools to provide students the business curriculum and preparation for a job in the industry. Locating a sport management program within a business school automatically infers that a business curriculum is included, but locating it in the kinesiology unit does not automatically preclude a sport business/management focus. Differences certainly will exist among schoolwide requirements such that students in a sport management program within a business school will typically be required to satisfy core business coursework as a part of accrediting body requirements. However, if a consistent sport management accrediting system gains momentum (i.e., COSMA), we will find much more commonality regardless of the home unit. Still, many argue that we must focus more on the business side of sport (e.g., Slack, 1996; Zakrajsek, 1993), which indicates a business home unit may be a better fit. However, is this a perfect match?

Typically business schools enjoy a high status relative to other schools and colleges within a university. The positive perceptions of central administration, and subsequent elevated status, are a result of student demand for a business education, alumni stature within the business world, and fundraising potential. Business schools are usually at the forefront of an institution's fund development campaign due to alumni earning power. All of these characteristics tend to produce greater resources from central administration.

Business schools are also entrepreneurial in finding external sources of revenue beyond their institutional funding. These include online program offerings, executive education programs, consulting activities, fee-based business projects, and alumni donations. The Association to Advance Collegiate Schools of Business (AACSB) reports that in 2008–09 the mean operating budget for a business school in the United States was $15,906,478. The mean endowment amount for a U.S. business school in 2008–09 was $25,123,210 (Association to Advance Collegiate Schools, 2010). This means more resources may be available for items such as general operating funds for departments, doctoral student stipends, graduate student assistantships, faculty travel funds, research awards, speaker series, and student scholarships, to name just a few. Of course, how the sport management program is perceived within the unit will certainly play a role relative to resource availability and allocation.

Students may also view the degrees offered as advantageous. For example, if the undergraduate degree is a Bachelor of Business Administration (BBA) or a Bachelor of Science in Business Administration (BSBA), doors open not only in the sport industry, but also in the general world of business. In times of economic uncertainty and diminishing job opportunities, this can be a distinct advantage. At the University of Massachusetts Amherst, sport management students receive a Bachelor of Science (B.S.) degree in Sport Management. However, students have the opportunity to pursue a double degree (taking 150 credit hours to receive a BBA degree in a traditional business major, along with a B.S. in Sport Management) or a double major (completing 120 credit hours to receive a BBA degree in a traditional business major, with sport management listed as a double major on the transcript). The master's program is similar. Regardless of structure, graduating from a business school may yield more job opportunities for the sport management graduate if he or she is willing to work outside of a sport setting.

This may be especially true at the doctoral level. For example, the Ph.D. offered at the University of Massachusetts Amherst is a Ph.D. in Business with a concentration in Sport Management. This is enticing to students because they can obtain employment within business schools (teaching traditional business disciplines as well as sport management classes) or kinesiology units. The benefits of completing doctoral work in business as opposed to kinesiology or education include not only more job options (as a result of being able to teach core business courses as well as sport management courses) but also a higher starting salary, because business school faculty are usually offered higher salaries than those in kinesiology or education. Faculty member salaries are market-driven, but for comparison purposes the average salary for a new assistant professor in marketing is $108,900 while a new assistant professor in management receives $104,400 (Business School Data Trends, 2010). The average salary for an assistant professor in kinesiology at research universities is $60,502 (American Kinesiology Association, 2010).

In contrast to the pressures that may exist for sport management faculty members located within a kinesiology unit, business schools typically do not stress grant funding to achieve tenure and promotion. Although some business school faculty acquire grant funding to support their research activities (including grant funding through the highly competitive National Science Foundation and National Institutes of Health), a grant funding requirement is not usually evident within a business school. Thus, a sport management program housed within a business school can bypass the pressure for grant funding that such faculty within a kinesiology unit may experience.

However, sport management programs housed in business schools have several disadvantages. Research journal outlets are of significant importance to many business schools, especially those at research intensive institutions. The traditional business school disciplines (i.e., accounting, marketing, finance, management) all have an established ranking system of journals (with some slight variations). These journal rankings are embraced by numerous business schools as a means of evaluating faculty for tenure and promotion, merit pay, and other rewards. For example, some institutions may require a junior faculty member to achieve at least one premier or A-list journal "hit" in order to achieve tenure. Various business journal ranking lists exist (for example, the *Financial Times* provides a list of 40 journals across traditional business disciplines, and the University of Texas at Dallas compiled a list of 24 premier business journals), and schools usually choose journals from these lists that fit their research expectations. These journals exhibit much influence due to the number of citations in other journals that refer to their articles (see Essay 7). Sport management journals are not found on these lists (Shilbury & Rentschler, 2007), which means that sport management faculty in business schools are under pressure to publish in A-list journals outside of sport. Because sport is viewed as an "outside" or "special" context, reviewers of these journals may be less apt to consider sport research as serious academic material. Furthermore, while a ranking system of sport management journals has commenced, with the *Journal of Sport Management* rated the highest in our field, these rankings are still in their infancy (Shilbury & Rentschler, 2007). And, as Shilbury and Rentschler (2007) argue, sport management's youth as a field of study results in its journals being included in few indices. Those that are included have fairly recently been added. As a result, our sport management journal publications are given far less credence than those of other disciplines.

A related disadvantage is the perception of sport as a not-so-serious topic of research. When the UMass Amherst Sport Management Department faculty were contemplating a merger into the Isenberg School of Management, one of the primary concerns was fitting in with the business school culture. Discussions often included the phrase "must be nice to do research within a sport context." Hallway conversations implied that we were more a faculty of physical educators or health and fitness experts. The underlying perception was that our research is "fun" but perhaps not valid or important to the business setting. The issues of cultural fit and a true understanding of our discipline are not limited to business school. Given the relative youth of sport management as an academic discipline, we argue that many in our discipline, no matter where their home units reside, are engaged in educating others as to what sport management truly means.

As stated earlier, higher faculty salaries are often noted as a reason to house a sport management program in a business school. After all, business school faculty traditionally have higher salaries than kinesiology unit faculty (see assistant professor salary above). However, a merger into a business school does not automatically mean sport management faculty salaries will rise. A business school typically will employ a market-driven, discipline-specific, salary approach. Faculty who can earn the most as practitioners in their field receive the highest salaries (e.g., accounting, finance). Given the relatively low salaries in the field of sport management, faculty will typically be "low on the totem pole" in terms of salaries. Further compounding this issue is the lack of respect sport management receives as a discipline (see above), which is also reflected in business school pay scales.

Recently, some programs housed in business units, such as the one at Arizona State University, have been eliminated. One reason for their demise is that the sport management graduates adversely impacted the unit's national rankings due to their low starting salaries. These lower salaries are reflected in the ranking calculations, and officials felt it was better to drop the program than suffer a fall in the rankings.

CONCLUDING THOUGHTS: DOES THE HOME UNIT REALLY MATTER?

We have delineated the advantages and disadvantages of kinesiology and business as the home unit for sport management programs as seen through our eyes and experiences. However, we are in complete agreement with Chalip (2006) and Mahony (2008), who contend that the debate over where sport management is housed is less important than the discussion regarding the status of our field. Mahony (2008) notes that "the respect and quality of treatment that sport management receives is more often based on people than structures" (p. 6). Support and respect for sport management can be found in both units—it has to do with *who* makes the decisions, not *where* that decision maker is housed. Chalip (2006) says that "our status ultimately derives not from our institutional location, but rather the research that we do and the students we attract" (p. 2). Of course, we can conduct better research and attract better students when we receive more resources, but his point is important. It is absolutely imperative for sport management faculty to produce quality research and to prepare our students to be successful professionals.

Sport management's growth has produced a variety of tensions within our field (Inglis, 2007), and "these tensions can feel intensely personal and political" (p. 2). The debate over which is the best home unit is just one of them. As our discipline grows, certainly these tensions will increase. Rather than allowing them to cause fragmentation, we must focus on our commonalties. Sport management is not large enough, nor firmly established enough in the academy, to withstand significant division. We must handle our tensions with mutual respect and recognize the value that each of our specialties contributes to our common goal of strengthening sport management as an academic discipline.

REFERENCES

American Kinesiology Association. (2010). AKA survey report. Retrieved from http://www.americankinesiology.org.

Andrews, D. L. (2008). Kinesiology's *Inconvenient Truth* and the physical cultural studies imperative. *Quest, 60,* 45–62.

Association to Advance Collegiate Schools. (2010). Business school data trends and 2010 list of accredited schools. Retrieved from http://www.aacsb.edu/.

Boucher, R. L. (1998). Toward achieving a focal point for sport management: A binocular perspective. *Journal of Sport Management, 12,* 76–85.

Chalip, L. (2006). Toward a distinctive sport management discipline. *Journal of Sport Management, 20,* 1–21.

Chalip, L., Schwab, K., & Dustin, D. (2010). Bridging the sport and recreation divide. *Schole: A Journal of Leisure Studies and Recreation Education, 25,* 1–10.

Chelladurai, P. (1992). Sport management: Opportunities and obstacles. *Journal of Sport Management, 6,* 215–219.

College programs in sports business. (2010, December 6–12). *Street and Smith's Sports Business Journal, 13*(32), 41–50.

Inglis, S. (2007). Creative tensions and conversations in the academy. *Journal of Sport Management, 21,* 1–14.

King, B. (2009, August 24). New lessons to learn. Sport management programs evolve to meet student demand, economic realities. *SportsBusiness Journal.* Retrieved from http://www.sportsbusinessjournal.com.

Mahony, D. F. (2008). No one can whistle a symphony: Working together for sport management's future. *Journal of Sport Management, 22,* 1–10.

NASSM. (2010). Sport management programs. Retrieved from http://www.nassm.org.

Parkhouse, B. L. (2001). *The management of sport: Its foundation and application.* (3rd ed.). Boston: McGraw Hill.

Parks, J. B. (2002). Scholarship: The other "bottom line" in sport management. *Journal of Sport Management, 6,* 220–229.

Shilbury, D., & Rentschler, R. (2007). Assessing sport management journals: A multi-dimensional examination. *Sport Management Review, 10,* 31–44.

Slack, T. (1996). From the locker room to the board room: Changing the domain of sport management. *Journal of Sport Management, 10,* 97–105.

U.S. Department of Commerce. (2008). U.S. Bureau of Economic Analysis. Retrieved from http://www.bea.gov.

Zakrajsek, D. B. (1993). Sport management: Random thoughts from one administrator. *Journal of Sport Management, 7,* 1–6.

Sport Management Accreditation

3

WHY IT IS AN IMPERATIVE STEP FORWARD

"The best defense against excessive regulation is a trustworthy system of self-regulation."

B. BRITTINGHAM (2008, P. 36)

A coauthor introduces the essay

Jay Gladden INDIANA UNIVERSITY–PURDUE UNIVERSITY INDIANAPOLIS

Jay Gladden is Dean of the School of Physical Education and Tourism Management at Indiana University–Purdue University Indianapolis. He received an M.A. in Sport Management from The Ohio State University and a Ph.D. in Sport Management from the University of Massachusetts. He was a founding board member of COSMA.

Jo Williams UNIVERSITY OF SOUTHERN MAINE

Jo Williams is an Associate Professor of Sport Marketing in the School of Business at the University of Southern Maine. Her research interests include sport marketing, particularly the use of social media. Additional interests focus on curricula innovation and student engagement. She also served as the first Chair for COSMA.

Introduction

In July 2008, the North American Society for Sport Management and the National Association for Sport and Physical Education partnered to create the Commission on Sport Management Accreditation (COSMA).The establishment of COSMA, an organization independent of NASSM and NASPE, represented the first attempt at accrediting sport management education programs. It was the culmination of a conversation about the need for accreditation that dates back to at least 1991 and a debate about quality in sport management programs that goes back to the late 1970s (Fielding, Pitts, & Miller, 1991).

In a time of ever-increasing public and political scrutiny of higher education, it seems logical that the field of sport management would move toward a formal accreditation process. In fact, sport management was one of the few professional fields that did not have a specialized accreditation process in place. Now several years into the process, COSMA has gained some traction, with 46 of 303 institutions listed on the NASSM website (NASSM, 2010) having committed resources toward becoming institutional members of COSMA. However, this represents only 15 percent of all programs, suggesting that there has not been widespread acceptance of COSMA. There are likely a host of reasons for this, including resource constraints and the ability to demonstrate quality. Additionally, many programs may see sport management accreditation as unnecessary because they are housed in academic units that are already accredited by a more visible specialized accrediting body such as the National Council for Accreditation of Teacher Education (NCATE), the Association to Advance Collegiate Schools of Business (AACSB), or the Council on Accreditation of Parks, Recreation, Tourism and Related Professions (COAPRT).

In this paper we argue the importance of COSMA accreditation. We also outline the overarching context in which this debate occurs and discuss the typical benefits and motivations for accreditation. Where applicable, we also make recommendations and predictions with respect to the success of COSMA. As two of the original COSMA commissioners (one of us having served as chair for the first three years), we clearly believe in the underlying need for sport management accreditation. It is the next logical step for a field in which there are no established markers of quality or common expectations of professionalism. Furthermore, the COSMA requirements allow for differences among programs. COSMA is focused on program outputs rather than inputs, which makes it current with the national accrediting philosophy. However, we also realize there are many skeptics and detractors who for a variety of reasons either do not plan to seek COSMA accreditation or intend to take a wait-and-see approach. We provide a review of the pressures facing academe in general and sport management programs in particular in illustrating the need for programs to pursue accreditation.

THE EVOLUTION AND RELEVANCE OF ACCREDITATION

ccreditation in U.S. higher education happens at three levels. At the highest level, the Council for Higher Education Accreditation (CHEA) serves as the accreditor of all accrediting agencies. CHEA specifies guidelines and standards to which an accrediting organization must adhere if they wish to be formally recognized and endorsed. The next level is the institutional or regional accrediting agencies, which exist to evaluate the performance of institutions as a whole. For example, the Southern Association of Colleges and Schools (SACS) serves as the accreditor for colleges and universities in the southern United States. These organizations are currently facing significant scrutiny from federal regulators and politicians, who suggest the accreditors are not sufficiently ensuring quality in their reviews of institutions. The last level is the discipline-based or specialized accreditors who evaluate programs in specific academic disciplines. For example, the Accreditation Board for Engineering and Technology (ABET) is the accrediting body for engineering programs, and the Association to Advance Collegiate Schools of Business (AACSB) is one of the accrediting agencies for business and management schools. As indicated earlier, COSMA is the specialized accrediting body for sport management programs.

Accreditation of higher education institutions and programs is not a new phenomenon. According to Judith S. Eaton, president of CHEA, accreditation dates back more than 100 years (Eaton, 2009). Regional accrediting bodies, such as the Higher Learning Commission (for the North Central Association of Colleges and Schools) and the New England Association of Schools and Colleges, trace their history to before the turn of the twentieth century. Specialized accrediting bodies possess similar histories; the AACSB, for example, was founded in 1916 and offered its first standards for accreditation in 1919 (AACSB, 2010). Similarly, the premier accreditor of teacher education programs, NCATE, was founded in 1954 (NCATE, 2010).

Since the inception of accrediting groups, increasing quality in education has been their focal point. If an institution or academic program is accredited, this theoretically signifies that it meets a requisite level of quality as determined by peer review. The process of accreditation is typically the same regardless of the level or discipline. The institution or program completes a self-study in which it articulates how it meets the standards for accreditation. Standards requiring documentation typically include strategic planning, resources, faculty sufficiency, and an outcomes assessment plan. The self-study is reviewed by a team of outside peer evaluators who add scrutiny to the process by conducting a campus visit. Following the campus visit, the peer review team makes a recommendation to a governing board, which then either grants or denies accreditation. Once received, accreditation is reviewed periodically, usually every three to ten years. Standards vary, but typically have evolved from a significant focus on inputs (what is being taught) to outputs (what students are learning). Furthermore, according to CHEA, the manner in which institutions and programs fulfill the standards must be consistent with their mission (i.e., "mission-driven"). Therefore, how an institution demonstrates quality may vary depending on its mission

(CHEA, 2009). The focus on outputs and the resources required to achieve them can serve as a deterrent to schools seeking accreditation. Referring to the AACSB, White, Miles, and Levernier (2009) suggest "the rigor of the AACSB accreditation standards have historically been sufficiently high that many business schools did not have the resources or even the desire to gain accreditation" (p. 408).

RECENT HISTORY: POLITICAL PRESSURES FORCING MORE RIGOR

For nearly 30 years, higher education has been in the crosshairs of the federal government, driven significantly by concerns from the public about the quality and costs of higher education. In 1983, the National Commission on Excellence in Education published the report "A Nation at Risk," which argued that the U.S. education system was in need of significant reform (Wise, 2005). In 1992, Congress made student achievement a priority of accreditation, and in 1998, made it the highest priority (Golden, 2006). These calls for improvement, particularly related to accountability, have become more acute in the last decade. Margaret Spellings, Secretary of Education under President George W. Bush, created the Commission on the Future of Higher Education, often referred to as the Spellings Commission. The commission had two focal points: improving the quality of higher education and controlling the costs of higher education. One of the commission's key recommendations was the creation of an accountability system to be managed by the federal government (Sandmann, Williams, & Abrams, 2009).

This recommendation represented a potential sea change for institutions and their accreditors. In calling for more transparency and comparability between institutions on consistent metrics related to student learning outcomes, the commission challenged one of the fundamental premises of accreditation, namely that "institutional autonomy is essential to sustaining and enhancing academic quality" (CHEA, 2009, p. 3). According to Brittingham (2008), the "accreditors' approach to assessment has hitherto been to support the quality-improvement function; by understanding student learning in light of program and institutional goals, the institution can judge its own effectiveness and have information useful for improvement" (p. 34). Requiring institutions to measure student learning using comparable metrics challenges the widely accepted practice of allowing the mission to drive the learning outcomes for students. The current paradigm allows institutions and programs to set learning outcomes that are consistent with their stated mission. The Spellings Commission recommendations would have required specific learning outcomes be consistent for all institutions.

While the Spellings Commission's recommendation for standardized learning outcomes was not enacted, it has greatly contributed to the conversation around outcomes assessment. Governmental scrutiny of accrediting entities' processes has increased, often focusing on the degree to which institutions are managing outcomes assessment. As Reeve (2010) notes, following the Spellings Commission, there has been "an increased awareness by institutions to be more transparent and consistent in describing the nature of their programs and the learning outcomes achieved by their students" (p. 17). The most notable and tangible step toward this increased transparency has been the increased use of standardized tests, which permit performance comparisons between institutions (Basken, 2007). For example, the Educational Testing Service offers Major Field Tests in a variety of disciplines. Additionally, universities have become much more proactive in providing evidence of the outcomes assessment process on their websites. A partnership between the Association of Public and Land-Grant Universities and the American Association of State Colleges created the Voluntary System of Accountability to provide comparable information on costs and outcomes assessment (Reeve, 2010). In essence, institutions of higher learning have realized what Brittingham (2008) suggested: "The best defense against excessive regulation is a trustworthy system of self-regulation" (p. 36) and adapted accordingly by demonstrating depth and effort in the collection of data to document student learning linked to specific goals.

Against this backdrop, sport management programs have not been immune from scrutiny. In fact, scrutiny might eventually be more intense than for some other academic areas, given the large number of sport management programs and what may be perceived as a small number of jobs, many of which do not pay extremely high salaries. Furthermore, sport management programs are behind related disciplines, such as business and education, in focusing accountability around outputs such as learning outcomes, at least in part because there was no formal accreditation process until 2008. Given these factors, it is incumbent on the field to stress their dedication to student learning by documenting learning outcomes and systematically collecting and analyzing relevant data. The COSMA guidelines for accreditation require an outcomes assessment process be in place. Thus, institutions that gain accreditation through COSMA have demonstrated an assessment plan, data from assessment efforts, and action plans related to improving student performance in all areas.

HOW WE ARRIVED AT THIS POINT

Throughout the advancement of sport management as a field of study, faculty and scholars have consistently emphasized the need to provide meaningful, quality programs and a core curriculum that ensures students become well-qualified and prepared professionals (Chelladurai, 1992; Fielding et al., 1991; Kelley, Beitel, DeSensi, & Blanton, 1994; NASPE–NASSM Joint Task Force, 1993; Ziegler, 1987). Assessing excellence and relevancy among sport management programs has been a concern for parents, prospective students, and employers who must choose from numerous programs. Scholars within the field have examined quality issues and considerations in a range of curricula areas including the "professional core" and internships/field experiences (Cuneen & Sidwell, 1994; Fielding et al., 1991; Kelley, Beitel, DeSensi, & Blanton, 1994; Irwin, Southall, & Sutton, 2007; Masteralexis & McDonald, 1997; Pitts & Danylchuk, 2007; Spence, Hess, McDonald, & Sheehan, 2009). These authors considered areas such as international dimensions, experiential learning, internships, and differentiated core curricula for a variety of specializations and the relevancy of various curricula components in the context of providing a strong professional preparation for students. Input from sport industry personnel regarding the development of sport management curriculum has also been recognized as an important factor in providing a quality education and relevant course content and programmatic experiences (DeSensi, Kelley, Blanton, & Beitel, 1990; Parks & Quain, 1986; Stier & Schneider, 2000; Ulrich & Parkhouse, 1982). In 2009, Petersen and Pierce conducted additional work in this area focusing on the perceived importance of curricular content areas to potential employers in professional sports leagues. Petersen and Pierce's findings are consistent with previous studies that identified internship experiences and the development of communication skills as two of the most important elements of sport management programs.

The First Attempt at Quality Assurance: Sport Management Program Review Council

External quality assurance and formal evaluation of sport management programs have received widespread attention for many years. During the 1980s, NASPE formed a number of task forces to examine curriculum standards for the sport management discipline (NASPE, 2008). Based on these efforts, a joint task force from NASPE–NASSM was formed to develop curricula guidelines for the discipline. In the early 1990s, curriculum standards were endorsed by NASPE and NASSM, and further work continued to refine the model. As mentioned in Essay 1, the first step toward excellence in sport management came with the formation of the Sport Management Program Review Council (SMPRC), which was a collaboration between NASPE and NASSM, in 1993. The purpose of SMPRC was to review and approve (not accredit) sport management programs according to the standards developed by NASSM and NASPE. For the first time there were clearly articulated standards around high-quality curriculum content and a process by which programs could be measured against these standards. By 2008, the SMPRC had further revised the model and set a protocol for a seven-year cycle aimed at continuous improvement and relevancy.

SMPRC program approval was an extremely important step toward quality assurance in sport management programs. It stimulated discourse about excellence in sport management within both NASSM and NASPE and provided a mark of excellence for those programs that successfully completed the review process. Universities whose sport management programs received program approval could market this designation, and the NASSM website made note in its listings of which programs had received approval. At the time program approval was suspended for the move to accreditation, 53 undergraduate programs, 32 masters programs, and 4 doctoral programs had been approved (SMPRC, 2008). Such participation clearly indicated the need and demand for quality assurance.

While SMPRC provided a valuable first step, many institutions felt that the financial and time costs involved in the process outweighed the benefits. There were a variety of reasons for this. First, the process led to program approval rather than accreditation. While some external stakeholders misinterpreted it as an accreditation process, it was never presented as such and thus may not have had as much internal currency as accreditation did within the university systems. Second, the process was focused on inputs instead of outputs. The most significant part of the process was demonstrating (through course syllabi) that the courses in the program met a very long list of curricular requirements. Rather than allow for individuality of programs that would focus on specialized areas of the field while providing adequate coverage in others, SMPRC mandated in-depth coverage of all of the key curricular areas. The intention was to spell out what constituted a strong sport management curriculum. However, it was not consistent with current accreditation practices that focus on what students learn rather than what is being taught. A third reason that SMPRC was not optimally successful was that it did not require a site visit. In the typical accreditation process, a written self-study is just the first step. A site visit can be illuminating, allowing the institution to answer reviewers' questions face-to-face rather than through written correspondence. Some programs wondered how a full review could occur without a site visit. Finally, SMPRC did not achieve widespread acceptance because a number of the programs perceived to be leaders in the field did not participate. This was likely due to the reasons above, but almost certainly resulted in other programs believing that the process was not necessary to obtain a reputation for quality.

Specialized Accreditation—COSMA

Given the limitations of SMPRC and the environmental (i.e., political) factors at work, specialized accreditation began to be considered in the sport management field in the early 2000s. The general issues and concerns impacting the accreditation process in other disciplines were examined in the work of Fielding et al. (1991). In this study, the researchers noted that the academic structure and the home unit of sport management programs as well as the relationships between departments were important components that may have an underlying association with curriculum quality. In addition, Fielding et al. (1991) found that even though faculty were aware of the challenges associated with accreditation, it was also seen as "a double-edged sword" with no guarantees of quality. Faculty also expressed concerns about the process's management and logistical considerations.

In 2005 and 2006, two joint NASPE/NASSM task forces, the Accreditation Task Force and the Standards Task Force, were formed to conduct independent investigations into the need for specialized accreditation and the potential accreditation models that could most appropriately serve the discipline (COSMA, 2010). Following significant work, including a roundtable discussion and feedback from NASSM members, the task forces recommended a move to full accreditation that resulted in the suspension of the SMPRC approval process in 2007. NASSM and NASPE members received draft accreditation manuals, and their feedback was solicited through discussion sessions at the annual conferences of both organizations (COSMA, 2010).

In 2008, the Commission on Sport Management Accreditation was launched to provide specialized accreditation for the sport management discipline (COSMA, 2010). Based on the recommendation of the NASPE–NASSM Standards Task

Force, the COSMA model and process was designed to be outcomes-based and mission-driven. According to COSMA (2010), the underlying philosophy of the accreditation model is based on "characteristics of excellence in sport management education and assessment of educational outcomes as a basis for accreditation decisions, rather than the prescriptive input standards approach." In this manner, COSMA is consistent with other specialized accreditation processes that use outcomes-based, mission-driven accreditation models to address curricula concerns and provide flexibility and focus when measuring quality (CHEA, 2006).

As stated earlier, since the launch of COSMA in 2008, 46 institutions have become members. Of these members, 10 have completed the candidacy process and are currently in the process of creating a self-study and preparing for the accreditation site visit. Two institutions have completed the process and were awarded accreditation in 2010 (COSMA, 2010). The initial response to COSMA has been favorable in terms of membership growth that includes both large and small and public and private institutions. Attendance at COSMA meetings and training sessions also indicates a positive response to the accreditation model. In addition, the COSMA Board of Commissioners has worked to continually improve the model and ensure that the quest to provide "excellence in sport management education" drives decision-making throughout the process. Yet COSMA is still in its infancy and its success will be dependent on overcoming some of the same challenges that SMPRC faced, as well as some new contextual changes. However, before discussing these challenges, it is important to put forth the best case for accreditation.

THE CASE FOR COSMA ACCREDITATION

The purposes and benefits of accreditation include quality control, allocation of resources, indication of quality to stakeholders, and outcomes assessment. Each of these will be discussed below.

Quality Control

First and foremost, the purpose of an accreditation process is to identify high quality programs. This quality assurance is multifaceted. According to Brittingham (2008), "accreditation serves two functions: institutional quality improvement among its members (the 'private' function) and quality assurance (the 'public' function)" (p. 32). Nearly all accreditation processes require a focus on continuous improvement, frequently achieved through outcomes assessment and strategic planning. In this way, the accreditor ensures programs employ dynamic rather than static processes to achieve quality in order to adapt to the rapidly changing world. Such a requirement is pertinent to ensure the careful, regular scrutiny and planning for sport management programs. Because sport management programs are housed in a variety of schools (business, education, kinesiology, etc.), the risk is that strategic planning occurs at the school or college level, but not at the program level. While this is not to suggest that school plans and evaluation processes ignore sport management programs, it does raise the likelihood that careful scrutiny occurs too seldom. For a field less than 50 years old that is still trying to define its value in an institutional context, regular planning is extremely important. Furthermore, many sport management programs have grown rapidly without agreement on the appropriate number of students given its faculty resources. Rapid growth also generates more administrative work, which potentially detracts from the more holistic strategic work that needs to occur on a regular basis.

Allocation of Resources

Another way the accreditation process ensures quality is by carefully scrutinizing the resources allocated to the program. Again, this is extremely relevant to the field of sport management. Because a number of programs have been created as instruments for enrollment growth, there has not always been a concomitant allocation of resources to operate the program. Thus, a purpose of the accreditation process for sport management programs is to ensure the institution provides sufficient resources to the program. The most clear manifestation of this resource commitment is in the faculty assigned to teach the classes in the program. While institutional accreditors commonly require newly hired faculty to be current in the fields in which they teach and to hold a degree one level above the level at which they are teaching, discipline-based accreditors typically go further. For example, AACSB requires 50 percent of all faculty in a business program to possess a terminal degree in their field and make some form of regular intellectual contribution to their field in order to be academically qualified. Standards like this one, which essentially mandate a certain level of doctorally qualified faculty, seem prudent for sport management programs for two reasons. First, the supply of faculty with relevant doctoral degrees has not traditionally been sufficient to meet the demand of institutions with programs needing faculty. The second reason is related to the first in that the gap between supply and demand has only been exacerbated by the number of programs whose enrollment has significantly outpaced a similar investment in faculty resources. In this context, programs exist and offer classes despite insufficient faculty numbers.

The resources requirement presents another more subtle reason why sport management program accreditation is needed. In cases of insufficient investment, institutions can use established accreditation guidelines to argue for initial investment. Alternatively, an institution, by virtue of membership with an accrediting institution, can use the accreditation findings to bolster the resource investment in programs. If, for example, a program goes through the accreditation process and COSMA finds the program lacking in faculty or other resources, COSMA would typically submit a finding that in some cases would have to be rectified before the institution can be accredited without any qualifiers. This strategy is risky for the program, because the institution may choose to discontinue the program rather than satisfy the accreditation requirements. In fact, the global financial crisis of 2008 saw the first significant willingness of institutions to discontinue sport management programs. Therefore, this may be a viable strategy only for those programs that are somewhat established but under-resourced in a particular area.

Importance to Stakeholders

Brittingham (2008) also points out the importance of accreditation to external stakeholders. Effective, discipline-based accreditation can be important to prospective students and their parents. Given the more than 300 programs listed on the NASSM website, prospective sport management students need markers of quality to help them make informed decisions. Because there are no official rankings of sport management programs, there are no completely objective quality measures for prospective students. COSMA accreditation can provide such an indicator. In doing so, it would complement other more subjective measures currently used, such as the entity in which the program is housed (i.e., business school, non-business school), the types of courses offered by the program, the expertise of the faculty, and the depth and influence of the program's alumni and industry network. Influence from prospective students and their parents may also work in favor of COSMA. If enough prospective students and parents use COSMA accreditation as a deciding factor, then even well-established programs, which might otherwise be reluctant to seek accreditation, may seek accreditation for competitive reasons.

Accreditation can also assure industry members who must evaluate the credentials of students from a wide variety of programs (CHEA, 2009). Among those in the sport industry who did not earn a sport management degree, there is some skepticism regarding the value of such a degree. An accreditation process will alleviate some of that skepticism by applying objective standards (many of them consistent with best practices in business) in evaluating programs. Additionally, COSMA accreditation can be a useful tool for sport industry organizations when seeking to expand their human resource base. If the industry views COSMA accreditation as a mark of legitimacy, then employers will be more likely to contact accredited programs when seeking to fill internships and job openings. This could represent another case of where market forces impact the prominence of the accreditation process. Admittedly, sport management and COSMA are far from achieving this perspective among members of industry, and much work remains to be done.

Focus on Outcomes Assessment

Perhaps the most compelling and immediate reason for programs to seek accreditation is COSMA's focus on outcomes assessment. The COSMA standards set forth high expectations with respect to programs articulating learning objectives, employing specific tools to measure student progress toward learning objectives, and adjusting curricular efforts based on assessment findings. This will provide two significant benefits to institutions. First, it will ensure that a formal, sport management-specific outcomes assessment process is implemented. This will be very useful to substantiate the significant learning that occurs within sport management programs during this time of ever-increasing scrutiny on the outputs of higher education. Secondly, COSMA standards and subsequent accreditation will provide the type of proactive and preemptive reporting that Brittingham refers to as being the best defense against governmental scrutiny. COSMA-compliant assessment plans would also provide the transparency sought by the Spellings Commission as well as comparability across institutions.

WILL COSMA SUCCEED? THE CHALLENGES

The long-term success of COSMA will be based on how key stakeholders perceive its credibility. Faculty, administrators, employers, parents, and prospective students must be assured that the process is rigorous and its standards bona fide. In 2009, Williams and Colles investigated faculty and administrator perceptions of the COSMA model and found that the most important elements in establishing a credible accreditation model are linked to the involvement of sport industry professionals, the mission-driven focus of the model, the quality of COSMA leadership, the focus on outcome-assessment data, cost control, and recognition by CHEA. Respondents in this study were also asked to consider the benefits of becoming accredited by COSMA. Interestingly, the marketing benefits associated with accredited status were rated significantly higher for respondents that had joined COSMA when compared to those that had not.

Lack of Involvement of Industry Professionals

To date, COSMA has had little formal involvement with industry professionals either in reviewing standards related to curriculum content, faculty qualifications, and strategic planning, or in the accreditation decision-making process. This lack of involvement presents a potential threat to the organization, and COSMA should consider following the example set by such accrediting agencies as AACSB and the Council on Aviation Accreditation (CAA) to ensure that industry professionals' perspectives are included. Sport industry professionals should be added to the Board of Commissioners and Board of Directors. They could also be used in an advisory capacity to review curricula content standards. Additional research examining industry perspectives related to accreditation would also provide value. Significantly incorporating the voice of industry may also serve to enhance the visibility and credibility of the process in the eyes of the sport industry.

COSMA Leadership Credibility

Leadership from the COSMA Board of Commissioners is also an important consideration in establishing and maintaining the organization's credibility. Difficult decisions are certain to arise within this process and the commissioners will be required to act in a manner that protects the integrity of the accreditation process and standards. Prather (2006) investigated the accreditation model used by the Council of Aviation Accreditation (CAA) and reports the perception that the organization's leadership does not make quality distinctions. The perception among stakeholders was that once an organization received candidacy status, accreditation was the inevitable next step. COSMA should recognize this situation because it clearly highlights the problems caused by a lack of distinctiveness among programs. Perhaps one of the greatest tests facing COSMA is its ability to deny accreditation to programs of insufficient quality. Certainly, many programs will be accredited, and deservedly so. But COSMA's credibility will be compromised if it fails to make difficult judgments when the information warrants such a conclusion.

Program Participation

On a related yet contrasting point, COSMA must ensure full participation by established and respected programs. As noted earlier, one of the problems experienced by SMPRC was that too many respected programs were either skeptical of the process or did not participate at all. Optimal success requires that all noteworthy programs buy into the process. This may be particularly challenging, because many of these programs exist in schools where they are already a part of another specialized accreditation process as stated earlier. Programs located in schools/colleges of education and business are already participating in an accrediting process either through NCATE or AACSB. These programs, and their respective dean's offices, might question why the program needs to have a sport management accreditation. The question has multiple answers. First, as a leader in the field, it is incumbent on the program to also be a leader in validating sport management as a stand-alone discipline. Second, if the process succeeds, it will be a true marker of quality, which can be used for marketing purposes with both prospective students and employers. In essence, programs that are not accredited will be at a competitive disadvantage with respect to recruitment and placement. Finally, the COSMA standards challenge the program to continuously improve and innovate with much more depth than the overarching education or business accreditation processes.

Cost Control

A consistently highlighted concern in program-level specialized accreditation is cost control (Prather, 2006; Roller, Bovee, & Andrews, 2003; Williams & Colles, 2009). Annual membership fees and the costs associated with hosting site visits are often considered prohibitive by faculty and administrators. In addition, the costs are often perceived to outweigh the benefits of becoming accredited (Kelderman, 2009). Many departments support multiple specialized accreditations (NCATE, AACSB, International Assembly for Collegiate Business Education [IACBE], etc.), which increases the total cost of supporting all programs and may potentially impact the decision to support a new accrediting body. Accreditation cost concerns may also be impacted by the fact that a number of other accreditors have the potential to include sport management. For example, in providing business accreditation IACBE also recognizes and accredits sport management as a sub-discipline. In this instance, an institution may see greater value in pursuing one accreditation that covers additional programs, even if it lacks the expertise necessary to fully assess sport management program quality.

CONCLUDING THOUGHTS

COSMA accreditation is an important step forward for the field of sport management. Governmental scrutiny of higher education outcomes is likely to persist for the foreseeable future. Such examination has already challenged institutions, schools, and programs to demonstrate their effectiveness and will continue to do so. In some cases, a level of comparability across institutions may be expected. Rather than have specific measures imposed on sport management programs, programs would be prudent to adopt a level of scrutiny from a specialized accrediting body that allows for some uniqueness and safeguards the mission of both the institution and the program. Specialized accreditation through COSMA provides the groundwork and data for programs to document their effectiveness. Even with a recently created accreditation process, the field of sport management is behind. Nearly every comparable field (with the exception of kinesiology) has a widely accepted accrediting program that also exhibits external validity. While we are just starting the process, early results suggest there is significant interest in the COSMA process. However, more needs to be done. In particular, industry acceptance must be sought, which in turn may help eliminate any reservations top programs have to aligning with COSMA. Difficult decisions are ahead, particularly for the COSMA Board of Commissioners. The organization has a good start in gaining significant legitimacy.

REFERENCES

AACSB. (2010). Accreditation. Retrieved from http://www.aacsb.edu/accreditation/aacsb.asp.

Basken, P. (2007, September 28). A year later, Spellings report still makes ripples. *Chronicle of Higher Education*, A1–A22.

Brittingham, B. (2008, September/October). An uneasy partnership: Accreditation and the Federal Government. *Change*, 32–39.

CHEA. (2006). Council on Higher Education: Fact Sheet #1. Retrieved 6/15/2008 from http://www.chea.org/pdf/fact_sheet_1_profile.pdf.

CHEA (2009). An overview of U.S. Accreditation. Washington, D.C.

Chelladurai, P. (1992). Sport management: Opportunities and obstacles. *Journal of Sport Management*, 6(3), 215–219.

COSMA. (2010). Philosophy of accreditation. Retrieved 6/15/2008 from http://www.cosmaweb.org/philosophy.

Cuneen, J., & Sidwell, M. (1994). *Sport management field experiences*. Morgantown, WV: Fitness Information Technology.

DeSensi, J., Kelley, D., Blanton, M., & Beitel, P. (1990). Sport management curricula evaluation and needs assessment: A multi-faceted approach. *Journal of Sport Management*, 4, 31–58.

Eaton, J. S. (2009). An overview of U.S. accreditation. Council for Higher Education Accreditation. Retrieved 7/21/2011 from http://www.chea.org/pdf/2009.06_Overview_of_US_Accreditation.pdf.

Fielding, L. W., Pitts, B. G., & Miller, L. (1991). Defining quality: Should educators in sport management programs be concerned about accreditation? *Journal of Sport Management*, 5, 1–17.

Golden, D. (2006, November 13). Colleges, accreditors seek better ways to measure learning. *Wall Street Journal*, B1.

Irwin, R. L., Southall, R. M., & Sutton, W. A. (2007). Pentagon of sport sales straining: A 21st century sport sales training model, *Journal of Sport Management Education, 1*(1), 18–39.

Kelderman, E. (2009). Struggling colleges question the cost—and worth—of specialized accreditation. *Chronicle of Higher Education, 56*(7), A14–A15.

Kelley, D. R., Beitel, P. A., DeSensi, J. T., & Blanton, M. D. (1994). Undergraduate and graduate sport management curriculum models: A perspective. *Journal of Sport Management, 8*(2), 93–101.

Masteralexis, L. P., & McDonald, M. A. (1997). Enhancing sport management education with international dimensions including language and cultural training. *Journal of Sport Management, 11*(1), 97–110.

NASPE. (2008). An abridged history of NASPE–NASSM sport management program approval. Retrieved 7/21/2011 from http://www.aahperd.org/naspe/pdf_files/SMPRC_HIstory.pdf.

NASPE–NASSM Joint Task Force on Sport Management Curriculum and Accreditation. (1993). Standards for curriculum and voluntary accreditation of sport management education programs. *Journal of Sport Management, 7*(2), 159–170.

NASSM. (2010). Sport management programs: United States. Retrieved 10/29/10 from http://www.nassm.com/InfoAbout/SportMgmtPrograms/United_States.

NCATE. (2010). About NCATE. Retrieved 10/28/10 from http://www.ncate.org/public/about-NCATE.asp.

Parks, J. B., & Quain, R. J. (1986). Curriculum perspectives. *Journal of Physical Education, Recreation and Dance, 57*, 22–26.

Petersen, J., & Pierce, D. (2009). Professional sport league assessment of sport management curriculum. *Sport Management Education Journal, 3*(1), 110–121.

Pitts, B. G., & Danylchuk, K. E. (2007). Examining the body of knowledge in sport management: A preliminary descriptive study of current sport management textbooks. *Journal of Sport Management Education, 1*(1), n.p.

Prather, C. D. (2006). The Council of Aviation Accreditation: Part two—contemporary issues. *Journal of Air Transportation, 11*(3), 34–60.

Reeve, T. G. (2010). Assessment, accreditation, and accountability: Using the A-list to promote kinesiology programs in higher education. *Quest, 62*, 15–34.

Roller, R. H., Bovee, S. L., & Andrews, B. K. (2003). Specialized accreditation of business schools: A comparison of alternative costs, benefits, and motivations. *Journal of Education for Business, 78*(4), 197–204.

Sandmann, L. R., Williams, J. E., & Abrams, E. D. (2009, April–June). Higher education community engagement and accreditation: Activating engagement through innovative accreditation strategies. *Planning for Higher Education*, 15–26.

SMPRC. (2008). Sport management program review approved program. Retrieved 6/15/2008 from http://www.aahperd.org/naspe/pdf_files/approvedPrograms08.pdf.

Spence, K., Hess, D., McDonald, M., & Sheehan, B. (2009). Designing experiential learning curricula to develop future sport leaders. *Journal of Sport Management Education, 3*(1), 1–25.

Stier, W. F., & Schneider, R. C. (2000). Sport management curricular standards 2000 study—undergraduate level. *International Journal of Sport Management, 1*, 56–69.

Ulrich, D., & Parkhouse, B. L. (1982). An alumni oriented approach to sport management curriculum design using performance ratings and a regression model. *Research Quarterly for Exercise and Sport, 53*(1), 64–72.

White, J. B., Miles, M. P., & Levernier, W. (2009). AACSB international and the management of its brand: Implications for the future. *Journal of Management Development, 28*(5), 407–413.

Williams, J., & Colles, C. (2009). Specialized accreditation of sport management programs: Perspectives of faculty and administrators. *Sport Management Education Journal, 3*(1), 26–46.

Wise, A. E. (2005). Establishing teaching as a profession: The essential role of professional accreditation. *Journal of Teacher Education, 56*(4), 318–331.

Zeigler, E. F. (1987). Sport management: Past, present, future. *Journal of Sport Management, 1*(1), 4–24.

Program Rankings in Sport Management

4

A CRITICAL ANALYSIS OF BENEFITS AND CHALLENGES

Consumers of sport management education (prospective students and their parents) are demanding accessible and interpretable data on the quality of programs.

A coauthor introduces the essay

Daniel F. Mahony KENT STATE UNIVERSITY

Daniel Mahony is the Dean of the College of Education, Health, and Human Services at Kent State University. Mahony has a Ph.D. in sport management from The Ohio State University and has published over 50 articles in various refereed journals, several book chapters, and one book. He served as President of NASSM in 2003–2004 and is a NASSM Research Fellow. He received the Earle F. Zeigler Award in 2007.

Anita M. Moorman UNIVERSITY OF LOUISVILLE

Anita Moorman is a Professor and Program Director of the Sport Administration Program at the University of Louisville. She holds a law degree from Southern Methodist University and an M.S. in Sport Management from the University of Oklahoma. Moorman has published more than 35 articles, over a dozen book chapters in sport management texts, and is co-author of the textbook *Sport Law: A Managerial Approach*.

Timothy D. DeSchriver UNIVERSITY OF DELAWARE

Timothy DeSchriver is an Associate Professor of Sport Management in the Lerner College of Business & Economics at the University of Delaware. He earned his Ed.D. in Sport Administration from the University of Northern Colorado in 1996. His teaching focuses on the areas of sport finance and sport marketing, and his research interests are sport consumer demand, pro sport ownership incentives, and sport facility financing.

Marion E. Hambrick UNIVERSITY OF LOUISVILLE

Marion Hambrick is an Assistant Professor at the University of Louisville. He holds a Ph.D. in Educational Leadership and Organizational Development with an emphasis in Sport Administration from the University of Louisville. His research interests include examining social media usage in sports and the diffusion of innovations in the sporting goods industry.

Introduction

The ranking of academic programs has become common around the world. Although there are not currently any formal rankings of sport management programs, the growing popularity of sport management as a major and the increasing number of academic rankings would suggest that future rankings are certainly possible. In fact, one major for-profit publication, *ESPN The Magazine,* attempted in 2007 to identify top programs in the United States for various sport management sub-specialty areas (e.g., college athletics, sport marketing). While the criteria the magazine used were unclear, the report did get the attention of sport management faculty and likely some current and potential students. Therefore, this seems to be an appropriate point to discuss program rankings in the discipline of sport management, including the advantages and disadvantages, and suggestions for how rankings may be compiled in sport management. However, we believe it is important to first examine the general history of academic rankings.

HISTORICAL APPROACHES TO RANKINGS

While some cite Raymond Hughes' rankings of graduate school departments in 1925 as the beginning of academic quality rankings (Webster, 1986), rankings in higher education actually started in the 19th century (Meredith, 2004; Webster, 1986). The U.S. Bureau of Education issued rankings of universities based on statistical information in their annual reports as early as 1870 (Meredith, 2004). During the 140-year history of these rankings, however, the only constant has been controversy. For example, the classification system developed by Kendric Babcock for the Association of American Universities in 1910 was suppressed by two U.S. presidents because of the controversy it generated (Meredith, 2004). The reasons for the controversies include the subjectivity involved with reputational rankings, the perceived biases of those doing the rankings, the inclusion of certain factors that may not be good measures of quality (e.g., percentage of alumni who donate), the relative weight given to various factors, and the difficulty in accurately assessing key factors (e.g., how well does a university or program teach its students).

However, these factors were less significant in the early years because most people did not pay much attention to the college rankings (McDonough, Antonio, Walpole, & Perez, 1998). The groups who focused on them tended to be college administrators and faculty, government officials, and graduate school applicants, but the general public and undergraduate students did not pay attention to them so their impact on institutions was minimal. This changed dramatically in the 1980s. In particular, *U.S. News & World Report*'s college rankings gained national attention and became big business. In fact, the magazine's "best colleges" issue is very popular and has been labeled its "swimsuit issue" because of its impact on the overall circulation of the magazine (Machung, 1998; McDonough et al., 1998; Meredith, 2004). In addition to its overall institutional rankings, *U.S. News & World Report* offers a separate issue that ranks colleges, schools, and individual programs at the graduate level.

The *U.S. News & World Report* rankings differed from many of the prior rankings in several aspects. First, the rankings were compiled by an independent for-profit organization. While this likely improved the impartiality of the rankings, it also meant the incentives for doing the rankings were different. *U.S. News & World Report*'s goal is to sell their publication. Perhaps in part because of this goal, they actually ranked institutions numerically. Prior assessments of universities generally either grouped them into categories such as Class I, Class II, etc. (Webster, 1986), or classified them into groups. For example, many research universities refer to the Carnegie Classifications as a ranking, but the Carnegie Foundation does not actually say that one group of institutions is better than another; they simply place institutions into different groups based on various criteria (e.g., research, program levels). Regardless, few, if any, previous ranking systems attempted to present the level of precision that exists in the *U.S. News & World Report*. However, many suggest this precision is an illusion, because such fine distinctions between universities do not truly exist (Clarke, 2004).

The popularity of the *U.S. News & World Report*'s rankings has since led other magazines to publish independent national rankings of higher education institutions (e.g., *Money*) and academic units (e.g., *Business Week*) (Meredith, 2004). *Kiplinger's* also ranks select four-year undergraduate universities in its "100 Best Values in Public and Private Colleges" issue (Sponsler, 2009). Rankings beyond the United States began with *Maclean's* inaugural rankings of Canadian institutions in the early 1990s ("20th Annual University," 2010). In fact, the rankings have gone worldwide with Shanghai Jiao Tong University's "Academic Ranking of World Universities" and the *Times Higher Education Supplement*'s "World University Rankings" (Ioannidis, Patsopoulos, Kavvoura, et al., 2007).

People debate the validity (whether the rankings measure what they purport to measure) and reliability (whether they provide a consistent measurement over time) of rankings, questioning whether an aggregated score can accurately gauge the educational quality provided by the institutions. In response to these concerns the Institute for Higher Education Policy has published two issue briefs addressing the role and relevance of ranking in higher education and evaluating the impact rankings have on institutional decision making (IHEP, 2009; Sponsler, 2009). However, colleges and universities recognize that few viable alternatives to the rankings exist and view them as a somewhat necessary evil (Ehrenberg, 2003).

While the impact of these rankings is not completely clear, some research indicates an improved ranking may impact applications, enrollment, quality of the students, and socioeconomic and racial demographics (Meredith, 2004; Monks & Ehrenberg, 1999). In fact, one recent study found that over half of prospective students reportedly use rankings when making a decision about which colleges and universities to attend (Bowman & Bastedo, 2009). Discussions with recruiters indicate the impact is even greater for international students who have less access to informal assessments, such as word of mouth. For example, Chinese recruiters charge families different rates depending on the rank of the institutions to which the student is admitted (i.e., higher rankings cost more), and they indicate that institutional ranking is often the most important or only factor to consider when the student has more than one option. Given the weight placed on rankings by some students, the criteria used in determining rankings is important.

CURRENT APPROACHES TO RANKINGS

Overall, ranking criteria vary widely. While *U.S. News & World Report* began by using only subjective assessments, it now uses a combination of subjective factors, such as peer assessment and employer assessment, and objective factors, such as student test scores, student–faculty ratios, admissions acceptance rates, grant dollars, and faculty awards. The factors are different for undergraduate versus graduate and across various graduate programs. The *Times* ranking is similar in its approach, while the Shanghai rankings focus on objective factors (Ioannidis et al., 2007). The Faculty Scholarly Productivity Index developed by Academic Analytics relies entirely on measures of faculty productivity to rank doctoral programs (Fogg, 2007). While this approach may seem limited, research has found that even rankings of undergraduate business programs are highly correlated with faculty research productivity (Siemens, Burton, Jensen, & Mendoza, 2005).

In September 2010, the National Research Council (NRC) published its long awaited rankings of doctoral programs, which used two separate sets of rankings. The first ranking was a reputational measure the NRC used previously, based on faculty perceptions of quality. The second, newer formula asked faculty members to rank the most important characteristics out of a group of 21, and the NRC developed the new rankings based on this information (Basken, 2010).

Across the various approaches to rankings, the categories and their respective weightings have generated considerable debate and analysis. <u>Some of the controversy surrounding the rankings deals with the validity, reliability, and comparability (whether they can be used to make comparisons across programs and academic institutions) of the rankings</u> (Clarke, 2002; Cremonini, Westerheijden, & Enders, 2008; Tsakalis & Palais, 2004).

The concerns about validity are multiple. First, Ehrenberg (2003; 2005) argues that no mix of variables can provide a comprehensive and accurate picture for a student deciding which college or university to attend. Each student is different and should consider factors that are generally not included in the rankings, such as the fit of the university to the individual's educational and extracurricular needs, budget, location and environmental preferences (e.g., rural or urban), and ability to pursue research. Second, others assert the ratings fail to consider less quantifiable but no less important variables, such as the cultural diversity of the institution and how these variables align with the student's previous experiences as well as his or her educational and personal background (Cremonini, Westerheijden, & Enders, 2008). In contrast, many of the variables (e.g., alumni giving rate) may have been chosen because of their ease of quantification. Third, each of these concerns can impact the educational experience. Only students can know for themselves the appropriate weight to give to each ranking assessment (Ehrenberg, 2003; 2005).

Reliability concerns are tied to the fact that criteria and the relative weight assigned to them often change over time. While Clarke (2002) argues for the importance of rankings, colleges and universities have called the rankings a "shifting yardstick" (Machung, 1998, p. 12). A university may rise or fall in the rankings without any changes occurring at the university, simply because the criteria have changed. Therefore, making comparisons over time requires caution (Clarke, 2002). In fact, studies have pointed to the sensitivity of the variables chosen for the rankings, whereby a small change in one variable can have a more significant influence on the overall ranking (Clarke, 2002; Tsakalis & Palais, 2004). The fact that "the choice of weights is . . . a value judgment and thus can vary depending on who is making the decisions" (Clarke, 2002, p. 446) adds to the measurement concerns.

The comparability concerns relate to the fact that the criteria of interest to the user may vary across institution types (e.g., public versus private) or degree level (e.g., bachelor's versus doctoral) (Bowman & Bastedo, 2009). For example, a business doctoral student will likely have different needs and use different evaluation criteria than an MBA student. The doctoral student may be more interested in a faculty-to-student ratio or the research productivity of faculty members, while an MBA student may be more concerned with placement rates and starting salaries of recent graduates (Urbancic, 2008). Likewise, there may be differences in the criteria used in rankings across various programs at a given university. For example, federal grant funding received may be a more appropriate criterion for programs in engineering or the natural sciences than for programs in a business school.

Questions regarding measurement issues and the various approaches to rankings have not diminished their popularity, and rankings do not seem to be going away (Fogg, 2007; Ioannidis et al., 2007). In 2007, Ioanndis and colleagues found that the term *university rankings* garnered over 42 million hits on Google. Another indication of the rankings' viability is that many universities paid $30,000 for the detailed data in the Faculty Scholarly Productivity Index despite the criticism of rankings among higher education administrators.

It appears clear that rankings in higher education are here to stay, so what are the implications for the academic discipline of sport management? The purpose of this essay is to explore the touted advantages and disadvantages associated with rankings in general and to evaluate how these factors would impact a proposed ranking process in the sport management discipline. Finally, to the extent the field of sport management opts to embrace program rankings, this essay discusses the elements and criteria that should be included in any sport management program ranking plan.

ADVANTAGES TO SPORT MANAGEMENT PROGRAM RANKINGS

There are many reasons to support the development of a ranking system for sport management programs. As mentioned earlier, methods of ranking are already popular and prevalent across higher education and other segments of society in general. Numerous publications annually rank colleges and universities (Webster, 1992), and rankings systems now even extend to specific academic disciplines such as business, medicine, and engineering. Beyond higher education, rankings are a popular part of society. For example, *USA Today* ranks the healthiest cities in which to live, the most beautiful vacation beaches, and the best college towns in the United States. Additionally, some informal rankings of sport management programs, such as those that appeared in the 2007 issue of *ESPN The Magazine,* have already appeared. In short, academic rankings are an inevitable and logical next step in the development of sport management as an academic discipline. Additionally, several aspects of academic rankings will allow for the continued growth of sport management as a respected field of study.

Development of the Field

When considering the use of rankings for sport management programs, first, a couple of questions must be posed. What exactly is a "quality" in these programs, and how should "quality" be measured? The overall discussion of higher education rankings devotes a great deal of time to the topic of quality in academia. For example, the *U.S. News & World Report* rankings rely heavily on the academic achievements of the students that a university recruits (SAT score, class rank, grade point average), alumni giving, library holdings, and endowment levels (Moore, 2004). With respect to sport management, what criteria should be used to determine quality? In answer to this question, some possible quality factors will be offered later in this essay. Perhaps more importantly, the development of a ranking system could be a first step in spurring discussion on the topic of quality and its measurement. All programs should strive for quality, but how can it be defined and measured? The development and implementation of a ranking system, if done properly, would be a significant and positive step forward for the field (Harvey, 2008).

Control over the Ranking System

A ranking developed by faculty in the sport management discipline would be preferable to one developed by those outside the field. Allowing other groups to develop a ranking system presents several dangers; this has recently become very clear to our colleagues in teacher education. In 2011, *U.S. News & World*

Report announced it would partner with the National Council on Teacher Quality (NCTQ) to rate teacher education programs. This resulted in widespread complaints from education deans across the United States who were upset by what they perceived to be poor methodology, and also because NCTQ is an organization that has had an adversarial relationship with education programs for several years (Jaschik, 2011). One conclusion to draw from this situation is that it is better to develop your own rankings than to wait for others to do it, because the results could be damaging to your field.

Benefits for Stakeholders

Another reason for developing a ranking system is that academic rankings can serve as an important signal for a variety of stakeholders in sport management. The potential oversupply of sport management programs and graduates has received a great deal of attention within the field over the past decade. The number of institutions offering sport management at both the undergraduate and graduate levels has risen dramatically over the past 10 to 15 years (see Essay 1). Some question how so many academic programs can properly educate these students and place them in the highly competitive sport industry. The situation is the result of sport management having developed into a "hot" major that easily attracts students. At some institutions, increased enrollment is academicians' response to waning student interest in traditional physical education programs.

While the popularity of sport management as an academic field is a positive for sport management academicians in the short term, it may have several long-term negative ramifications. Currently, it is difficult for students to determine the institutional objective for a sport management program. Does a university have a sport management program because it desires to provide a quality educational experience, or is it offering a program simply to attract students and their tuition dollars? A properly designed and administered ranking system may be another tool for students deciding on which program to attend. It could also be helpful to employers who are deciding on which universities to focus their recruiting efforts.

Perhaps the most important stakeholder group is potential students and their parents (Harvey, 2008). The current trend in the marketing of higher education favors the development of a ranking system. Consumers of sport management education (prospective students and their parents) are demanding accessible and interpretable data on the quality of programs. Sport management programs must develop multiple methods for satisfying this need. Rankings provide a concise, and presumably informed, assessment of colleges and universities and may play a key role in the decision-making process for students (Bowman & Bastedo, 2009). Rankings will allow students to determine which programs are most appropriate for them by providing important information on the quality of a program's faculty, availability of financial aid, the academic profile of its students, and the ability of that program to place its students with internships and jobs in the sport management industry. This is especially true given that more students than ever are seeking programs that may be a considerable distance from their homes.

As sport management's global reach grows, a rankings system may be a key decision-making component for international students who may not have as much access to the quantity and quality of program information that domestic students have. Lastly, a ranking system can also aid high school guidance counselors who advise prospective students on their college choices (Webster, 1992).

Additional stakeholders who may be greatly aided by academic ranking systems are college and university department chairs and administrators. Rankings can provide these groups with impartial data on the quality of their programs, thus allowing them to make well-informed decisions on issues such as resource distribution (Bowman & Bastedo, 2009; Urbancic, 2008; Webster, 2001) and the performance of faculty (Webster, 1992). In other words, administrators are more likely to invest in sport management programs if they believe the investments will impact rankings, and thereby enhance the reputation of the department, school, college, and/or university. Programs and departments at a given institution are in a continual battle for scarce resources. These resources can be finances, space, equipment, faculty lines, and graduate assistantships, just to name a few. A program's ranking could be leveraged to accumulate internal resources that can, in turn, be used to make further programmatic upgrades.

Yet other stakeholder groups that may be positively influenced by a sport management ranking system include external philanthropic groups and grant providers. It can be difficult for these groups to determine which universities they should consider funding and which universities can provide the research support they need. Rankings would serve as their tool for determining the top programs on a variety of criteria, including which programs produce quality research.

Competition Within the Discipline

A ranking system also has the potential to stimulate competition within the discipline. Some are critical of viewing sport management programs from a competitive standpoint, but others would appreciate rankings' potential to differentiate the strong programs from the weak. Over time, the weaker programs may take steps to improve their quality, or possibly face elimination. For example, most ranking systems rely in part on the academic profile of students. If a program's ranking can be improved by attracting better students, as measured by high school GPA or SAT/ACT scores, all programs would be expected to place greater emphasis on recruiting and attracting better students. Competition for the best students should raise the median profile of the sport management major. In turn, students may have more successful professional careers, which will ultimately increase the reputation of sport management as an academic discipline.

Marketing and Publicity

Lastly, a worldwide or national sport management academic ranking system could serve an important marketing and publicity role for the field. Annual academic rankings in publications such as *U.S. News & World Report* and *Barron's* are read by millions of people. These are some of the best-selling issues of the publications (Kersten, 2000). The top universities, in turn, continually cite these rankings when promoting themselves. The same could be true for a future sport management ranking system. For example, if a sports publication such as *Sports Illustrated,*

ESPN The Magazine, or *Street & Smith's SportsBusiness Journal* published a thorough and unbiased edition dedicated to ranking all sport management programs, it could be very popular. This popularity would help market not only individual programs, but also the overall academic discipline. Programs could advertise their ranking on websites, promotional brochures and materials, and media outlets.

DISADVANTAGES OF PROGRAM RANKINGS IN SPORT MANAGEMENT

The benefits of ranking academic programs must be balanced against the limitations, flaws, and inherent dangers associated with program rankings. Thus, a sport management program ranking requires stakeholders to exercise great caution.

Challenge to Existing Systems for Program Comparisons

Ranking academic programs poses limitations even greater than those associated with ranking universities and colleges. Many benefits to student consumers associated with university and college rankings simply do not trickle down to the program level. Rankings provide consumers with useful information that helps them differentiate among seemingly similar types of institutions. This benefit makes sense when consumers are literally faced with hundreds or even thousands of choices. For example, in selecting a business school or college of engineering, a consumer faced with more than a thousand potential choices can be greatly aided by sorting them according to an independent ranking. However, sport management is still a relatively small discipline with fewer than half as many programs as there are for business. Student consumers already have access to information through the NASSM degree program listing, the NASSM/NASPE program approval list, and the new and expanding COSMA list of accredited programs. In fact, these resources may be more useful than rankings to consumers for distinguishing among programs.

Historically, the NASSM/NASPE sport management program approval process allowed consumers to evaluate program differences and refine their selection process. Student consumers could quickly identify sport management programs within their geographic region of interest and the degrees they offered (bachelor's, master's, or doctorate) and link directly to the program's website for more information. This process does not offer specific selection criteria to the student consumer, but it does enable him or her to identify differences among programs fairly quickly and easily. In addition, this information is free from the type of advertising and sponsorship common in the *U.S. News & World Report* online directory. Such advertisements and sponsorships may only serve to confuse consumers rather than to inform their selection process.

The newly established accreditation process should provide an even greater benefit than a program ranking system to prospective students and administrators because it incorporates student learning outcomes and ongoing assessment (see Essay 3). This information is arguably more useful to prospective students and administrators than a potentially misleading ordinal ranking. IHEP (2009) observed that rankings may be beneficial where other, formal quality control measures are lacking. However, in an area such as sport management where a formal accreditation system is in place, but in its early stages, rankings could serve to undermine that process and do more harm than good. Instead, the sport management discipline may be better served by creating incentives for programs to go through the COSMA accreditation process. This could be accomplished by working with industry media outlets, in addition to NASSM, to publish lists of approved and/or accredited programs rather than rankings of programs. Most administrators would expect an academic program to obtain and maintain positive accreditation status; thus, accreditation could become the standard. After the sport management discipline fully embraces accreditation, ranking programs may be the logical next step. However, ranking programs prematurely could undermine the accreditation process.

Flaws in Methodology and Rationale

As discussed previously, ranking critics note the many flaws in ranking methodology and rationale. These flaws may not be overcome in a sport management ranking process. In fact, the infancy of the sport management field combined with its interdisciplinary nature may make these flaws more difficult to surmount than flaws in other, more established programs. For example, one study examining the ranking of business schools on the management of technology found that virtually all rankings are based on research productivity in peer-reviewed journals (Linton, 2004). In traditional fields of study this is not a problem because there is relative agreement regarding the quality and impact of the journals in the field. Although the field of sport management has already produced a number of unique scholarly journals, there is no widely accepted agreement on the quality of these journals in comparison to one another and certainly not in comparison to the journals of the parent discipline. For example, *Sport Marketing Quarterly* may be perceived as the highest quality scholarly journal in sport marketing, but it would not necessarily be perceived as the highest quality journal in the field of sport management nor in the field of marketing, the parent discipline. Thus, it would be difficult to control for these varied perceptions in order to accurately assess the relative research productivity of faculty.

Over-Reliance of Policy Makers and Stakeholders

Additionally, rankings are inherently dangerous due to the inclination of policy makers and stakeholders to rely on them too much in making resource allocation decisions and internal assessment plans (Sponsler, 2009). Rankings can perpetuate an arms race within institutions as programs compete for resources. This may create more vulnerability among sport management programs than opportunity. We have seen many examples of a university president setting extreme and probably unrealistic goals to become a Top 25 Public Research University and then directing resources toward that goal, only to succumb to a poor economy and faculty dissatisfaction with shrinking or nonexistent raises and resources (McMurray, 2010). This propensity of administrators to target an arbitrary ranking as a strategic goal and then to base resource allocation solely on that goal should be carefully considered in any move toward sport management program rankings. Ultimately, sport management programs that are not ranked in the top 10, or that fail to meet some other desired target, could be forced to shift their focus and resources toward improving their ranking rather than improving their program.

Also, institutions may tend to shift resources from teaching to research. A common strength of sport management programs in seeking institutional support is the size of our programs in terms of credit hour production and number of majors. Programs with large student enrollments require significant resources for teaching. As noted previously, rankings of doctoral programs and business programs are highly correlated with faculty research productivity (Fogg, 2007; Siemens et al., 2005). Thus, if the rationale for establishing rankings is based on the goal of influencing allocation decisions, its success will be dependent upon developing a system that does not overemphasize research in order to achieve higher rankings.

In addition, even if rankings enabled sport management programs to become more entrepreneurial in pursuing outside contracts with sport organizations, as has been proposed by some (see Essay 9), this would only be beneficial if the industry partners truly understood the ranking criteria. Furthermore, the ranking criteria would need to include precise measures of research expertise and competence. Because the ranking criteria would likely only rank faculty productivity in terms of number of publications per faculty person or number of publications in selected journals, this measure may be of little use to an industry partner in identifying potential research partnerships. Thus again, if an industry partner used the ranking as a substitute for investigating the actual expertise and ability of the faculty and sport management program to conduct the desired research, the ranking could be misleading.

While sport management program rankings may help stimulate recognition of sport management both within our discipline and among students and external stakeholders, the limitations associated with program rankings suggest this endeavor should be pursued cautiously.

ELEMENTS FOR A PROPOSED RANKING SYSTEM IN SPORT MANAGEMENT

Some ranking of programs may be inevitable as sport management continues to grow in popularity. So, while we are not convinced that rankings in sport management are a good idea at this point, we do believe we should proactively discuss ranking systems in order to be prepared if they appear necessary. Thus, our primary question is: How can we develop a sport management ranking system that limits potential flaws? We have the following suggestions:

1. A good ranking system should be multidimensional (Webster, 1986). A system that ranks programs based on one criterion is problematic because it is unlikely to capture all of the important aspects of a program. In addition, it is likely that users of the ranking system will not all be focused on the same criterion (Ehrenberg, 2003; 2005). While it may be impossible to identify every variable that would be important to users (Ehrenberg, 2003; 2005), a system that includes multiple criteria is likely to be more valid and more useful.

2. Because the users of the ranking system may be more or less interested in specific criterion (Rehmeyer, 2008), the system should allow users to examine categorical rankings (i.e., they could see rankings of programs on each criterion). This would allow programs that may not be at the top or in the top 25 overall to focus on being at or near the top for a specific criterion.

3. The system should allow users to develop their own ranking by adjusting the relative weight given to each criterion. Not all of the criteria will be important to all users, and the importance of each may vary. For example, one user may be primarily concerned with faculty research productivity, while another may place more value on peer assessments. The users could decide for themselves the weight for these factors (e.g., 40%, 60%, 75%) and develop a customized ranking that takes into account what is important to them. This would be easy to do if the ranking is set up on an interactive website.

4. The ranking system should be different for different degree levels. Some of the criteria may be the same, but different factors are clearly more important at the doctoral level than at the bachelor level. Research productivity, for example, would be more important in the former than the latter.

5. Per capita numbers should be used as opposed to aggregate numbers whenever possible (Webster, 1986). For example, measures of faculty research productivity would better assess quality if the focus were on publications per faculty member as opposed to total number of publications. The latter would provide too much of an advantage to larger programs, which could have a large aggregate number but a relatively small average per faculty member.

6. The data provided for putting together the rankings should be obtained from the most accurate source. For example, much of the program data at universities should be obtained from offices of institutional research, as opposed to faculty in sport management programs.

7. Unbiased individuals should collect and analyze the data and develop the ranking system. The ranking system could be devised by retired sport management faculty or others with knowledge of the area, but who have little vested interest in the outcome of the rankings. The data could be collected and analyzed by individuals with expertise in research and evaluation and who are not associated with a sport management program.

8. Those developing the criteria should consider the unintended consequences of rankings. For example, an emphasis on SAT, ACT, or GRE scores often discourages minority students, who tend to do worse on these exams. So, if test scores are one of the criteria used, another criterion should be one that encourages minority recruitment (e.g., part of the ranking may be percentage of students who are minorities).

9. Some have questioned the use of subjective criteria (Clarke, 2002; Standifird, 2005), but it is difficult to ignore that we are still a relatively small field and know a lot about each other and our programs. In addition, we know that attempts in sport that ignore opinions do not lead to better rankings (e.g.,

computer rankings in college sports). Therefore, we must accept that a mix of subjective and objective data is likely to result in a better ranking system.

10. The first attempt at ranking programs will likely have some difficulties. A pilot program in the first year may work out some of these problems. A good pilot program could enhance reliability and validity of later revisions.

11. The ranking system should be voluntary. As discussed earlier, there are a number of good reasons against ranking programs, so those programs that do not wish to be included should be able to opt out.

Exhibit 4.1 offers some preliminary criteria that could be used in a ranking of sport management programs.

EXHIBIT 4.1

Possible criteria for ranking sport management programs.

Peer assessment. Sport management is a small field. Faculty know a lot about each other and can provide input that other criteria may miss. In order to make this input easier for the reviewers to assess accurately, programs may want to list their full-time faculty along with a few sentences about their program highlights.

Sport management faculty/student ratio. This provides a measure of the resources available to meet students' needs. This can be provided overall (e.g., full-time faculty per total students) and at certain levels (e.g., tenure-track faculty per doctoral student). As this criterion is developed, we should make sure it is aligned well with the new sport management program accreditation criteria. In addition, we will need to make decisions about the importance of tenure track positions compared to other full-time positions, terminal degree faculty versus full-time faculty without a terminal degree, etc. Because the rankings will likely impact resource allocations, these are critical decisions.

Research productivity. There are a number of ways to calculate research productivity, including citations, refereed journal articles per faculty member, publications in top-tier journals, and percentage of faculty who are research fellows. It may include one of these criteria or several criteria. Much of this information is now available online.

Incoming student data. This would include test scores and undergraduate GPA (graduate students only). These are commonly used measures based on the theory that the best programs attract the best students. Similar measures could also be used at the undergraduate level, but programs do not have much control over the admissions process and criteria at their universities so this may not be a fair criteria.

Program diversity. This will likely include the percentage of students who are minorities (African, Latino, Asian, and Native American—ALANA). Including this criterion will help offset potential biases in the test scores. This factor is also likely to be important to many users of the rankings. It might also be advantageous to include the percentage of international students.

Acceptance rates (graduate programs only). This is another measure of the reputation and appeal of the program.

Percentage of alumni finding jobs in the field. This criterion is perhaps the most important to many students and their parents. Unfortunately, it may prove to be the most difficult to obtain. Those developing the system will need to create surveys and work with programs to develop a distribution list.

Alumni and/or student satisfaction. This factor is also likely to be important to future students, but difficult to obtain. However, if we can survey graduates about their jobs, we can also gather information about their satisfaction with the program. Likewise, we can obtain lists of current students and survey them.

CONCLUDING THOUGHTS

We admittedly have reservations about ranking sport management programs, but we believe the topic deserves to be explored more thoroughly. Having discussed the background and approaches to rankings and its advantages and disadvantages, we have offered suggestions for how a good ranking system could be developed. We hope this provides a starting point for the conversation and an outline of factors that may prove useful in developing a ranking system.

REFERENCES

Basken, P. (2010, September 30). New rankings formula elevates Physics program U. of Hawaii. *The Chronicle of Higher Education.* Retrieved October 1, 2010 from http://chronicle.com/article/New-Rankings-Formula-Elevates/124764/?sid=at&utm_source=at&utm_medium=en

Bowman, N. A., & Bastedo, M. N. (2009). Getting on the front page: Organizational reputation, status signals, and the impact of *US News and World Report* on student decisions. *Research in Higher Education, 50,* 415–436.

Clarke, M. (2002). Some guidelines for academic quality rankings. *Higher Education in Europe, 27,* 443–459.

Clarke, M. (2004). Weighing things up: A closer look at the *U.S. News and World Report*'s ranking formulas. *College and University Journal, 79*(3), 3–9.

COSMA. (2010). *About COSMA.* Retrieved May 25, 2010 from http://www.cosmaweb.org/about.

Cremonini, L., Westerheijden, D., & Enders, J. (2008). Disseminating the right information to the right audience: Cultural determinants in the use (and misuse) of rankings. *Higher Education, 55,* 373–385.

Ehrenberg, R. (2003). Reaching for the brass ring: The *U.S. News & World Report* rankings and competition. *Review of Higher Education, 26,* 145–162.

Ehrenberg, R. (2005, September). Method or madness? Inside the *USNWR* college rankings. CHERI Working Paper 39. Retrieved July 21, 2011 from http://www.ilr.cornell.edu/cheri.

Fogg, P. (2007, January 12). A new standard for measuring doctoral programs. *Chronicle of Higher Education,* A8–A13.

Harvey, L. (2008). Rankings of higher education institutions: A critical review. *Quality in Higher Education, 14,* 187–207.

Institute for Higher Education Policy. (2009, May). Issue brief: Impact of college rankings on institutional decision making: Four country case studies. Washington, D.C: Institute for Higher Education Policy. Retrieved on September 29, 2010 from http://www.ihep.org/Publications/publications-detail.cfm?id=126.

Ioannidis, J. P. A., Patsopoulos, N. A., Kavvoura, F. K., Tatsioni, A., Evangelou, E., Kouri, I., Contopoulos-Ioannidis, D. G., & Liberopoulos, G. (2007). International ranking systems for universities and institutions: A critical appraisal. *BMC Medicine, 5,* article 30.

Jaschik, S. (2011, February 8). Anger over new rankings. *Inside Higher Ed.* Retrieved February 17, 2011 from http://www.insidehighered.com/news/2011/02/08/education_deans_object_to_us_news_methodology_for_new_rankings.

Kersten, G. (2000, January). Grading on the curve: College ratings and rankings. *Points of Reference,* pp. 2–4.

Linton, J. D. (2004). Ranking business schools on the management of technology. *Journal of Product Innovation Management, 21,* 416–430.

Machung, A. (1998). Playing the rankings game. *Change, 30,* 12–16.

McDonough, P. M., Antonio, A. L., Walpole, M., & Perez, L. X. (1998). College rankings: Democraticized college knowledge for whom? *Research in Higher Education, 39,* 513–537.

McMurray, J. (2010, September 20). Universities rethink goals amid recession. *Kypost.com.* Retrieved October 12, 2010 from http://www.kypost.com/dpp/news/state/UniversitiesEconomy_78303001.

Meredith, M. (2004). Why do universities compete in the rankings game? An empirical analysis of the effects of the *U.S. News & World Report* college rankings. *Research in Higher Education, 45,* 443–461.

Monks, J., & Ehrenberg, R. G. (1999). The impact of the *U.S. News & World Report* college rankings on admissions outcomes and pricing decisions at selective private institutions. *NBER Working Paper No. W7227.*

Moore, R. (2004). Do colleges identify or develop intelligence? *Journal of Developmental Education, 28,* 28–34.

Rehmeyer, J. (2008, October 3). Rating the rankings. *Science News.*

Siemens, J. C., Burton, S., Jensen, T., & Mendoza, N. A. (2005). An examination of the relationship between research productivity in prestigious business journals and popular press business school rankings. *Journal of Business Research, 58,* 467–476.

Sponsler, B. A. (2009, September). Issue brief: The role and relevance of rankings in higher education policymaking. Washington, D.C: Institute for Higher Education Policy. Retrieved on September 29, 2010 from http://www.ihep.org/publications/publications-detail.cfm?id=130

Standifird, S. S. (2005). Reputation among peer academic institutions: An investigation of the *U.S. News & World Report*'s rankings. *Corporate Reputation Review, 8,* 233–244.

Tsakalis, K. S., & Palais, J. C. (2004). Improving a school's *U.S. News & World Report* ranking. *Journal of Engineering Education, 93,* 259–263.

20th Annual University Rankings. (2010, November 10). *Macleans.com.* Retrieved February 17, 2011 from http://www2.macleans.ca/2010/11/10/macleans-20th-annual-university-rankings/.

Urbancic, R. (2008). A multiattributes approach for PhD programs. *Journal of Education for Business, 83,* 339–346.

Webster, D. S. (1986). *Academic quality rankings of American colleges and universities.* Springfield, IL: Charles C. Thomas.

Webster, D. S. (1992). Academic rankings: First on a list of one. *Academe, 78*(5), 19–22.

Webster, T. (2001). A principal component analysis of the *U.S. News & World Report* tier rankings of colleges and universities. *Economics of Education Review, 20,* 235–244.

Is Sport Management a Unique Discipline?

HOW THIS QUESTION CAN INFORM OUR PEDAGOGY

essay

5

"The process for success in development of sport management curricula is one of dynamic change."

BETTY VAN DER SMISSEN (1984, P. 16)

A coauthor introduces the essay

Dianna P. Gray UNIVERSITY OF NORTHERN COLORADO

Dianna Gray is a professor who has expertise in sport marketing and consumer behavior and the scholarship of teaching and learning. She is the Founder and Director of the Sport Marketing Research Institute (SMRI) at the University of Northern Colorado. Gray received her Ph.D. from The Ohio State University and has worked in interscholastic, collegiate, and private-sector sport.

Linda A. Sharp UNIVERSITY OF NORTHERN COLORADO

Linda Sharp received her J.D. from Cleveland Marshall College of Law and practiced corporate law for seven years. She is in her second decade at the University of Northern Colorado as a faculty member in the Sport Administration graduate program. Sharp is a recognized scholar in legal issues pertaining to K–12 and higher education athletic programs, club sport, recreational activities, and physical education. She is co-author of the textbook *Sport Law: A Managerial Approach*.

Introduction

As the world changes, so does the classroom. Teachers in the twenty-first century work in classrooms quite unlike those that they entered as students; therefore, they must

57

regularly update their skills to meet the challenges of a changing educational system and a more diverse student population. So too is the management and sport business changing; sport managers today must be capable of dealing with the myriad challenges of a dynamic global marketplace and increased competition. Future sport managers must be prepared to succeed in a rapidly changing world, armed with a toolbox of knowledge and skills, fully aware of the complex and dynamic relationship between sport, business, and management. Delivering quality sport management education, therefore, is an important step in developing high-quality, well-prepared sport managers.

Certainly one of the hallmarks of a respected discipline is the rigor of its research and its accumulated body of knowledge. Another hallmark, albeit one less widely hailed, is the quality of the professors who teach in sport management programs and contribute to the pedagogical literature. In this essay we offer a review of the current status of sport management pedagogy. We address the historical debate on whether sport management is a unique discipline within the academy and the resulting implications for its pedagogy. Best practices in sport management pedagogy are presented, and we conclude with commentary on future direction of scholarship, teaching, and learning in the discipline.

SPORT MANAGEMENT AS A UNIQUE DISCIPLINE

As discussed in Essay 1, sport management academic programs are a relatively recent development. The birth of any new academic discipline raises questions that will help shape its curricular development and the research agenda for years to come. What does our discipline entail? Is it a unique discipline? The answers to these questions guide the curricular content deemed appropriate for students in sport management. They also set the framework for the research agendas of the discipline's scholars. We continue to struggle with the issues raised above, which is simply indicative of the evolution of this young discipline.

To appreciate the argument of the discipline's "uniqueness," one must understand the evolution of the sport management academic program. In 1984, van der Smissen, a recognized scholar in a number of disciplines related to sport, recreation, and physical activity, wrote a book chapter entitled "Sport management curricula—An idea whose time has come!" (van der Smissen, 1984). This chapter was visionary in that van der Smissen cogently argued that sport management curricula should be separate from and different than traditional curricula for physical education and recreation programs. Although the pragmatic genesis of the sport management program may have been due in part to declining enrollment in physical education and recreation programs, van der Smissen understood that sport management was a different type of program and should "be responsive not only to a changing society but also to changing institutions of higher education" (p. 7). After discussing the impact of societal trends analyzed in the then-current bestseller *Megatrends* by John Naisbitt (1982), van der Smissen urged university departments to make sport management a separate program "in terms of a core of required courses selected in accord with the competencies needed by persons going into Sport Management positions" (p. 11). Furthermore, those who attained a degree in sport management should be considered to be qualified for "a career in itself" (p. 10) and not simply rely on it as an alternative for the lack of jobs in physical education teaching or public recreation.

In further discussion, van der Smissen (1984) noted that in order to prepare students for a career in sport management, the curriculum must comprise three areas: (1) a professional core; (2) general education; and (3) practica and internships. Curricular development needs to be an ongoing process, adapting to the needs of the market and society. "The process for success in development of sport management curricula is one of dynamic change" (p. 16).

Another vital contribution to the early literature concerning the uniqueness of sport management as a discipline was a 1987 article by Zeigler entitled "Sport management: Past, present, future." Zeigler has made innumerable scholarly contributions to the discipline of sport management; in recognition, the most highly regarded award given by NASSM is named for him.

Zeigler noted that three precipitating factors led to his analysis of sport management: (1) the establishment of NASSM in 1985–86; (2) criticisms of the management practices engaged in by professional and educational sport organizations; and (3) the increasing complexity of management theory and practice. After reviewing the history of sport management, he also observed that there was a lack of awareness by those who taught in sport management programs concerning the theoretic literature in management. "One can only speculate about the intellectual level of these programs when the professors and instructors have typically been such reluctant, unproductive scholars themselves" (p. 10). His charge to professionals was that research developed and disseminated in the field of sport management must "increasingly strive for a theoretical basis" (p. 11).

Zeigler's plan for the future of professional preparation involved a competency-based approach to management development, which is a requirement in all professional preparation programs. He argued that if sport management programs were to develop sport managers who were effective in a changing environment, then the development of management competencies based on sound management theory was a necessity.

Both van der Smissen (1984) and Zeigler (1987) made strong arguments for the development of curricula based on the competencies needed by sport managers operating in a complex and ever-changing landscape. Zeigler (1987) asserted that sport managers need a strong grounding in current managerial theory, and van der Smissen (1984) argued for distinct curricular requirements based on the needed competencies of the sport manager.

A decade later, Slack (1998) wrote a thought-provoking article entitled, "Is there anything unique about sport management?" Slack, who was known as an intellectual provocateur, essentially argued that "there is really nothing unique about the body of knowledge within the field of sport management that could not be delivered equally well or better by any reasonable business school whose staff members are conversant with the sports pages of any major newspaper" (p. 22). He explained this self-proclaimed "heretical claim" (p. 22) as follows.

The two essential components of sport management as set forth by Parkhouse (1996) are, of course, *sport* and *management*. Slack commented that this combination of terms "suggest[s] that those of us who research and teach in this area are responsible for generating knowledge about the wide array of organizations that exist in the sport industry and for training the managers who operate these organizations" (p. 22). However, in his view we, as sport management academicians, failed on both counts.

In regard to research, Slack asserted that our scholarship was too narrow in focusing largely on educational sport and professional sport. Scholarship also was confined to organizational behavior issues and ignored the subdisciplinary issues that are a part of management. "We are then as sport management researchers restricting ourselves to a narrow range of organizations and an equally narrow range of management topics" (p. 24). Based on this observation, he concluded that sport management did not have a unique body of knowledge because sport settings are not unique and we have not generated any innovative approaches to management theory. To those who posited that this state of affairs was simply indicative of an emerging field of study, he pointed out that the field of organizational strategy had made many more substantial contributions to its body of knowledge in a shorter period of time than had sport management. The sport management curriculum literature, he suggested, appeared to have a "bolt on" flavor. The essential curricular requirements referenced as necessary competencies for managers in the sport industry were akin to those found in a business school with nothing really unique to set sport managers apart.

Slack concluded with a challenge to those of us in sport management: "In that we are unable to lay claim to unique knowledge I believe that those of us in the field we call sport management are vulnerable" (p. 27). We are vulnerable, he stated, to being "colonized" by business schools that could offer "a more rigorous and publicly acceptable product than we currently do" (p. 27). In order to overcome this threat he urged us to become more "reflexive and self critical" about what we do and to contribute to theory development by using sport organizations as a test of existing theory and "as a site to extend current theory" (p. 27). Finally, Slack urged sport management academicians to expand the type of organizations that we study and to expand the subdisciplinary areas of our work with the purpose of forging stronger links with sport industry practitioners.

This call to arms was an interesting commentary from Slack, who at the time was the editor of the *Journal of Sport Management,* the discipline's leading journal. Although he acknowledged the "heretical" nature of this article, it was a catalyst for other sport management scholars to reflect upon and discuss the essential question of our "uniqueness." This issue continues to inform the scholarship and critique of our discipline.

Scholars continued to engage in debates and discussions regarding our identity. Costa (2005) added to the literature with "The status and future of sport management: A Delphi study." She queried experts on a number of issues concerning the status and future of the field and used the Delphi technique to analyze differences in perception relating to these issues. Regardless of the specific point of inquiry, the experts had "markedly different perspectives about the field's assumptions and beliefs" (p. 127). These differences were apparent in comments pertaining to the field's uniqueness. "The majority of comments hinged on derivatives of the field's definition and identity; who we are, what is unique, what differentiates us from other fields of study, and what, specifically, is sport management theory?" (p. 127). The essential dichotomy was apparent in how some panelists felt that sport management existed only to apply existing theory to sport, and how others believed that sport management does build unique theory.

The uniqueness argument is integral to our discipline. Divergent views on this point lead to discussions about where our programs should be housed (see Essay 2), what our curricula should contain, what our research agendas should include in terms of methodology, the relative value of basic versus applied research, and at its core, "a concern about whom the field should serve, and what it should seek to achieve" (Costa, p. 133). This essential question also informs the decisions we make about the "diversity of topics" our field should address. "These insights, and the debates from which they derive, have significant implications for the training of researchers for the field" (p. 133). The identity issues that continue to beset us need to be considered when training future researchers who must understand more than research methods and analytic techniques.

Chalip (2006) contributed to the discourse in the *Journal of Sport Management* article, "Toward a distinctive sport management discipline." He acknowledged the "substantial malaise among sport management scholars about the field's status, direction, and future" (p. 1), and put this frustration into perspective by noting that our experience is typical of young disciplines. According to Chalip, our malaise is simply reflective of the maturation process.

Chalip also referred to the work of Costa discussed above and noted that the debate about sport management and its future is healthy insofar as it "nurtures the field's growth and development" (p. 2). He asserted that it was his desire to respond to Costa's challenge to "consider the pathways by which sport management can mature as a distinctive discipline—pathways that will enable our field to assert unabashedly its significance as an academic endeavor and its relevance to the practitioner's world" (pp. 2–3).

In order to carve out our distinctiveness as a discipline, we need to engage in two complementary models of sport management research: the derivative model to ascertain the degree to which mainstream theories are applicable to sport phenomena and the sport-focused model to "search for theory that is grounded in sport phenomena" (Chalip, p. 3).

The quest for our uniqueness as a discipline is an ongoing one that will engender debate for the foreseeable future. Chalip believed that this debate is healthy and necessary for a young discipline and not a cause for concern. Although Slack took a "heretical" position, it was only to serve as a catalyst for further discussion. As Costa pointed out, the debate about who we are and what contributions our field can make will continue to have significant implications for our research agendas and in our preparation of future sport management scholars and for practitioners in the sport industry.

HOW THE QUESTION OF UNIQUENESS INFORMS PEDAGOGY

The question of uniqueness in the sport management discipline needs to inform our pedagogy as well as our research agendas. In a 1991 perspectives contribution in the *Journal of Sport Management,* Slack noted that sport management graduates need to appreciate more than the technical skills of management and "understand sport as a social product that is intimately tied to other social organizations and to larger social processes" (p. 95). For undergraduates, therefore, he suggested that students need instruction in four content areas: (1) a strong knowledge base in management; (2) a comprehensive understanding of the nature of sport; (3) electives from other social science areas such as history, sociology, political science, and philosophy; and (4) a well-supervised practicum program. Slack also suggested that it would be wise to improve our links as sport academicians with other academic areas and, if possible, to obtain teaching experience in a business school to re-examine some of the central work in a particular area of management.

Frisby (2005) argued that "if we are to fully understand all dimensions of sport management, we need research to be conducted from multiple paradigms" (p. 2). She also stated that we need to use a critical lens to inform our research and called management a "messy, ambiguous, political, and fragmented" activity (p. 5). How can we do justice to teaching our students about the inherent "messiness" of management if all we do is address the traditional functions of the manager in terms of planning, organizing, coordinating, and controlling?

Frisby also noted the impossibility of having our students become strong critical thinkers if sport management professors are not well-versed in critical social science theories. If we are to integrate critical social science into our pedagogy, we need to use the tools of insight and critique in our teaching. She concluded that "embracing critical social science and exposing students, future researchers and managers to it opens up a new world that, up to this point, has been inadequately explored" (p. 9).

BEST PRACTICES IN SPORT MANAGEMENT PEDAGOGY

While many in our field have called for greater attention and rigor in regard to research, others have also called for a focus on teaching and learning (Cuneen, 2004; Frisby, 2005; Mahony, Mondello, Hums, & Judd, 2004). Many institutions of higher education emphasize teaching as their primary focus, and all espouse that teaching is important. Although the pedagogical literature abounds with studies on the relationship of teaching to research, there is still little clarity on the universal priority of research over teaching (Allen, 1996; Feldmann, 1987; Hattie & Marsh, 1996). Boyer, in *Scholarship Reconsidered* (1990) stimulated discussion throughout higher education about the nature of scholarship, particularly in regard to teaching, and suggested that teachers who devise and assess better ways to help students learn, or who research methods of teaching are indeed, scholars. We owe a debt of gratitude to Boyer. As a result of the ensuing debate over his ideas, there has been an increasing acceptance that good teaching involves much scholarly activity.

Teaching sport management is a challenging endeavor, and fortunately the body of literature specific to sport management pedagogy is growing. The sport management curriculum has matured over the last twenty years with the initiation of program approval by the Sport Management Program Review Council (SMPRC), which was sponsored jointly by NASPE/NASSM and, more recently, with accreditation (COSMA, 2010) initiatives providing benchmarks for the structure and content of academic degree programs. A review of the NASSM conference abstract archive (2007–2010) in the program area of teaching reveals that 60 papers have been presented covering topics ranging from experiential learning, case studies, and technology in the classroom, to civic engagement and the sociological imagination's relevance to sport management (NASSM, 2007–2010). The literature only recently reflects the need to evolve from *what* we teach (or include in our curriculum) to *how* we teach.

The sport management teaching and learning literature has evolved since the late 1980s and the establishment of a formal academic journal in sport management. Early works, as evidenced by a review of the *Journal of Sport Management* (which debuted in 1987), reveal an emphasis on the development of curricular models, or the assessment of sport management curricula, and content-driven competency-based approaches to sport management (see Exhibit 5.1). The studies were largely descriptive; they helped to define sport management programs and laid the groundwork for program approval by the SMPRC and COSMA two decades later. Subsequent work has focused more on critical pedagogy, the preparation of doctoral students, and teaching excellence (see Exhibit 5.2). However, it was not until the 2007 introduction of the *Sport Management Education Journal* (SMEJ), a joint publication of NASSM and NASPE, that a greater emphasis on teaching and learning research was realized. Also in 2007, *Sport Management Review,* the journal of the Sport Management Association of Australia and New Zealand (SMAANZ), published a special issue on sport management education and teaching and learning for the future.

Textbooks and Pedagogy Books

According to Pitts and Danylchuk (2007), a primary source of information for students and teachers alike is textbooks. The textbook is arguably the most commonly used tool and greatly influences how content is delivered. At the time of the article's publication, a total of 129 books published from 1990 through 2006 had been analyzed, and the authors identified 14 categories, with management, marketing, law, finance, and event management representing the largest categories (pp. 43–44). They identified no texts with content focused on teaching and learning or sport management pedagogy (Pitts & Danylchuk, 2007). It was not until 2010 that the first books dedicated to the teaching and learning of sport management were published: *Teaching Sport Management* (Gentile, 2010) and *Experiential Learning in Sport Management*

EXHIBIT 5.1

Early teaching and learning literature published in the *Journal of Sport Management*, 1987–1995.			
Article Title	**Author(s)**	**Publication Info**	**Pedagogy Type**
Competency-based Approaches to Sport Management	Jamieson, L.	1987, 1(1), 48–56	Competency-based education
Sport Management Curricula: Current Status and Design Implications for Future Development	Parkhouse, B.	1987, 1(2), 93–115	Curriculum
Guidelines for Programs Preparing Undergraduate and Graduate Students for Careers in Sport Management	Brassie, P.	1989, 3(2), 158–164	Curriculum
Sport Management Curricular Evaluation and Needs Assessment: A Multifaceted Approach	DeSensi, J., Kelley, D., Blanton, M., & Beitel, M.	1990, 4(1), 31–58	Curriculum
Defining Quality: Should Educators in Sport Management Programs Be Concerned About Accreditation?	Fielding, L., Pitts, B., & Miller, L.	1991, 5(1), 1–17	Accreditation; Educational quality
A Study of Curricular Preparation Needs for Sport Club Managers	Lambrecht, K.	1991, 5(1), 47–57	Curriculum
Graduate-Level Professional Preparation for Athletic Directors	Cuneen, J.	1992, 6 (1), 15–26	Curriculum
Standards for Curriculum and Voluntary Accreditation of Sport Management Education Programs	NASPE—NASSM Joint Task Force	1993, 7(2), 159–170	Curriculum
Some Insights on Meaningful Internships in Sport Management: A Cooperative Education Approach	Chouinard, N.	1993, 7(2), 95–100	Cooperative education/internships
Undergraduate and Graduate Sport Management Curricular Models: A Perspective	Kelley, D., Beitel, M., DeSensi, J., & Blanton, M.	1994, 8(2), 93–101	Curriculum
Toward a Critical Pedagogy in Ethical Decision Making in Sport Administration: A Theoretical Inquiry into Substance and Form	Malloy, D., & Zakus, D.	1995, 9(1), 36–58	Critical pedagogy

EXHIBIT 5.2

Later teaching and learning literature published in the *Journal of Sport Management*, 1996–2009.			
Article Title	**Author(s)**	**Publication Info**	**Pedagogy Type**
Content Analysis of the Introductory Course in Sport Management	Li, M., & Cotten, D.	1996, 10(1), 87–96	Course content
Enhancing Sport Management Education with International Dimensions Including Language and Cultural Training.	Masteralexis, L., & McDonald, M.	1997, 11(1), 97–110	Competency-based education
Managing Program Excellence During Our Transition from Potential to Merit	Cuneen, J.	2004, 18(1), 1–12	Zeigler Lecture: Teaching excellence
Are Sport Management Doctoral Programs Meeting the Needs of the Faculty Job Market? Observations for Today and the Future	Mahony, D., Mondello, M., Hums, M., & Judd, M.	2004, 18(2), 91–110	Preparation of doctoral students
The Good, the Bad, and the Ugly: Critical Sport Management Research	Frisby, W.	2005, 19(1), 1–12	Zeigler Lecture: Critical social science paradigm in teaching
The Status and Future of Sport Management: A Delphi Study	Costa, C.	2005, 19(2), 117–142	Preparation of doctoral students
Can Gender Equity Be More Equitable?: Promoting an Alternative Frame for Sport Management Research, Education, and Practice	Shaw, S., & Frisby, W.	2006, 20(4), 483–509	Implications of gender equity conceptual framework for teaching, research and practice
The Conscience and Commerce of Sport Management: One Teacher's Perspective	Hums, M.	2009, 24(1), 1–9	Good citizens; sport management educators; curriculum

(Foster & Dollar, 2010). In *Teaching Sport Management,* Gentile provides techniques and tips, along with activities and ideas, to incorporate technology in traditional, online, and hybrid courses. Foster and Dollar (2010) focus on experiential learning, including classroom assignments, volunteering, practica, and internships. The authors present a five-step learning model (p. 13) that emphasizes the importance of gaining experience in the sport industry prior to applying for a full-time position.

Experiential Learning

While the value of internships will be discussed at greater length in Essay 13, there is considerable support in the sport management literature regarding the development and benefits of formal experiential learning practices (Cuneen & Sidwell, 2003; Cunningham & Sagas, 2004; Jowdy, McDonald, & Spence, 2004; Pauline & Pauline, 2008; Southall, Nagel, LeGrande, & Han, 2003; Spence, Hess, McDonald, & Sheehan, 2009; Young & Baker, 2004). Kolb (1984) describes experiential learning as "knowledge created from the combination of grasping experience and transforming it" (p. 41), and Jowdy et al. (2004) state that effective experiential models should stimulate students' "vertical development" and help them make the leap from textbook concepts to real-world applications. Sheehan, McDonald, and Spence (2009) outlined classroom-as-organization pedagogy and the complementary experiential learning activities used to develop students' emotional competency in a sport event management class. The authors reported that one of the most important lessons learned from this experience was the significant role that reflection played in students' development, particularly as it pertained to the instructor's ability to provide relevant feedback. They contend that the classroom-as-organization approach to learning is the preferred pedagogy to maximize development of students' emotional competency. There are many proponents of experiential learning among those in the academy, and it is no surprise that this model enjoys much support in the applied field of sport management. Of the 60 papers listed in the NASSM Conference Abstract Archive: Teaching, six focused on experiential learning.

Case Studies

The case method has been a staple of management, marketing, and legal education for over a century. However, despite its prevalence in business schools, case pedagogy has not gained similar favor in sport management. Zeigler was an early proponent of the use of the case method in sport management instruction. Dixon (2008), in his comprehensive piece on case pedagogy, notes that Zeigler (1959) advocated for the use of the case method in our discipline nearly fifty years ago. In the preface to his then-groundbreaking text, which included thirty cases on the administration of physical education and athletics, Zeigler (1959) claimed that "serious consideration should be given to the case method of teaching human relations and administration in our field . . . it is the ideal method in a democratic country" (cited in Dixon, p. 147).

In support of its goal to provide a platform for the dissemination of sport management pedagogical work, a section of the *Sport Management Education Journal* is devoted to publishing teaching cases. As Pitts (2003) and McDonald and Milne (1999) illustrate with case books focusing on sport marketing, Foster, Greyser, and Walsh (2006) and Chadwick and Arthur (2008) have also demonstrated that there is a market for textbooks that include a variety of general sport-business cases. There are also online sites that contain sport business-related cases, including Harvard Business Publishing for Educators (http://hbsp.

harvard.edu/product/cases) and CasePlace.org (www.caseplace.org/). Sport management academics can apply for educator access to the Harvard cases, which includes educator copies of case studies along with teaching notes. While sport management is not a dedicated content area on the Harvard site, sport-specific cases can be found among the content areas of competitive strategy, finance, marketing, and service management. CasePlace.org is an online library of reading materials, multimedia content, and teaching modules that focuses on social, environmental and ethical issues in business and is a project of the Aspen Institute Center for Business Education.

Technology and Web-Based or Online Instruction

Sport management educators have addressed the importance of integrating technology into sport management programs to enhance student learning experiences (Smith, 2010; Walker & Haffner, 2009). Smart classrooms—those that are equipped with computers, multimedia projectors, Internet connections, document cameras, and Classroom Response Systems (sometimes called clickers)—are fast becoming the norm in higher education. Gone are the days of delivering lectures via chalkboards and overhead projectors. Ostensibly, technology allows us to engage our students using methods that were unavailable in the past. The use of clickers in classes has been shown to decrease absenteeism (Smith, 2010) and provide direct and indirect opportunities to assess students' recall of facts and higher-order thinking skills (Bruff, 2009). Simulations (e.g., Oakland A's Baseball Business Simulator) and hyperpedagogy (e.g., Second Life) are yet other methods that combine technology and experiential learning.

Sport management academics are also designing, developing, and delivering online (or web-based) courses. Web-based instruction (WBI) has mushroomed in recent years as administrators and students alike seek to redefine the traditional classroom. Course management platforms such as Blackboard/WebCT have helped popularize online course delivery. Even though the adoption of WBI has evoked considerable scholarly debate in regard to its effectiveness as a learning tool (Bennett, 2002), the realities of higher education in the twenty-first century mandate that at a minimum, sport management faculty be exposed to some web-based instructional models. Bennett, Henson, and Connaughton (2001), and Bennett (2002), conducted research on students' satisfaction with web-based classes and found that students are satisfied with their online experiences, including the interaction they received from the instructor of the class and the convenience of taking a class via the Internet (Bennett, 2002, p. 45). The authors' findings also indicate that when compared with traditional face-to-face course delivery, the students' rated their online class experience quite favorably. When compared with the conventionally delivered sport management class, the web-based students scored equally well on quizzes and examinations. However, Bennett (2002) also found that students reported negative experiences with web-based quizzes and the lack of social interaction with class peers. Despite this, it appears that online course delivery (or distance education) will continue to be a factor in the delivery of sport management courses.

CONCLUDING THOUGHTS: FUTURE DIRECTIONS FOR TEACHING AND LEARNING IN SPORT MANAGEMENT

In light of the rapidly changing social, cultural, and economic conditions faced by educational institutions, the challenge to remain relevant is considerable. The prevailing view of learning as a simple process of internalizing a fixed body of knowledge is outdated and has largely been removed from the millennial student experience (Cuneen, Gray, Verner, et al., 2008; Light & Dixon, 2007). Given the increasingly rapid pace of social and economic change arising from advances in information technology, the traditional emphasis on content has become less important than helping students learn *how to learn,* critically analyze, and adapt to changing environmental and market conditions. As other fields, such as chemistry education and psychology, have established a well-researched body of literature on teaching and learning specific to their disciplines, so too should sport management educators research and develop a pedagogical literature specific to our field. Then, as a field, we must make a commitment to teaching and sharing what we have learned.

REFERENCES

Allen, M. (1996). Research productivity and positive teaching evaluations: Examining the relationship using meta-analysis. *Journal of the Association for Communication Administration, 2,* 77–96. Retrieved from http://www.comm.unt.edu/Journal/jaca.htm.

Bennett, G. (2002). Web-based instruction in sport management. *Sport Management Review, 5*(1), 45–68. DOI:10.1016/S1441-3523(02)70061-2

Bennett, G., Henson, R., & Connaughton, D. (2001). Student perceptions of an online course in sport management. *International Journal of Sport Management, 2*(3), 205–215.

Boyer, E. (1990). Scholarship reconsidered: Priorities of the professoriate. Princeton, NJ: The Carnegie Foundation for the Advancement of Teaching.

Bruff, D. (2009). *Teaching with classroom response systems: Creating active learning environments.* San Francisco: Jossey-Bass.

Chadwick, S., & Arthur, D. (2008). *International cases in the business of sport.* Burlington, MA: Butterworth-Heinemann.

Chalip, L. (2006). Toward a distinctive sport management discipline. *Journal of Sport Management, 20,* 1–21.

College programs in sport business (2010, December 6–12). *Street and Smith's Sports Business Journal, 13*(32), 41–50.

Commission on Sport Management Accreditation (2010). Retrieved from http://www.cosmaweb.org/.

Costa, C. A. (2005). The status and future of sport management. *Journal of Sport Management, 19,* 117–142.

Cuneen, J. (2004). Managing program excellence during our transition from potential to merit. *Journal of Sport Management, 18,* 1–12. Retrieved from http://journals.humankinetics.com/JSM.

Cuneen, J., & Sidwell, M. J. (2003). *Sport management field experiences.* Morgantown, WV: Fitness Information Technology.

Cuneen, J., Gray, D. P., Verner, M. E., Baker, R. E., Hoeber, O., & Young, D. (2008). Teaching the millennial student redux: A discussion on connecting with Generation Me. Paper presented at the North American Society for Sport Management 2008.

Cunningham, G. B., & Sagas, M. (2004). Work experiences, occupational commitment, and intent to enter the sport management profession. *Physical Educator, 61*(3), 146–156. Retrieved from http://www.phiepsilonkappa.org/public.html.

Dixon, J. C. (2008). "Making the case" for using the case method in sport management education. *International Journal of Sport Management and Marketing, 4*(2/3), 146–164. DOI:10.1504/IJSMM.2008.018646

Feldman, K. A. (1987). Research productivity and scholarly accomplishment of college teachers as related to instructional effectiveness: A review and exploration. *Research in Higher Education, 26,* 227–298. DOI:10.1007/BF00992241

Foster, S. B., & Dollar, J. E. (2010). *Experiential learning in sport management: Internships and beyond.* Morgantown, WV: Fitness Information Technology.

Foster, G., Greyser, S. A., & Walsh, B. (2006) *The business of sports: Cases and text on strategy and management.* Mason, OH: Thomson South-Western.

Frisby, W. (2005). The good, the bad and the ugly: Critical sport management research. *Journal of Sport Management, 19,* 1–12.

Gentile, D. (2010). *Teaching sport management: A practical guide.* Sudbury, MA: Jones & Bartlett.

Hattie, J., & Marsh, H. W. (1996). The relationship between research and teaching: A meta-analysis. *Review of Educational Research, 66,* 507–542.

Jowdy, E., McDonald, M., & Spence, K. K. (2004). An integral approach to sport management internships. *European Sport Management Quarterly, 4*(4), 215–233. DOI: 10.1080/16184740408737478.

Kolb, D. A. (1984). *Experiential learning: Experience as the source of learning and development.* Englewood Cliffs, NJ: Prentice-Hall.

Light, R., & Dixon, M. A. (2007). Contemporary developments in sport pedagogy and their implications for sport management education. *Sport Management Review, 10,* 159–175. DOI: 10.1016/S1441-3523(07)70009-8.

Mahony, D. F., Mondello, M., Hums, M., & Judd, M. (2004). Are sport management doctoral programs meeting the needs of the faculty job market? Observations for today and the future. *Journal of Sport Management, 18*(2), 91–110. Retrieved from http://journals.humankinetics.com/JSM.

McDonald, M. A., & Milne, G. R. (1999). *Cases in sport marketing.* Sudbury, MA: Jones & Bartlett.

Naisbett, J. (1982). *Megatrends: Ten new directions transforming our lives.* New York: Warner Books.

NASSM. (2007–2010). NASSM conference abstract archives: Teaching. Retrieved from http://www.nassm.com/Archive/Category/Teaching.

Parkhouse, B. L. *The management of sport: Its foundation and application.* St. Louis: Mosby.

Pauline, G., & Pauline, J. S. (2008). Teaching sport sponsorship activation through a client-based experiential learning project. *Sport Management Education Journal, 2*(1), 19–37.

Pitts, B. G. (2003). *Case studies in sport marketing.* Morgantown, WV: Fitness Information Technology.

Pitts, B. G., & Danylchuk, K. E. (2007). Examining the body of knowledge in sport management: A preliminary descriptive study of current sport management textbooks. *Sport Management Education Journal, 1,* 40–57.

Sheehan, B. J., McDonald, M. A., & Spence, K. K. (2009). Developing students' emotional competency using the classroom-as-organization approach. *Journal of Management Education, 33*(1), 77–98. DOI: 10.1177/1052562908328920.

Slack, T. (1991). Sport management: Some thoughts on future directions. *Journal of Sport Management, 5,* 95–99.

Slack, T. (1998). Is there anything unique about sport management? *European Journal for Sport Management, 5,* 21–29.

Smith, B. (2010). Classroom response systems: Using technology to enhance sport management instruction. Paper presented at the North American Society for Sport Management.

Southall, R. M., Nagel, M. S., LeGrande, D., & Han, P. (2003). Sport management practica: A metadiscrete experiential learning model. *Sport Marketing Quarterly, 12*(1), 27–31, 34–36.

Spence, K. K., Hess, D. G., McDonald, M., & Sheehan, B. J. (2009). Designing experiential learning curricula to develop future sport leaders. *Sport Management Education Journal, 3*(1), 1–25.

van der Smissen, B. (1984). A process for success: Sport management curricula—an idea whose time has come. In B. K. Zanger & J. B. Parks (Eds.), *Sport management curricula: The business and education nexus* (5–18). Bowling Green, OH: Bowling Green State University.

Walker, S., & Haffner, E. (2009). An interdisciplinary competency-based approach to technology instruction in the sport management curriculum. Paper presented at NASSM.

Young, D. S., & Baker, R. E. (2004). Linking classrooms to professional practice: The internship as a practical learning experience worthy of academic credit. *Journal of Physical Education, Recreation, & Dance, 75*(1), 22–30. Retrieved from http://www.aahperd.org/publications/journals/joperd/.

Zeigler, E. F. (1959). *Administration of physical education and athletics: The case method approach.* Englewood Cliffs, NJ: Prentice-Hall.

Zeigler, E. F. (1987). Sport management: Past, present, future. *Journal of Sport Management, 1*(1), 4–24.

Theory versus Practice

6

A BALANCING ACT

"It is inspired teaching that keeps the flame of scholarship alive."

E. L. BOYER (1990, P. 24)

David K. Stotlar UNIVERSITY OF NORTHERN COLORADO

David Stotlar has an Ed.D. from the University of Utah and serves as the Director of the School of Sport & Exercise Science at the University of Northern Colorado. He has written over 70 articles and more than 40 textbooks and chapters in sport marketing and management. He served as a board member and president of NASSM and is a NASSM Research Fellow. He is also a founding member of the Sport Marketing Association.

Lori L. Braa UNIVERSITY OF MOUNT UNION

Lori Braa is an assistant professor at the University of Mount Union in Ohio. She earned her Ph.D. in Sport Administration from the University of Northern Colorado in 2011. Before completing her degree, Braa worked as the recreation manager for the City of Farmington, New Mexico. She also spent over 13 years as a collegiate athletic administrator, working at Messiah College, Mesa State College, and the NCAA national office.

Introduction

Few dilemmas in academe have resulted in as much animosity and camaraderie as the one of theory versus practice. Since the inception of the sport management discipline, staunch supporters have argued both sides of the dilemma. One sport management professor said that he and a colleague were so far apart on the issue that the curvature of the earth kept them from seeing eye-to-eye on the topic. Academicians have

noted that without theoretical underpinnings, sport management cannot constitute a scholarly discipline. Those who favor a focus on practice question the
utility of theory in the daily routine of sport managers. The purpose of this chapter
is to present the issues, discuss the evolution of the field, and provide the reader
with substance about the debate.

BACKGROUND

A look at the history of sport management and the framework of theory
versus application is helpful in understanding where the discipline
is today. Sport management as we know it is a relatively new field of study.
Organized sport and management practices date back to 1000 B.C.E., when
Chinese officials wrote about how to manage and control human activity
(Black & Porter, 2000). Although the practice and study of management can
be traced back to ancient times, it was not until the twentieth century that the
art and science of management was the focus of extensive academic examination. Today most universities offer an academic program in administration
of some kind, whether it is business administration, public administration, or
sport administration.

According to Earle Zeigler, one of the founders of the discipline, sport
management began as an ancillary area in the field of education, mostly within
physical education. As far back as the 1890s, coursework concerning facility
maintenance and organizing and conducting sporting events fell under what was
known as the administration of physical education (Zeigler, 1951). In 2009,
Chelladurai examined three significant factors that elevated the status of sport
management as a field of study: (1) the expansion of sport management degree programs, (2) the development of professional associations, and (3) the
creation of scholarly journals. Sport management has become extremely popular
on college campuses across the country as both an academic discipline and a
professional occupation.

The Expansion of Sport Management Programs

Today, sport plays an increasingly important role within society and educational
institutions in most countries around the world. For example, in 2009 the median total expense of individual institutions in a major U.S. intercollegiate athletic
conference was over $59 million (Equity in Athletics Disclosure Act, 2009). Ac-
cording to the European Union's White Paper on Sport in Europe (2007), sport
generated €407 billion in 2004, representing 3.7 percent of EU GDP, and accounted for 15 million jobs, or 5.4 percent of the workforce.

Sport clearly qualifies as big business. Zeigler made the point that the rapidly growing field needed good managers and administrators. Too often in sport
history, particularly in the United States, former coaches were cast in administrative roles woefully unprepared for the increasing demands of the job. To
fill this void, more universities began offering programs in sport management

with the intent to prepare professional managers in amateur, professional, and intercollegiate sport.

As with many industries, fast expansion of sport management programs raised a variety of issues (see Essay 1). Leaders in the sport management field accepted the challenges and achieved success in a short period of time. In that light, it is important to examine the realities of where we are as a discipline, looking not only at our achievements, but also at our mistakes and disappointments as we move forward (Costa, 2005).

The Development of Professional Associations

As noted by Chelladurai (2009), the establishment of professional associations is an indication of the maturity of a profession. It represents the coming together of collective ideas from both practitioners and scholars to generate guidelines of self-regulation for those in the profession (Chelladurai, 2009). The creation of the North American Society for Sport Management in 1985 became the foundation of the many associations in existence today. Pitts (2001) states, "It is ironic that one of the world's oldest professions is one of the world's newest fields of study." Since 1985, the associations within the field of sport management have gained respect. The creation of the Sport and Recreation Law Association (SRLA) quickly followed NASSM in 1986. The Sport Marketing Association (SMA) was founded in 2002. As noted in Essay 3, the Commission on Sport Management Accreditation (COSMA) was established in July of 2008 as an independent body to provide services and accreditation of sport management programs in colleges and universities across North America. Sport management has also made its mark beyond our borders. Countries and regions that developed professional organizations include Japan (Japan Sports Management Association, JaSMA), New Zealand and Australia (Sport Management Association of Australia and New Zealand, SMAANZ), Europe (European Association for Sport Management, EASM), Asia (Asian Association for Sport Management, AASM), Latin America (Latin American Organization in Sport Management, LAOSM), and Africa (African Sport Management Association, ASMA).

The Creation of Scholarly Journals

In the first edition of the *Journal of Sport Management,* Parks and Olafson note that "the growth of sport management as an academic area of study has been accompanied by the express desire of many academicians and practitioners for a professional publication that would, among other functions, 'disseminate pertinent information, research developments, trends and issues, and relevant professional articles'" (Parks & Olafson, 1987, p. 2).

The rift over theory versus practice within the profession has been reflected in the purpose of the professional journals. According to its mission statement:

> *The Journal of Sport Management* publishes research and scholarly review articles; short reports on replications, test development, and data reanalysis (Research Notes);

editorials that focus on significant issues pertaining to sport management (Sport Management Perspectives); articles aimed at strengthening the link between sport management theory and sport management practice (From the Field); journal abstracts (Sport Management Digest); and news items of interest to professionals in sport management (Management Memos)." (North American Society for Sport Management, n.d.)

In 2007, NASSM responded to the needs of the profession by establishing the *Sport Management Education Journal.* This journal is a joint refereed publication of NASSM and NASPE. The stated purpose of the journal is to "advance the body of knowledge in pedagogy as it relates to sport management education and disseminate knowledge about sport management courses, curricula, and teaching." The journal editors noted that "manuscripts may address a wide range of issues concerning graduate and undergraduate education such as: curriculum planning, curriculum design, future employment requirements, trends and their impacts, course content, fieldwork, internships, experiential learning, teaching methods, accreditation, community education, and tenure and promotion" (North American Society for Sport Management, n.d.).

International journals also flourished during the development of the profession. Published by SMAANZ, the *Sport Management Review* is published as a service to sport industries worldwide. It is a multidisciplinary journal concerned with the management, marketing, and governance of sport at all levels and in all its manifestations—whether as an entertainment, a recreation, or an occupation. The journal encourages collaboration between scholars and practitioners. It welcomes submissions reporting research, new applications, advances in theory, and case studies (SMAANZ, 2010). The journal clearly states that it "encourages collaboration between scholars and practitioners," a concept evident in the content of each issue. Similarly, the *European Sports Management Quarterly* (*ESMQ*, formerly *EJSM* and the official journal of EASM) "covers a wide range of sport management topics and ensures a balance of practical application and theory" (EASM, 2010).

Specialized professional journals also emerged as the discipline matured. Journals such as the *International Journal of Sport Management and Marketing, Sport Marketing Quarterly* (the preferred publication of the Sport Marketing Association), the *International Journal of Sport Management, Journal of Sport Marketing and Sponsorship,* and the *Journal of Sport Finance,* and others expanded outlets for our research.

Trade journals aimed primarily at practitioners also developed during the evolution of the profession. In the early 1980s, *Athletic Purchasing and Facilities* (later *Athletic Business*) was one of the first publications to provide guidance to those managing sport organizations. *Sport, Inc.* was a short-lived publication in the late 1980s to early 1990s that focused on management, marketing, and sales practices in the sport industry. Although it was a great contribution to the field, perhaps the discipline just was too young to support the journal. The 1990s brought the two most widely read practitioner-oriented publications, *SportsBusiness Journal* and the *SportsBusiness Daily.* Other popular trade journals of the day included *Fitness Management, Athletic Administration, NCAA News,* and *Athletic Management.*

Professional Conferences

Another key factor in the evolution of a discipline is the establishment of forums (i.e., conferences) where scholars and practitioners meet to disseminate the best thinking in both theory and practice. At the first NASSM conference, in his president's address, Bob Boucher (1986) noted that "sport management is a field that cannot divorce itself from practical and professional concerns. In effect, the proof of administrative theory and practice is in the pudding, and therefore we should make every effort to bridge this 'gap' whether it be real or mythical" (Boucher, 1986, p. 5). A question we must ask ourselves as we move forward is, "Is the gap between theory and practice so great that it cannot be bridged" (Boucher, 1998, p. 80).

At many NASSM conferences, practitioners have been invited as keynote speakers. Attendees are often split on the merits of those decisions. Some speakers are good, while others come unprepared and reinforce the academy's opinion that practitioners are simply uninterested in and uninformed about the knowledge base in the field. Others in the academy are a bit more kind and accepting of such naiveté. Over the years, NASSM conference organizers have invited fewer industry speakers and filled the program with more academic research.

One of the earliest conferences to welcome both industry professionals and academicians was the International Sport Business Conferences, started by discipline pioneer Guy Lewis in the late 1980s. Hosted for many years by the University of South Carolina, this conference eventually evolved into the Sport Entertainment & Venues Tomorrow conference.

The Sport Marketing Association (SMA) offered its first conference in 2003. Paramount in the establishment of the conference was the integration of theory and practice with a focus on balancing academics and practitioners. A review of SMA conference programs shows that such integration was achieved.

Practitioner-focused conferences have been around since the early 1980s as well. The Athletic Business Conference has been a staple provider of information regarding facilities and equipment. In collegiate sports, the National Association of Collegiate Directors of Athletics and its sub-groups (NACMA, CoSIDA, CABMA, & CEFMA) have provided a variety of forums. The International Association of Assembly Managers (IAAM) has also hosted numerous professional conferences since the 1980s. IAAM started as a practitioner-only conference and expanded to include more academic and research sessions. The Sport Lawyers Association organized meetings in the late 1980s principally composed of lawyers but open to others to disseminate legal information with a focus on professional sport. A more recent conference, the National Sport Forum, specializes in attracting marketing personnel from across the sport industry. Since its first conference in 1995, more academicians have joined the forum each year.

FRAMING THE DEBATE THROUGH BOYER'S MODEL OF SCHOLARSHIP

In his 1990 book, *Scholarship Reconsidered: Priorities of the Professorate*, Ernest Boyer notes that today when we speak of *scholarship*, it is defined by one's rank within a college or university as well as by research and publications. Parks & Bartley (1996) state that "in the academy, scholarship is the currency with which credibility is purchased." Respect in the academy rests on the credibility and scholarship of our sport management faculty and the programs we offer within higher education (Parks & Bartley, 1996).

The first college was founded on the North American continent more than 350 years ago. As higher education continued to grow and change, the educational and social issues surrounding the academy have profoundly changed (Boyer, 1990). Interestingly, the word *scholarship* did not enter the lexicon of higher education until 1906, when D. C. Gilman introduced it as the ability to think, communicate, and learn (Boyer, 1990). Today, scholarship is viewed through a more focused lens, which regards research as the most essential form of scholarly activity. Boyer believes that knowledge is not necessarily linear, in that "theory leads to practice" and "practice to theory" (p. 16) and that teaching shapes both research and practice. His objective is to enhance this relationship by suggesting that the work of the professoriate might be thought of as having four separate, yet overlapping, types of scholarship. These are "the scholarship of *discovery*, the scholarship of *integration*, the scholarship of *teaching* and the scholarship of *application*" (p. 16).

Scholarship of Discovery

The scholarship of discovery is the most familiar facet of the Boyer model; it is what the academy defines as research. It begs us to consider the question, "What is to be known, what is yet to be found?" (1990, p. 19). It provides the basis for investigation and inquiry—two essential elements within higher education. The scholarship of discovery is not just about outcomes, but also about the passion and process in the advancement of knowledge. Boyer contends that "scholarly investigation is at the heart of academic life" (p. 18) and the discovery of new knowledge is crucial not only to the academy but to the world. Investigation and research contribute to the discipline and advance the body of knowledge through the dissemination of this knowledge. Within sport management, examples of the scholarship of discovery are the publication of articles, manuscripts, and books and the presentation of research at professional meetings (Commission on Sport Management Accreditation, 2010).

Scholarship of Integration

The scholarship of integration asks, "What do the findings mean? Is it possible to interpret what's been discovered in ways that provide a larger, more comprehensive understanding?" (Boyer 1990, p. 19). Integration is the ability to make a connection across disciplines, it means "fitting one's own research—or the research of others—into a larger intellectual pattern" (p. 19). It is essentially the ability to amalgamate ideas and apply them to the real world. COSMA defines it as the "interpretation, synthesis, and connection of theories, ideas, and concepts across disciplines that results in new insights, broader perspectives, a more comprehensive understanding of those disciplines" (Commission on Sport Management Accreditation, 2010, p. 45). Examples of the scholarship of integration include the development of new multidisciplinary courses and curricula, the development of multidisciplinary seminars and workshops, and textbook authoring. In many ways, it seems as though the scholarship of integration is the key link between theory and practice.

Scholarship of Teaching

The scholarship of teaching evolved from Aristotle's proposition that teaching is the highest form of understanding. Boyer (1990) states that "the work of the professor becomes consequential only as it is understood by others" (p. 23). His contention is that a well-informed and knowledgeable professor is able to communicate his or her knowledge while advancing student learning; "it is inspired teaching that keeps the flame of scholarship alive" (p. 24). In the end, "without the teaching function, the continuity of knowledge will be broken and the store of human knowledge dangerously diminished" (p. 24).

Rigorous scholarship of teaching begins with what a teacher knows: he or she must be "widely read, current, and intellectually engaged in [his or her] fields" (COSMA, 2010, p. 43). The scholarship of teaching not only requires knowledge in the field but also includes the understanding of how best to convey the information to students. Some examples of the scholarship of teaching include curriculum review and revision; development of new teaching materials; development and evaluation of new methods of instruction; and presentation of these methods in workshops, seminars, and professional meetings devoted to improving teaching skills (p. 43).

Scholarship of Application

The scholarship of application, or the application of knowledge, asks, "How can knowledge be responsibly applied to consequential problems? How can it be helpful to individuals as well as institutions?" (Boyer, 1990, p. 21). It is here that service comes into the academy. Though service has traditionally been one of three criteria used to evaluate and promote faculty, it is often given little attention. On many campuses the term *service* is vague and defies clarity. It covers anything from campus activities to sitting on committees to participating in local community activities. Boyer points to the importance of service as it relates to scholarship, yet he notes that the scholarship of application must relate to one's field of expertise and knowledge, not public service in the broader community. The scholarship of application requires both creativity and critical thought in analyzing significant problems. New understanding and knowledge evolve from this scholarly investigation and research. The scholarship of application consists of, but is not limited to, consultation, policy analysis, program evaluation, and technical assistance (COSMA, 2010, p. 44). This function is also a fiercely contended area in the discipline (see also Essay 9). Faculty who actively engage in consulting with sport organizations believe that those activities keep them grounded and provide real-life examples to enhance both teaching and learning. They believe that such collaboration deepens the core learning experience. Others, who concentrate principally on the theory, do not feel the obligation to apply the results of their research. This may also emerge as a function of the type of institution at which they teach. Traditional Carnegie research institutions may reward faculty who engage in theoretical work, while faculty in undergraduate-only institutions may be rewarded for outreach activities with sport organizations.

Sport Management and Boyer's Model of Scholarship

So how does sport management fit into Boyer's (1990) model of scholarship? Since the inception of sport management as a field of study, its scholars have been continually challenged by the debate between theory and practice. Boyer's model may help our discipline bridge the gap between what practitioners expect and what academicians expect. Parks (1992) states that "Boyer's perspective on scholarship could appropriately be adopted by sport management scholars to examine the contemporary landscape in sport to investigate many of the concerns with which we are all familiar" (p. 222). She is referring to the practitioners' concern for best practices and researchers' focus on theory as it relates to the advancement of knowledge within the sport management field. The fact that Parks's comments are twenty years old shows the persistence of this dilemma.

COSMA promotes and recognizes excellence in sport management education in colleges and universities at the baccalaureate and graduate levels. In their principles they have adopted Boyer's model as a standard for scholarly and professional activities: "Excellence in sport management education requires faculty members to be involved in scholarly and professional activities that enhance the depth and scope of their knowledge, especially as it applies to their teaching discipline" (COSMA, 2010, p. 43).

It is apparent from the sport management literature that there is no clear consensus on the applied versus theory debate. We suggest that instead of concentrating on our differences, we should be mindful that both theory and practice play integral roles in our field of study. As viewed though Boyer's model, one cannot be successful without the other. As long as institutions continue to train both sport managers and professors within sport management, we will need both theory and practice. Perhaps this is where an institutional mission can provide guidance. The contemporary thinking in sport marketing suggests that there is no room in the market for a product that everyone likes a little. Rather, success in the market demands that a product or service be actively sought by a passionate segment. In relation to the aforementioned concept, homogenization of institutional purpose is not necessary or even desirable.

Specialization within the discipline may warrant further investigation. In fact, it may actually already be in place. Some institutions are known more for the production of scholars while others are recognized within as producing skilled practitioners. This dichotomy reflects the larger debate in higher education about whether colleges and universities should produce classically educated individuals or vocationally trained individuals. Administrators and faculty may seriously debate the issues, yet in the end, just as in sport marketing, the consumer may ultimately decide the outcome. If the institution cannot provide the empirical research that garners grant support and research funding, the academy may fail. On the other hand, if the industry does not believe that hiring credentialed employees will add value to their enterprise, again, the academy may fail.

Ultimately, the debate may be resolved with opposing, yet mutually defendable, positions. Some institutions and faculty will continue to value pure research and theory for theory's sake. Some institutions will continue to produce well-trained practitioners to satisfy the needs of the sport industry. Finally, other institutions will attempt to do both. Success for faculty will depend on finding the right fit for their personality and professional qualifications. Structures, systems, and strategies must be analyzed for congruency within the subject institution.

DEBATE WITHIN THE DISCIPLINE AND INDUSTRY

Costa (2005), finds that experts in the field of sport management are concerned about how to apply research and theory. Some of her academically minded panelists note that when research has an applied use, the notion of theory development is primarily ignored. One panelist went so far as to state, "When we say, 'linking theory to practice,' what we mean is forget the theory and focus on the practice" (p. 130). Criticism also comes from the industry based on the type of research being conducted. Many from this group believe that the research produced by faculty often has little application or utility in practice. However, the researchers counter argue that they are not obligated to conduct research that has immediate practical application.

Institutions of higher education, the faculty who reside there, and their students must understand that their role in society will be judged by their contribution. Therefore, those who seek to investigate, analyze, and create theory do so at the pleasure of society and a free market. Those who seek career training for jobs in the sport industry do so under the watchful eye of seasoned practitioners. If the products of the modern university do not meet the requirements of society, those universities, like any business, risk elimination or worse yet, irrelevance. The increasing entrepreneurial focus in higher education can be achieved whether the focus is on research or application. Those programs concentrating on research can generate external funding essential to their enterprise, while those focused on career training can attract business-minded students and their tuition dollars. However, institutional ambiguity can create problems for programs and faculty.

There is clearly a struggle between those doing the research and those applying the knowledge (Parks, 1992). From its beginning, the field of sport management has had an applied nature based on an important link with practitioners. What has become a common question within our field—with no agreed upon answer—is "how best to translate theory into practice" (p. 221). Many believe the purpose of academia is to prepare professionals for careers, while others believe that the purpose is more esoteric. There is a belief that theory is developed and exists for theory's sake, not fundamentally as a utility to guide practice. Thus, we see a gap between theory and practice within both academia and the practice of sport management.

QUALITATIVE VERSUS QUANTITATIVE RESEARCH

A related debate about the kind of research conducted in the discipline also continues. Early on, much of the research was descriptive in nature because little was known empirically about the discipline. Although quantitative in nature, the data did not lend itself to more sophisticated analysis. Gradually the type of research and the sophistication of data analysis elevated the research base. However, some researchers feel that only rigorous quantitative research will advance our field and that qualitative research is merely "fluff." Others attest to the fact that qualitative research has been underutilized, underappreciated, and results in "thicker and richer" information for the field. For example, much of the early quantitative research on sport sponsorship looked broadly across sponsors to garner information on sponsor objectives and outcomes. More recently, qualitative investigations have put aside the broad generalizations from quantitative studies to understand the intricacies unique to the specific objectives and outcomes sponsors seek. As the discipline continues to examine this topic, it may not really matter which kind of research is done but only that we continue to do research, both quantitative and qualitative (Costa, 2005; Chalip, 1989; Yauch & Steudel, 2003). To gain acceptance and recognition, the research produced by sport management professionals should be of the highest caliber in order to add to the body of knowledge and improve practice.

Collectively building a distinct body of knowledge within sport management depends on multiple outlets. Original research such as doctoral dissertations, peer-review journal articles, and textbooks are a few of the forums for written dissemination of our body of knowledge. Reviews of dissertation topics reveal that most of research being conducted is in the fields of marketing, organizational theory, and organizational behavior, with very little work done in other areas (Dittmore, Mahony, Andrew, & Phelps, 2007; Soucie & Doherty, 1996). Pitts and Pedersen (2005) completed a study on content areas published in the *Journal of Sport Management*. Their findings show the management and organizational skills in sport content areas produce the highest percentage of articles (38%). Their study also finds that intercollegiate athletics is the most written about segment (40%), with participation sport and professional sport trailing at 13 percent and 12.8 percent respectively.

SPORT MANAGEMENT FACULTY

As the discipline began to develop, Chelladurai (1992) noted that many of the newly minted programs were one-person programs where faculty was "spread too thin to be able to specialize in one aspect and create a unique body of knowledge in that specialization" (p. 216). Mahony (2008) investigated issues addressing the lack of faculty to teach in our ever expanding discipline and the disparity between the program demands.

Researchers have noted that the number of qualified faculty and discipline-prepared doctoral students have not been able to keep pace with the increased number of position vacancies. For example, during times of rapid program expansion (1997–1999) there were approximately 200 entry-level faculty openings and approximately 15 doctorate students graduating per year (Mondello, Mahony, Hums, & Moorman, 2002). Although the upward trend on the demand side has continued, higher education in the 2010s has experienced a period of budget cuts, downsizing, and reorganization, threatening to further reduce the supply of qualified teaching faculty.

We must also address the qualifications of those faculty. Depending on the nature of the institution, university faculty typically need to have a terminal degree to maintain their position over the long term. Adjunct or part-time faculty must have at least a master's degree and do not generally have long-term or tenure-track appointments. Requiring a Ph.D. would most likely preclude practitioners from joining the faculty at many institutions. Furthermore, those with a master's degree would have little job security in higher education and receive considerably less pay. Yet, it is our belief that the students could benefit from instruction from both. As noted earlier, the COSMA Accreditation Principles and Self Study Preparation Manual suggests that faculty should be actively engaged in consulting with sport organizations and industry-based practice to enhance both teaching and learning (COSMA, 2010, p. 44).

CONCLUDING THOUGHTS

As the sport management field continues to grow and develop, the most debated issue is probably that of application versus theory. As with any good debate, some are not so sure this is a problem (Costa, 2005). One individual asked, "Is this integration [of theory and practice] always necessary and desirable?" Others are concerned about the tension between theory and practice. Another individual stated, "our dialogue maintains the distinction between theory and practice, and thereby mitigates against real and meaningful integration. . . . Theory and practice can be jointly obtained" (Costa, 2005, p. 130). The debate over basic and applied research fails to recognize the value of both and the effect they have on one another. There is extensive literature revolving around the questions "whom the field should serve and what it should seek to achieve" (Costa, 2005, p. 133). The question becomes whether, as a discipline, we concern ourselves with looking at the issue strictly from an academic stance or if we are open to consider all positions and views.

For years applied researchers have competently applied theory and their findings to assist those in the field of sport (Chalip, 1985, 1990; Ulrich, 2001). Sport management practitioners could equally benefit from applying the theoretical research results in their business lives (Edwards, 1999; Weiss, 1980). In other words, application can inform theory, and theory can inform application

(Costa, 2005). The true question may be how research is communicated to practitioners, whether it is through trade journals or by presenting the results in a way in which practitioners can apply them.

Advancement of the theory versus practice debate has also been a result of changes in the industry. Hiring authorities in the industry have begun to recognize the attributes and skills of sport management graduates. In return, those newly hired sport executives have brought with them a better understanding of theory and an increased appreciation of the academy.

In the end, it is not about who wins the argument, but rather the discussion we have (Brown, Isaacs, Vogt, & Margulies, 2002; Ulrich, 2001). The discussion began as early as the first edition of the *Journal of Sport Management* when Zeigler (1987) wrote, in his challenges for the future, about the need to maintain the theoretical base and at the same time make our knowledge sensible and useful. If, as students, faculty, administrators, and practitioners we keep Zeigler's words in mind, the dilemma of theory versus practice can become the integration of theory and practice.

REFERENCES

Black, J. S., & Porter, L. W. (2000). *Management meeting new challenges.* Englewood Cliffs, NJ: Prentice Hall.

Boucher, R. (1986). President's opening address. In C. F. Schraibman (Ed.), *Proceedings of the First Annual Conference of the North American Society for Sport Management* (3–7). Kent, OH: Kent State University.

Boucher, R. L. (1998). Toward achieving a focal point for sport management: A binocular perspective. *Journal of Sport Management, 12,* 76–85.

Boyer, E. L. (1990). *Scholarship reconsidered: Priorities of the professoriate.* Princeton, NJ: Carnegie Foundation for the Advancement of Teaching.

Brown, J., Isaacs, D., Vogt, E., & Margulies, N. (2002). Strategic questioning: Engaging people's best thinking. *Systems Thinker, 13*(9), 2–6.

Chalip, L. (1985). Policy research as social science: Outflanking the value dilemma. *Policy Studies Review, 5,* 287–308.

Chalip, L. (1989). The post-season assessment survey: A simple method for sports organisation development. *New Zealand Journal of Sport Medicine, 17*(2), 28–31.

Chalip, L. (1990). Rethinking the applied social sciences of sport: Second thoughts on the emerging debate. *Sociology of Sport Journal, 7,* 172–178.

Chelladurai, P. (1992). Sport management: Opportunities and obstacles. *Journal of Sport Management, 6,* 215–219.

Chelladurai, P. (2009). *Managing organizations for sport and physical activity.* Scottsdale, AZ: Holcomb Hathaway.

COSMA. (2009). History. Retrieved from http://www.cosmaweb.org/history.

COSMA. (2010, June). Accreditation principles and self study preparation. Retrieved from http://www.cosmaweb.org/sites/all/pdf_files/COSMA_Accreditation_principles.

Costa, C. (2005). The status and future of sport management: A Delphi study. *Journal of Sport Management, 19,* 117–142.

Dittmore, S. W., Mahony, D. F., Andrew, D. P. S., & Phelps, S. (2007). Is sport management research diverse? A five-year analysis of dissertations. *International Journal of Sport Management, 8*(1), 21–31.

Equity in Athletics Disclosure Act. (2009). Equity in athletics data analysis. Retrieved from http://ope.ed.gov/athletics/GetOneInstitutionData.aspx.

Edwards, A. (1999). Reflective practice in sport management. *Sport Management Review, 2,* 67–81.

Sport Management Association of Australia and New Zealand. (2010). Aims and scope. In *Sport Management Review.* Retrieved from http://www.elsevier.com/wps/find/journaldescription.cws_home/716936/description#description.

European Association for Sport Management. (2010). Journal. Retrieved from http://www.easm.net/index.php?option=com_content&view=article&id=15&itemid=38.

Isaacs, S. (1964). *Careers and opportunities in sports.* New York: Dutton.

Mahony, D. F. (2008). No one can whistle a symphony: Working together for sport management's future. *Journal of Sport Management, 22,* 1–10.

Mahony, D. F., & Pitts, B. G. (1998). Research outlets in sport marketing: The need for increased specialization. *Journal of Sport Management, 12,* 259–272.

Mondello, M., Mahony, D. F., Hums, M. A., & Moorman, A. M. (2002). A survey of search committee chairpersons: Candidate qualifications preferred for entry-level sport management faculty positions. *International Journal of Sport Management, 3,* 262–281.

NASSM. (n.d.). Mission statement. Retrieved from http://www.nassm.com/InfoAbout/JSM/Mission.

NASSM. (n.d.). Journal aim and scope. In *Sport Management Education Journals,* Retrieved from http://www.nassm.com/InfoAbout/SMEJ.

Parks, J. B. (1992). Scholarship: The other "bottom line" in sport management. *Journal of Sport Management, 6,* 220–229.

Parks, J. B., & Bartley, M. E. (1996). Sport management scholarship: A professoriate in transition? *Journal of Sport Management, 10,* 119–130.

Parks, J. B., & Olafson, G. (1987). Sport management and a new journal. *Journal of Sport Management, 1*(1), 1–3.

Pitts, B. G. (2001). Sport management at the millennium: A defining moment. *Journal of Sport Management, 15,* 1–9.

Pitts, B. G., & Pedersen, P. M. (2005). Examining the body of scholarship in sport management: A content analysis of the Journal of Sport Management. *Smart Journal, 2*(1), 33–52.

Soucie, D., & Doherty, A. (1996). Past endeavors and future perspectives for sport management research. *Quest, 48,* 486–500.

Ulrich, W. (2001). The quest for competence in systemic research and practice. *Systems Research and Behavioral Science, 18*(1), 3–28.

Weiss, C. (1980). Knowledge creep and decision accretion. *Knowledge Creation, Diffusion and Utilization, 1,* 381–404.

European Union. (2007). White Paper on Sport. Retrieved from http://ec.europa.eu/sport/white-paper/whitepaper8_fr.htm # 3_1 on 12/2010.

Yauch, C. A., & Steudel, H. J. (2003). Complementary use of qualitative and quantitative cultural assessment methods. *Organizational Research Methods, 6,* 465–479.

Zeigler, E. F. (1951). *A history of professional preparation for physical education in the United States, 1861–1948.* Eugene, OR: Microfiche Publications.

Zeigler, E. F. (1987). Sport management: Past, present, future. *Journal of Sport Management, 1*(1), 4–24.

essay 7

Publish or Perish?

*Publish or perish! That's the scheme. We must all play the game 'academe.'
Winning fame and acclaim; is the goal of that game.
It does wonders for one's self-esteem.*

SIMANEK & HOLDEN (2002, P. 209)

The author introduces the essay

John J. Miller TROY UNIVERSITY INTRODUCTION

John Miller is the Associate Dean of the College of Health and Human Services at Troy University in Alabama. He has served as President of the Sport and Recreation Law Association, the Safety and Risk Management Council of America, and as Chair of the Sport Management Council of the National Association for Sport and Physical Education. He has published over 70 articles and more than 40 textbooks and chapters and has served on seven editorial review boards.

Introduction

Traditionally, universities have been recognized as places for knowledge production. In his 1869 Harvard inaugural speech, Charles Eliot stated that "The prime business of American professors must be regular and assiduous class teaching (quoted in Boyer, 1996, p. 130). Eliot, who served as the president of Harvard for forty years, is credited with expanding the concept of diversity in higher education (Rudenstine, 1996). Although Eliot appreciated that diversity could generate levels of unrest, which would make the student experience more complex, he was resolute regarding the significance of having an open and diverse university. Eliot reasoned that a successful democracy required people to learn about and appreciate others from different backgrounds (Rudenstine, 1996).

In such an environment, challenging views would increase useful knowledge that would profit each student.

However, the debate over who delineates what is useful knowledge in higher education has raged for a long time (Delanty, 2001). Daniel Coit Gilman, who founded Johns Hopkins University in 1876, believed that knowledge should be attained not through teaching but rather through research (Boyer, 1990). Nearly twenty years later, William Rainey Harper, the first president of the University of Chicago, declared that "each appointee [must] sign an agreement that his promotions in rank and salary would depend chiefly upon his research productivity." (Cowley, 1980, p. 160). By the late 1800s, the view that knowledge was best attained through research had taken a substantial hold in American higher education (Boyer, 1990). Woodrow Wilson, as president of Princeton University, declared that "the discovery and dissemination of new truths were conceded a rank superior to mere instruction" (quoted in Muto, 1993, p. 6). In 1958, Caplow and McGee addressed the power struggle between teaching and research by indicating that while beginning faculty members were hired as teachers, they were evaluated primarily as researchers. As such, scholars were considered to be academics who conducted research, published their findings, and communicated their knowledge to their students (Boyer, 1990). However, a study by Miller, Chen, Hart, and Killian (1990) reported that higher education administrators strongly supported the belief that scholarship comprised more than just research.

The association between research and teaching has become more complicated and challenging in the present university environment. The emphasis on research has become the central tenant in defining professional recognition as well as promoting the identity of the university (Barnett, 2003). As a result, many universities have made publishing research an essential component for tenure and promotion of faculty (Barnett, 2003). In fact, "publish or perish" has become an accepted adage for many faculty members in institutions of higher education (Barnett, 2003; Gendron, 2008). This phrase implies that a faculty member's ability to attain tenure and promotion is mainly a function of his or her research publishing success (Barnett, 2003), eclipsing teaching in many cases (Porter & McKibbin, 1988).

CHALLENGES TO RESEARCH PUBLICATION

"Publish or perish" has become prevalent throughout higher academia, including sport management. The impact of publish or perish in terms of the application of research to the practitioner, the influence of journal reviews, and issues in performance measures of research publications will be discussed in this essay.

Impact of Publish or Perish

Even though teaching and service may be considered, the primary determinant at most universities for attaining promotion and tenure is ultimately research publication (Bedeian, 1996). For many years this emphasis on publishing worked well. The tenure and promotion decisions were based on the number of citations a faculty member had accumulated. More recently, however, faculty, especially those of junior status, have been forced to play a game in which tenure criteria is based on the number of articles published and the relative prestige of the publications in which they appear. Tenure and promotion appear to be progressively more difficult to attain as more institutions require decisions to be based on numerically driven research evaluation systems. Thus, academic productivity is increasingly measured by "hard" data such as the number of studies a faculty member has published in peer-reviewed journals and the number of times those studies have been cited by other researchers (Gendron, 2008).

In essence, the race starts at the time of hire and continues for a set period of time (typically six years), when the tenure and promotion decision is made. Indeed, as a chair or member of a hiring committee, I have either instructed others or been instructed to investigate the number of published research articles or the publishing potential of a candidate's research based on his or her curriculum vitae when recruiting new faculty members. This practice can result in a "graying" of doctoral students, due to the expectation that they publish research articles before they receive their Ph.D.s. "Graying" refers to a productivity climate that raises the demand on beginning researchers to accelerate publishing prior to graduation and as such lengthens the time it takes to complete their degree (Long, Bowers, Barnett, & White, 1998). Publishing research before graduation puts these scholars years ahead of their predecessors. For example, a sport management doctoral student who publishes a manuscript before completing his or her dissertation raises the bar for all other graduate students seeking employment in higher education as well as for established faculty researchers. Moreover, doctoral students involved with more than one publication team before graduation raise the bar even higher (Long et al., 1998).

Are the beginning scholars' publication expectations a reflection of the expectations of the graduate school? Or are they a reflection of the expectations of the hiring university for which the beginning researcher wishes to work? Long et al. (1998) report that the academic status of the scholar's graduating institution may not be a reliable indicator of the scholar's future research productivity. In fact, they find that individuals who graduate from non-research-oriented universities and attain positions at research institutions are the most productive researchers. This indicates a robust relationship between research productivity regarding publication counts, citation counts, and affiliation with other researchers (Long et al., 1998). This finding is supported by Reskin (1977), who contends that graduates who obtain positions at research institutions logically find themselves surrounded by others who trained to conduct research.

Williamson and Cable (2003) report that future research output can be predicted based on the dissertation advisor's qualifications. Specifically, early career research output is significantly enhanced when working under advisors who are themselves productive researchers.

Interestingly, Williamson and Cable find that hiring decisions are strongly influenced by the status of an individual's academic origin, despite it not being a predictive factor for future research productivity. Conversely, they report that hiring decisions do not consider advisor productivity, even though this has a significant effect on a researcher's productivity in the early years of his or her career. These findings are important for beginning scholars and administrators to consider in the "publish or perish" environment. If attaining a position in higher academia is paramount, a beginning sport management scholar should study under established researchers and later seek out departments that employ other prolific researchers in the field.

Although a tenure-track faculty member should conduct and publish on a regular basis, solely relying on one's number of citations to achieve tenure and promotion may be risky (more on this later). The pressure to publish research, particularly on those who are not tenured, makes academia a highly stressful career that can result in burnout (De Rond & Miller, 2005). Not many professions, for example, require well-educated individuals to work for months, often on multiple projects, to submit to journals that have only a 15 to 20 percent acceptance rate.

Another disadvantage of the publish-or-perish mentality is its negative effect on original research. Smith (1990) states, "One of the most negative aspects of the pressure to publish is that it discourages any bold or original work. When so much rests on not simply doing the research but, more important, getting it published, the risks of doing something unorthodox, something that might offend strongly held prejudices in a particular field, are great" (p. 191). Thus, any progress due to publication efficiency may come at the expense of innovation, boldness, heterogeneity, and scientific progress in the field (Bouchikhi & Kimberly, 2001). Scientific progress as it relates to the professional industry is the focus of the next section.

Applying Research to the Practitioner

Researchers often attempt to develop associations with business and industry outside of their universities. In developing these relationships, Berman (2008) indicates, researchers need to improve their comprehension of what research means to a business. Without a good understanding of the industry, a disconnect between researchers and practitioners may create distrust. Emphasizing methodology over results is one way in which researchers disregard industry needs. According to Bedeian (1989), "theory thin and method driven" academic research is created in two ways. First, too much attention to the structure of the study may result in neglect of its findings. Bedeian (1989) states that research should "be judged on the basis of the substantive enlightenment it has supplied, not on the basis of the methodological heat it has generated" (p. 3). In other words, industry professionals are interested in research results as they pertain to their ongoing business concerns and not in the methodology employed to arrive at the results.

A second concern expressed by Bedeian (1989) is that the meticulousness of the research methodology may lead to theoretical deficiency. Bedeian declares, "We seem to believe that truth will be discovered somehow through using more and more esoteric techniques of data manipulation rather than by looking for it in the real world" (p. 3). Weick (1989) reinforces this sentiment by stating, "Theorists often write trivial theories because their process of theory construction is hemmed in by methodological strictures that favor validation rather than usefulness" (p. 516). For whom are university researchers writing by employing a philosophy that emphasizes methodology over usefulness, their academic colleagues or the field practitioners? It is an interesting question to ponder given that many researchers also teach future sport management practitioners. It would seem that conducting research that applies to those who could best implement the research (the students in their future jobs) would make it more meaningful. However, this may not always be the case in sport management academia. Some practicing sport managers (especially our former students) appreciate the value of applied research as a source of potential competitive advantage. However, other practitioners may perceive academic research as having little value because they see their work and academic knowledge as unrelated. Rynes, Bartunek, and Daft (2001) report that practitioners and university researchers seldom meet because research findings lack relevant, practical application in the business world. Hambrick (1993) was even more to the point when he stated, "Each August, [academics] come to talk with each other; during the rest of the year we read each other's papers in our journals and write our own papers so that we may, in turn, have an audience the following August: an incestuous, closed loop" (p. 13).

In other words, who outside of the academic sport management field is in fact reading, much less implementing, the research being conducted? To extrapolate from Hambrick, do we come together to present to each other in March, April, or May; read each other's papers throughout the rest of the year; then propose research projects to those same conferences in March, April, or May to begin the whole loop over? Stressing rigorous, conventional methodology diminishes innovation and communication to the professional industry as the primary reasons for publishing research (De Rond & Miller, 2005). Day (1982) further elaborates on this issue in stating, "Although the ultimate goal of scientific research is publication, it has always been amazing to me that so many scientists neglect the responsibilities involved. A scientist will spend months or years of hard work to secure data, and then unconcernedly let much of their value be lost because of lack of interest in the communication process" (p. 32).

Research may be introduced, discussed, and studied in our classrooms, but has it been communicated to or influenced sports executives? Or has research in sport management become too incestuous? Are we publishing research to impress each other, journal editors, and reviewers? These are questions for readers to ponder as they read the next sections.

Impact of Journal Reviews

Based on the aforementioned concerns, faculty may become wary of conducting research that may not impress others or be quickly considered for publication. Publication outlets that include interdisciplinary, multidisciplinary, or longitudinal approaches, or those with a distinct philosophical orientation, may be rejected in favor of publication speed. Amis and Silk (2005) state that because sport management is "inherently multidisciplinary in nature, we envision an academic landscape that is not dominated by any single overarching meta-narrative that marginalizes and obfuscates alternative approaches" (p. 358). The emphasis on productivity and traditional publication outlets may decrease innovation and increase insignificant or unsubstantial research (Bedeian, 1989; Byrne, 1990). This may diminish the perception of sport management as a serious academic discipline.

Miller (1995) contends that because academicians have become increasingly restricted in their fields of inquiry, they have submitted to a Machiavellian attitude of "whatever it takes" to get published. The fear of rejection in the research community may result in scholars embarking on more narrowly defined projects, which are less risky for their careers. A dearth of academic boldness in pursuing viable applications of research may be due, in part, to the journal review process, which directly impacts those seeking promotion and tenure (De Rond & Miller, 2005).

The review process is conducted as an objective blind review in which feedback is sought to improve the final manuscript (Bedeian, 2003; Starbuck, 2003). Reviewers for peer-reviewed journals are usually unidentified experts who provide insights as to how manuscripts can be improved (Bedeian, 2003). This model is the ideal; however, some have reported that the blind review process is quite different. Phrases such as *overly disparaging reviewers* (Miner, 2003), *uninformed, biased, and destructive* (Frost & Stablein, 1992), and *political gamesmanship* (Bedeian, 2003) have been cited in studies of this process. While reviewing is considered a control mechanism for a journal, the process raises several concerns. Graham and Stablein (1985) state that "The perils of the publishing process [we]see include threats to idealistic values and humanistic instincts; rejection and/or ridicule of one's creative labor; thwarted career goals; and the perpetuation of a system which batters egos in the name of bettering human understanding" (p. 139).

As a result, "First-time critical reviews are a shock to newcomers in the field. Some may never try to submit a paper again" (Graham & Stablein, 1985, p. 146). Additionally, established researchers are not immune to scathing criticisms. Some established sport management researchers have told me of having received such comments as "the author must have an agenda against men"; "there is a fatal flaw in the study" (without explaining it); and "this study isn't very interesting." In these instances, the comments led the authors to assume that the reviewers either did not care about improving the product or were biased against the study area. While such comments may be in the minority, they suggest that the research process has become a language game resulting in an assortment of epistemological and ontological statements (Kaghan & Phillips, 1998; Putnam, 1996). This practice may result in a research review process where judgments about the quality of the paper are largely based on the reviewers' lack of reflexivity of the assumptions about the research area (Haley, Hardy, & Alvesson, 2004). Hardy, Phillips, and Clegg (2001) define reflexivity as an "awareness of the situatedness of the scientific knowledge and an understanding of the research and research community from which the knowledge has appeared. Whereas objective knowledge claims to be un-situated—true any time and any place—reflexive knowledge is situated and includes a recognition of the multiple translation strategies that bring it into being" (p. 554).

In these circumstances, reflexivity means recognizing that a research manuscript represents merely one interpretation among many possible interpretations (Jermier, 1985), even though the reviewer may disagree with the position the author has taken. When reviewers who lack reflexivity disagree with an author's perspective, they may not consider the merits of the research as the author applies it to the subject matter of the project. Instead, they may judge the project's merits on how they (the reviewers) believe the research *should* be applied. In contrast, a protocol that emphasizes reflexivity may increase different representations of a subject matter. In other words, the reviewer needs to consider the article as the author wrote it and not how the reviewer would prefer it to have been written. As Hardy et al. (2001) surmise, "knowledge is not created by the actions of individual researchers but by multiple interactions within research communities" (p. 536). Amis and Silk (2005) further elaborate on this point by stating:

> to avoid such one-sided reductionism, there is a need for a variety of ways of seeing and interpreting in the pursuit of knowledge; the more one applies, the more dimensions and consequences of the field can be illuminated. It is in this sense that we embrace an expansion of knowledge, of ways of seeing and interpreting through engagement with alternative ontological, epistemological, ideological, political, and methodological approaches to the study of sport management. (p. 361)

Reviewers must make decisions about the merits of a manuscript. Often they are put in the role of experts to provide feedback to the author(s) as to what is or is not good research (De Rond & Miller, 2005). While preferences may exist among reviewers, these preferences should not result in reflexive opposition of another person's choices for the foundations or scope of the research positions (Amis & Silk, 2005). Such positions could lead to research publications that correspond "to an orthodoxy defining what constitutes 'good' research" (Bedeian, 2004, p. 205).

The adoption of publication orthodoxy may be the result of two factors in the academic field of sport management. First, it may result from relative like-mindedness among the researchers. Menand (2010) states that those in higher education "tend increasingly to think alike because the profession is increasingly self-selected" (p. 155). As mentioned previously, the productivity of researchers may be affected by those with whom they work. If more than one of the researchers is pursuing a specific line of research, they may have had many articles published, resulting in even more investigators, both at other institutions as well as any doctoral students, following suit. This may result in publication orthodoxy.

Secondly, publication orthodoxy may result from the fact that the main research areas of journal editors are associated with the substance of the manuscripts they selected for publication (Martinko, Douglas, & Campbell, 2000). As the number of new, more specialized journals increases, the number of experts who may be qualified to review manuscripts for them may be limited by publication orthodoxy. Rejection or resubmission with major changes may not mean that an article is poor (although it may be); instead, it may be that the research is outside the journal's subject area. Often, veteran reviewers are associated with more than one established journals in a field. These reviewers are inundated with requests to review submissions for multiple journals. Having fewer reviewers not only places an excessive burden on those reviewers, but it may also result in the reviewers being less informed in the specific area addressed in the paper. For example, an individual may be called upon to review an article that is broadly, but not specifically, within their area of knowledge. As a result, the reviewer's comments may not reveal a sufficiently intricate understanding of the research topic. These comments could lead the article's author to wonder if the reviewer read and understood the purpose of the article.

Having more specialized journals and fewer individuals to review submissions also increases the length of the review process. Additionally, a smaller cadre of reviewers makes it more difficult to sustain the normal model of three reviewers per article, which may threaten the integrity of the review process.

Rejection or request for major changes and resubmission should be made so the author can re-evaluate and strengthen the paper. The author should consider whether the comments of the editor(s) and reviewer(s) are valid. Do the comments validate the request for broad-based revisions or new data analysis or sampling? An author needs to appreciate that the reviewer's insights will strengthen a paper, which in turn, will make it more likely to be accepted for publication.

Because research articles are often not accepted without revision, authors usually discuss which revision requests to accept with journal editors and reviewers. If the author chooses to re-submit to the original journal with major changes that impact the essence of the study, the question arises whether the author is maintaining the purpose of the study or whether he or she is subordinating its purpose to meet the criterion of the reviewers. In other words, is the author complying with the reviewers' comments because they strengthen the article or simply to get the paper published? If it is for the first reason, then the review process has been successful. However, if it is to receive a publication, then the article's novelty and impact may be diminished. If authors compromise their original research intent in order to achieve publication, they are increasing the potential for publication orthodoxy.

Authors who regularly refuse to accept the comments made by journal editors or reviewers likely will not publish a sufficient number of articles in refereed journals to survive in higher academia. However, they do have the opportunity to submit the article to a different academic journal. The potential dangers in new submissions are, at a minimum, two-fold. First, the review process begins all over again. The length of time it is in the hands of the new reviewers will not be distinctly different from the timeframe of the original journal. If the first journal allowed a six-week period for the reviewers to peruse and evaluate the article, so will the next journal. Along with the time involved in the review process, the author will need to factor in the one-to-two week period needed to identify the suitability of submitting to another journal as well as the two-to-three week period for revisions if accepted. As a result, the author has invested four months in getting the article accepted. Because the pressure to publish at many research-oriented institutions includes obtaining multiple publications per year as one performance measure, academics must multi-task on several research projects simultaneously, at least until attaining tenure and often beyond then to ensure that they adequately meet their performance measures.

Issues in Performance Measures of Research Publications

The growth of performance measurement practices, such as impact factors and journal rankings, has encouraged the establishment of research objectives related to the number of hits in well-regarded journals (Gendron, 2008). Performance measurement implies that a socially produced and shared classification system divides academic researchers into certain pecking orders. This process may be referred to as *mathesis,* or the creation of a social order using measurement that facilitates the recognition of a person's position within a specific population (Foucault, 1970; Townley, 1995). For example, performance measurement practices may mean a researcher in one area may question collaborating with researchers in another area simply because he or she perceives them to be inferior. As a result, some potentially outstanding research avenues are ignored. According to Gendron (2008):

> Performance measurement promotes the constitution of the academic performer especially through journal rankings used to make superficial judgments about the self and others—for instance, in tenure reviews or funding committees. Rankings also affect journal editors whose lives are increasingly regulated by the position of their respective journals in rankings, and the status of journals regarding shallow measures of performance such as the impact factor. (p. 119)

Unfortunately, as stated above, the proliferation of performance measurements, such as impact factors and journal rankings, may decrease intellectual innovativeness. Such a decrease may occur because the authors' attention is focused on the number of hits they can display on their vitae. Or they submit because of some narrow measure of performance that a journal reports, rather than considering whether the research content of the paper is a good fit with the journal. As stated in Essay 5, the number of sport management journals has increased substantially over the past fifteen years. There are now twenty-six journals specifically relating to sport management (see Exhibit 7.1).

Of these journals, 15 (60%) published their first issue in 2004 or later, including the *International Journal of Sport Management and Marketing* (2005); *Journal of Issues in Intercollegiate Athletics* (2008); and *Journal of Venue & Event Management* (2009). Because newer journals tend to have lower impact factors (as discussed in the next section) or lack recognition, beginning researchers may shy away from them in an attempt develop a tenure-worthy vita. In the sport management field, this may occur despite the fact that new sport management journals possess very high review standards and boast editorial boards with many thorough and experienced researchers.

EXHIBIT 7.1

Sport management journals established between 1977 and 2010.

Name of Publication	Year of First Issue
Journal of Sport and Social Issues	1977
Applied Research in Coaching and Athletics Annual	1986
Journal of Sport Management	1987
Journal of Legal Aspects of Sport	1991
Sport Marketing Quarterly	1992
European Sport Management Quarterly	1994
Sport Management Review	1998
International Journal of Sports Marketing & Sponsorship	1999
International Journal of Sport Management	2000
Journal of Sports Economics	2000
Journal of Contemporary Athletics	2004
International Journal of Sport Management and Marketing	2005
Journal of Quantitative Analysis in Sports	2005
SMART Online Journal	2005
Sport Management International Journal Choregia	2005
Journal of Sports Media	2006
International Journal of Sports Finance	2006
Journal for the Study of Sports and Athletics in Education	2007
Sport Management Education Journal	2007
International Journal of Sport Communication	2008
Journal of Issues in Intercollegiate Athletics	2008
Journal of Intercollegiate Sport	2008
Journal of Venue & Event Management	2009
Journal of Sport Administration & Supervision	2009
International Journal of Sport Policy	2009

Impact factors

Impact factors of journals have gained so much attention recently that they are becoming a major controlling factor in higher academia. In fact, some academics assert that impact factors have become *the* essential item in the promotion and tenure process at many universities. For example, the impact factor for Journal A is the number of citations (in other publications) in 2012 to articles published in Journal A during the previous two years (e.g., 2010–2011) divided by the total number of articles published in Journal A during those two years (see Exhibit 7.2). That so many educated people in academia rely on such a limited evaluation of journal performance denotes the absolute trust many individuals place in numbers (Porter, 1995).

Monstersky (2005) states that the phrase *publish or perish* may better be reworded as *publish in a high-impact journal or perish*. The impact factor was designed by Eugene Garfield so less recognized journals could contend with the more recognized ones. But the measurement is biased against fields that regularly cite research that is more than two years old. According to Monstersky (2005), the impact factor formula should include all citations, not just those in a given year. This would raise a journal's impact score and even the playing field for journals that regularly cite older research.

When members of tenure or hiring committees are not familiar with a candidate's sub-discipline, they may use the impact factors of the journals the candidate has published in to identify the quality of his or her research. This may cause committee members to give more weight to a research paper published in a high-impact journal than the quality of the paper's information warrants. Yet, even Garfield, originator of the impact factor, cautioned that it could be misused because there are broad disparities from article to article within a single journal (Garfield, 1998). Simply stated, the impact factor does not reflect the quality of any single paper or author in a given journal.

Thomson ISI's Web of Science, an electronic database that is often used to determine the numbers of citations for papers, only counts citations to papers that appear in the journals included in the database (Garfield, 1998). For example, I found that searching ISI's database produces an under-representation of the scientific output of sport management research. In other words, if your paper is not published in certain select journals listed in the database, the Web of Science will not count it. Thus, sport management academic researchers may not be fairly judged against other researchers in the sciences, even in their own departments.

EXHIBIT 7.2

Formula for determining impact factor.

$$\text{Impact Factor for } Journal\ A = \frac{\text{Citations in 2012 to } Journal\ A \text{ articles published in 2010 and 2011}}{\text{Total articles published in } Journal\ A \text{ in 2010 and 2011}}$$

Another resource that may be used to determine number of citations is Google Scholar. The Harzing Publish or Perish (PoP) software uses Google Scholar to break down academic citations assessing both author and journal impact. In contrast to the Thomson ISI Web of Science, which is accessible only at universities that subscribe to it, Google Scholar is free to anyone with an Internet connection. Pauly and Stergiou (2005) state that "free access to data provided by Google Scholar provides an avenue for more transparency in tenure reviews, funding and other science policy issues, as it allows citation counts, and analyses based thereon, to be performed and duplicated by anyone" (p. 34). Additionally, Google Scholar is cited as performing the fastest searches (Bosman et al., 2006). Finally, Google Scholar identifies a considerable number of unique citations, making it very helpful for those involved in the tenure and/or promotion process (Meho & Yang, 2007).

Bosman and colleagues (2006) provide a succinct synopsis of the disadvantages of Google Scholar and Thomson ISI Web of Science (see Exhibit 7.3).

The problems in Google Scholar indicate that until a method is developed that automatically and precisely parses results into error-free, meaningful, and usable data, it will be of limited use for large-scale comparative citation and bibliometric analyses (Meho & Yang, 2007). Due to its inherent problems, identifying citations via Google Scholar will most likely be deemed invalid at institutions of higher education (Meho & Yang, 2007).

Another circumstance that can affect impact factors is the average number of days it takes for a journal to process new submissions. Garfield (2005) states that the "time required to referee manuscripts may also affect impact. If manuscript processing is delayed, references to articles [in the manuscripts] that are

EXHIBIT 7.3

Synopsis of the disadvantages of Thomson ISI Web of Science and Google Scholar (Bosman et al., 2006).

Thomson ISI Web of Science

- General search is restricted to ISI-listed journals
- Cited reference is restricted to citations from ISI-listed journals
- Citations to non-ISI journals awarded solely to first author
- Web of Science has a limited collection of minor variations of the same title
- Narrow coverage of non-English sources

Google Scholar

- Includes some non-scholarly citations
- Not all scholarly journals are identified
- Coverage might be asymmetrical across dissimilar fields of study
- Unreliable for older publication information
- Algorithms sometimes generate senseless results
- May catalog more journals than the Web of Science, but may not result in those journals receiving higher impact factors

no longer within the *JCR* (*Journal Citation Reports*) two-year window will not be counted" (p. 9). As mentioned earlier, editors and reviewers are besieged to review an increasing number of sport management submissions, which leads to a longer review process and potentially compromises the two-year mandate for impact factor inclusion.

The editor of the *Journal of the American Medical Association* criticized over-reliance on the impact factor stating that it "has taken on a life of its own. There are wonderful journals that have impact factors lower than some of the higher citation journals, and they're perfectly appropriate for good scientists to publish in" (Monstersky, 2005). No wonder impact factor has been described as "dodgy evaluation criteria" (Lawrence, 2007).

Journal rankings

A number of departments have formulated journal ranking lists to identify the top journals in the field to assist in determining tenure and promotion. Such ranking lists usually include a number of criteria such as citation rates, acceptance rates, and circulation numbers. Lowry, Humphreys, Malwitz, & Nix (2007) reported that journal rankings can facilitate faculty effectiveness in important activities such as determining where to submit their research, assisting tenure and promotion committees in knowledgably evaluating candidates, and assembling academic collections. However, developing a journal ranking list can be contentious, especially when diverse populations, including sport management, exercise physiology, sport psychology, motor learning, and motor behavior faculty, are in one department. Additionally, because sport management relies on paradigms and knowledge from many other disciplines, ranking sport management journals may be contentious even among sport management faculty. The field's interdisciplinary nature may hinder the recognition and assessment of journals in which faculty publish.

Another disadvantage of journal rankings is that they encourage individuals to use them in judging their work as well as that of their colleagues. Gendron (2008) states that "Journal rankings and performance measurement schemes tend to become increasingly influential within many fields of research, thereby consolidating the prevalence of performativity on the life and research endeavours of many academics. The latter are nowadays often pressured to publish in 'top' journals to ensure they have a displayable level of performance" (p. 97).

Because most sport management journals do not have an impact factor, the department faculty may shy away from them. In earlier years I, as well as some of my sport management colleagues, was encouraged by department chairs to publish research in academic business journals. The rationale was that such journals looked better on my vita because of their rankings and impact factors. If this practice continues, beginning researchers in the field may avoid sport management journals, to a certain extent, in order to build their credentials for promotion. While this is a reasonable strategy for untenured faculty, it may slow the identification and distribution of new and innovative ideas into the research literature and smother academic discourse in the sport management field. To effectively determine journal rankings, departments should evaluate individual research articles rather than the journals in which they are published. As Hogler and Gross (2009) state, "it would be pertinent to consider whether a journal carries substantial influence in a field of study, whether an article appears in a widely circulated special issue, and whether the reputation of other scholars publishing in the journal enhances the general impact of a work" (p. 121).

Restricting supply to increase the price of a product may be a good strategy in ticket sales, but is it appropriate for the exchange of bold, new ideas in sport management higher academia?

CONCLUDING THOUGHTS

The publish-or-perish concerns affecting the academic field of sport management have already been experienced by other academic disciplines in science, medicine and humanities. While some of these concerns have been expressed in this essay, others, such as ethical practices in publication authorship, ghost writing, for-profit journal publishing, and grant writing expectations, have not. To include these items would create such a breadth of information as to overwhelm both the reader and author. The information provided is not a rant (so to speak) nor does it promote the idea that journal reviewers and editors should not be critical of poorly developed or written research. Moreover, this essay should not be construed as advancing the notion that doctoral students should not be involved in publishing research prior to graduation (they should). Rather, this essay describes paradigm shifts that may affect sport management researchers who are involved with the publish-or-perish environment as they "all play the game 'academe'."

REFERENCES

Amis, J., & Silk, M. (2005). Rupture: Promoting critical and innovative approaches to the study of sport management. *Journal of Sport Management, 19,* 355–366.

Barnett, R. (2003). *Beyond reason: Living with ideology in the university.* Buckingham, UK: Society for Research Into Higher Education.

Bedeian, A. G. (1989). Totems and taboos: Undercurrents in the management discipline. *Academy of Management News, 19*(4), 1–6.

Bedeian, A. G. (1996). Lessons learned along the way: Twelve suggestions for optimizing career success. In P. J. Frost & M. S. Taylor (Eds.), *Rhythms of academic life: Personal accounts of careers in academia* (pp. 3–9). Thousand Oaks, CA: Sage.

Bedeian, A. G. (2003). The manuscript review process: The proper roles of authors, referees, and editors. *Journal of Management Inquiry, 12,* 331–338.

Bedeian, A. G. (2004). Peer review and the social construction of knowledge in the management discipline. *Academy of Management Learning and Education, 3*(2), 198–216.

Berman, J. (2008). Connecting with industry: Bridging the divide. *Journal of Higher Education Policy and Management, 30*(2), 165–174.

Bosman, J., van Mourik, I., Rasch, M., Sieverts, E., & Verhoeff, H. (2006). Scopus reviewed and compared. The coverage and functionality of the citation database Scopus, including comparisons with Web of Science and Google Scholar. Retrieved on September 27, 2010, from http://www. citeulike.org/user/msampson/article/3481989.

Bouchikhi, H., & Kimberly, J. (2001). It's difficult to innovate: The death of the tenured professor and the birth of the knowledge entrepreneur. *Human Relations, 54*(1), 77–84.

Boyer, E. L. (1990). *Scholarship reconsidered: Priorities of the professoriate.* Princeton, NJ: Carnegie Foundation for the Advancement of Teaching.

Boyer, E. L. (1996). From scholarship reconsidered to scholarship reassessed. *Quest, 48,* 129–139.

Byrne, J. A. (1990, October 29). Is research in the ivory tower "fuzzy, irrelevant, and pretentious"? *Business Week,* 62–63, 66.

Caplow, T., & McGee, R. J. (1958). *The academic marketplace.* New York: Basic Books.

Cowley, W. H. (1980). *Presidents, professors, and trustees.* Donald T. Williams, Jr. (Ed.). San Francisco: Jossey-Bass.

Day, R. A. (1982). *How to write and publish a scientific paper* (2nd ed.). Philadelphia, PA: ISI Press.

De Rond, M., & Miller, A. N. (2005). Publish or perish: Bane or boon of academic life? *Journal of Management Inquiry, 14*(4), 321–329.

Delanty, G. (2001). *Challenging knowledge.* Buckingham, UK: Open University Press.

Foucault, M. (1970). *The order of things: An archeology of the human sciences.* London: Tavistock.

Frost, P. J., & Stablein, R. E. (1992). Themes and variations. In P. J. Frost & R. E. Stablein (Eds.), *Doing exemplary research* (pp. 243–269). London: Sage Publications.

Garfield, E. (1998, June). Letters to the editor: The impact factor and using it correctly. *Der Unfallchirurg, 48*(2), 413. Retrieved from http://www.garfield.library.upenn.edu/papers/derunfallchirurg_v101(6)p413y1998.pdf.

Garfield, E. (2005). The agony and the ecstasy—The history and meaning of the journal impact factor. Paper presented at the International Congress on Peer Review and Biomedical Publication, Chicago, IL.

Gendron, Y. (2008). Constituting the academic performer: The spectre of superficiality and stagnation in academia. *European Accounting Review, 17*(1), 97–127.

Graham, J. W., & Stablein, R. E. (1985). Newcomer's perspective on publishing in the organizational sciences. In L. L. Cummings & P. J. Frost (Eds.), *Publishing in the organizational sciences* (pp. 138–154). Burr Ridge, IL: Irwin.

Haley, B., Hardy, C., & Alvesson, M. (2004). Reflecting on reflexivity. Paper presented at the Academy of Management Conference, New Orleans, LA.

Hambrick, D. C. (1993). 1993 Presidential Address: What if the Academy actually mattered? *Academy of Management Review, 19*(1), 11–16.

Hardy, C., Phillips, N., & Clegg, S. (2001). Reflexivity in organization and management theory: A study of the production of the research subject. *Human Relations, 54*(5), 531–560.

Harley, S. (2002). The impact of research selectivity on academic work and identity in UK universities. *Studies in Higher Education, 27*(2), 187–205.

Hogler, R., & Gross, M. A. (2009). Journal rankings and academic research: Two discourses about the quality of faculty work. *Management Communication Quarterly, 23*(1), 107–126.

Jermier, J. M. (1985). When the sleeper wakes: A short story extending themes in radical organizational theory. *Journal of Management, 11,* 67–80.

Kagan, W. N., & Phillips, N. (1998). Building the Tower of Babel: Communities of practice and paradigmatic pluralism in organizational studies. *Organization, 5*(2), 191–217.

Lawrence, P. A. (2007). The mismeasurement of science. *Current Biology, 17*(15), R583–R585.

Long, R. G., Bowers, W. P., Barnett, T., & White, M. C. (1998). Research productivity of graduates in management: Effects of academic origin and academic affiliation. *Academy of Management Journal, 41*(6), 704–714.

Lowry, P. B., Humphreys, S., Malwitz, J., & Nix, J. (2007). A scientometric study of the perceived quality of business and technical communication journals. *IEEE Transactions on Professional Communication, 50*(4), 352–378.

Martinko, M. J., Douglas, S. C., & Campbell, C. R. (2000). Bias in the social sciences publication process: Are there exceptions? *Journal of Social Behavior and Personality, 15*(1), 1–18.

Meho, L. I., & Yang, K. (2007). A new era in citation and bibliometric analyses: Web of Science, Scopus, and Google Scholar. *Journal of the American Society for Information Science and Technology, 58*(13), 2105–2125.

Menand, L. (2010). *The marketplace of ideas: reform and resistance in the American university.* New York: W. W. Norton & Company.

Miller, H. (1995). *The management of change in universities.* Buckingham, UK: Open University Press.

Miller, R. I., Chen, H., Hart, J. B., & Killian, C. B. (1990). *New approaches to faculty evaluation— A survey, initial report.* Athens, OH: Ohio University. Report submitted to the Carnegie Foundation for the Advancement of Teaching.

Miner, J. B. (2003). Commentary on Arthur Bedeian's "The manuscript review process: The proper roles of authors, referees, and editors." *Journal of Management Inquiry, 12,* 339–343.

Monstersky, R. (2005, October 14). The number that is devouring science. *Chronicle of Higher Education.* Retrieved on August 27, 2010, from http://chronicle.com/free/v52/i08/08a01201. htm.

Muto, A. (1993). *The University of California Press: The early years, 1893–1953.* Berkeley, CA: University of California Press.

Pauly, D., & Stergiou, K. I. (2005, December 22). Equivalence of results from two citation analyses: Thomson ISI's Citation Index and Google Scholar's service. *Ethics in Science and Environmental Politics,* 33–35.

Porter, L. W., & McKibbin, L. E. (1988). *Management education and development: Drift or thrust into the 21st century?* New York: McGraw-Hill.

Porter, T. M. (1995). *Trust in numbers: The pursuit of objectivity in science and public life.* Princeton, NJ: Princeton University Press.

Putnam, L. (1996). Situating the author and the text. *Journal of Management Inquiry, 5*(4), 382–386.

Reskin, B. F. (1977). Scientific productivity and the reward structure of science. *American Sociological Review, 42,* 491–504.

Rudenstine, N. L. (1996). Why a diverse student body is so important. *Chronicle of Higher Education, 42*(32), B1–B2.

Rynes, S., Bartunek, J. M., & Daft, R. L. (2001). Across the great divide: Knowledge creation and transfer between practitioners and academics. *Academy of Management Journal, 44*(2), 340–356.

Simanek, D. E., & Holden, J. C. (2002). *Science askew: A lighthearted look at the scientific world.* Bristol, UK: IOP Publishers.

Smith, P. (1990). *Killing the spirit: Higher education in America.* New York: Viking Press.

Starbuck, W. H. (2003). Turning lemons into lemonade: Where is the value in peer reviews? *Journal of Management Inquiry, 12,* 344–351.

Townley, B. (1995). Managing by numbers: Personnel management and the creation of a mathesis. *Critical Perspectives on Accounting, 6*(6), 555–575.

Weick, K. (1989). Theory construction as disciplined imagination. *Academy of Management Review, 14*(4), 516–531.

Williamson, I. O., & Cable, D. M. (2003). Predicting early career research productivity: The case of management faculty. *Journal of Organizational Behavior, 24,* 25–44.

External Funding

GETTING A PIECE OF THE PIE

It is commonly held that it is more difficult to get external funding in sport management than many other disciplines. We should not blindly accept this assumption.

The author introduces the essay

Robert E. Baker GEORGE MASON UNIVERSITY

Robert Baker, Ed.D., is the Director of the Center for Sport Management at George Mason University. Prior to initiating academic programs at two different institutions, he had garnered extensive sport industry experience. His research interests include professional preparation in sport management, the dynamic relationships among sport industry stakeholders, and sport for development and peace. He has obtained approximately $2 million in external funding and has written dozens of scholarly and professional articles.

Introduction

Levin (2011) notes that a "crisis in academe" that extends beyond the current economic situation has been building for some time. He cites budget limitations, increasing costs, and international competition among the reasons why institutions have devoted increasing time and energy to the pursuit of external funding. Standard revenue streams for state-sponsored public institutions have been substantially reduced, accounting for a smaller and smaller percentage of operating budgets; therefore, competition for available external monies has intensified (Bowers, 2011). As such, grantors and financial partners providing external funding to institutions are central stakeholders in the future of higher education, including sport management. Grantors disperse funds, usually on a competitive proposal basis, within a specified area of interest. Partnering entities enter a contractual or cooperative agreement that is uniquely negotiated with an institution. Grantors and partners include governmental agencies, private non-profit foundations, or for-profit corporations.

Traditional revenue streams are no longer adequate to support our academic programs, including sport management. Therefore, higher education has diversified its sources of funding. Institutions of all types and sizes, whether public or private, have intensified their pursuit of external funding (Connolly, 1997; Gulbrandsen & Smeby, 2005; Liefner, 2003; Sanz-Menendez & Cruz-Castro, 2003). As part of this evolving institutional dynamic, the strategic quest for external funding has become a challenge for all academic disciplines. Sport management is not exempt, nor should it expect to be. However, are sport management academicians prepared to compete for external funds? Sorting through the myriad avenues of external funding can seem a daunting task. From a small award supporting a specific limited research project to multi-million dollar awards for specialized program delivery, external funding comes in a wide array of styles and sizes. Available from a variety of sources, and for an assortment of purposes, external funding is a complex element of ever-increasing importance in higher education generally, and in sport management as a result.

This essay presents some basic information about external funding, but it is not intended to be a "how to" guide to acquiring external funds. Rather, it is intended to address prominent interests and concerns associated with external funding, particularly in sport management, and in some cases, to suggest stakeholders' courses of action. It first provides a brief overview of the types of funds available, their sources, and the processes through which they are obtained. Based upon that foundation, multiple considerations are then presented, including the importance of external funding, benefits and pitfalls of external funding relevant to sport management, stakeholder interests in external funding, strategies to enhance funding opportunities, entrepreneurship in higher education, and more.

TYPES AND SOURCES OF EXTERNAL FUNDING

Revenue sources vary, as do the mechanisms for obtaining external funds. Externally acquired revenue can be gifted by an external entity, or it can be generated in the form of competitively awarded funds.

Donations

Often gifted monies come through development efforts. Development, including the solicitation of small donations and major gifts, has become a key element in every institution of higher education, with such responsibilities often filtering to the unit level. Development gifts emanate from individual donors, corporate do-nors, private philanthropic foundations, government agencies, and other private agencies or partners willing to contribute. Seeking donations is now a com-mon means of obtaining revenue from external sources. Donors must connect with the purpose and see value in their gift. For example, a sport management program, through its faculty members, could develop and manage a long-term relationship with its alumni. As time passes, a successful alumnus/a may be will-ing to donate a large sum of money, perhaps to establish a scholarship, endow a chair, or name a building, or maybe simply to support aspiring students by ap-plying the gift toward general program costs. Conversely, a sport management program's development strategy might be to manage alumni relationships that yield many small donations from a large number of alums. Regardless of the purpose or the magnitude of the gift, this clearly illustrates that the academy is in the business of development. It's called *development* for a reason: gifts result from relationships developed over time.

Development is a contact sport. Effectively managing contacts among alumni, prospective donors, and other stakeholders is essential in the develop-ment process. Engaging with those contacts is a crucial strategic and tactical activity in relationship building. The development of relationships ultimately fosters not only goodwill, but also giving.

Competitively Awarded Funds

In contrast to development gifts, competitively awarded funds (while they can encompass some of these elements) are generally less relationship-based. Grants, contracts, and cooperative agreements, all common manifestations of competi-tive awards of external funds, are each unique in their own right.

Types of awarded funds

A *grant* is any in-kind or cash payment, contribution, or subsidy conferred by an external organization, or grantor, to an eligible recipient, or grantee. Grant sponsors include both federal and state government agencies, private non-profit foundations, for-profit businesses, and everything in between. Grants are usually for a specified purpose and are most often awarded conditionally (BusinessDic-tionary.com, n.d.). For example, the U.S. Soccer Foundation might provide modest funding for an interested faculty member to work in cooperation with local youth soccer authorities to provide a specific program to improve coaching and enhance facilities in a given location. Another example might find the U.S. Department of Education funding a faculty team at an institution to conduct innovative research in sport management education that aligns with the broader interests of the DOE. In either case, there are specific stipulations as to how, and on what, the money is spent. The grant is consequently awarded to the most attractive proposal submit-ted, based on submission criteria established by the grantor.

Contracts, on the other hand, are often negotiated arrangements that need not be competitively awarded like grants. They are voluntary, deliberate, and binding agreements that consist of an offer, acceptance, and consideration (Business-

Dictionary.com, n.d.). For example, an island nation in South Asia may have a specific interest in using sport as a vehicle to address violence, nutrition, and poverty issues. A properly constructed team of experts, including sport management faculty, could obtain contractual funding to conduct appropriate research and deliver a program addressing such needs. Another scenario would see a professional sport franchise choosing to outsource on a contractual basis, to an individual faculty consultant, the evaluation of specific socially responsible programming to determine its cost-effectiveness. In this case, the faculty member serves as an independent contractor to the franchise when entering into an agreement to provide services for pay. (See Essay 9 for more information on industry contracts.)

Similar to yet distinct from contracts, *cooperative agreements* are a form of assistance in which the federal government provides funding authorized by public statute, and the government plays a substantial role in its use. It reflects a relationship between the government and a recipient serving as an intermediary. These agreements are used to assist the intermediary in the delivery of services, programming, or goods in support of the authorized end result. For example, the U.S. Department of State might choose, as grantor, to enter into a funded cooperative agreement with an institution, through uniquely qualified faculty members who are committed to working cooperatively with federal employees to plan, deliver, and evaluate desired Department of State programming. In one scenario, sport management faculty members may cooperate with the Department of State to host visiting sport-related groups of foreign visitors in various regions of the United States in order to promote cross-cultural understanding. Sport management faculty would work closely with Department of State personnel to ensure the goals of the program are met.

Grant process

Despite the ever-important solicitation of gift revenues, the following discussion centers on competitively awarded funds, because the process for obtaining these funds is often challenging and complex. Grant proposals take a great deal of a faculty member's time and energy, with no guarantee of reward. Yet, the pursuit of external awards has intensified throughout higher education.

How does the grant process work? The award process begins when a grantor issues a request for proposals (RFP), in which it solicits applications for funding from prospective grantees. The RFP usually includes the purpose and nature of the grant and outlines the parameters to which the proposal must adhere. Like the grantors themselves, grant proposals vary greatly. There is no typical proposal. Each is uniquely suited to match the corresponding RFP. That said, some critical elements commonly included in proposals are the budget, the budget justification, and the narrative (a description of the proposed work to be completed). Grantors often limit the length of the narrative, as well as specify the contents to be included. Maximum budget amounts and restrictions on how the amounts are spent are commonplace as well. For example, the grantor could specify the parameters of the narrative, restricting it to 25 pages. They may require contents to include sections on the need for the project, partnerships to support the project, evaluation components, reporting procedures, and so forth.

A grantor may cap a single grant award at $250,000, with a maximum of 25 percent to be spent on administrative costs, including a maximum of 10 percent on indirect costs. They may also prohibit indirect charges on participant costs. Most grants come with these strings attached; however, these strings, when taken seriously, clarify what the grantor is seeking.

Any competitive edge, such as writing the proposal to the exact standards of the RFP, is essential, as there are generally far more submissions than awards. For example, during the 1960s over 50 percent of all submitted proposals were funded at the National Institutes of Health (NIH). In the 1970s and 1980s, 30 to 40 percent of submitted proposals received funding. Now, the NIH funds only 15 percent of the total number of proposals submitted (Levin, 2011). A federal grant writing resource suggests that grant proposals submitted by a good professional grant writer are generally successful at a rate of approximately three in ten (FederalGrants.com, 2011). Professional grant writers can be hired as full-time institutional employees in support of faculty projects, or they can be contracted for specific pre-submission contributions such as proposal review. Institutions dependent upon external awards often make such investments in support of the grant writing process in order to increase the chances of success. Achieving a 30 percent success rate in grant writing depends on the purpose of the grant (e.g., research, training, program) and the review process (e.g., external peer, internal committee), but strictly adhering to the grantor's stated guidelines is indispensable.

IMPORTANCE OF EXTERNAL FUNDING

Why is external funding so important? As previously discussed, from a macro perspective it is important to tap into new revenue sources for institutions. Beyond the economic implications, external funding supports academic programming such as sport management programs, faculty, and research endeavors. Success in obtaining external funding is in part related to quality research output, making funding central to the work of the academy (Laudel, 2005). However, institutional autonomy can be impacted as micro-political systems, both public and private, direct the flow of revenue and thus the direction of research interests and institutional action (Vincent, 2006). Competitive allocation of external resources is central in funding strategies, often relying upon formula-based performance measures and/or the evaluation of specific project proposals. Competitive, performance-based resource allocation results in positive changes in academic work, but can also produce unintended consequences that will be discussed later in this essay (French, 2003; Liefner, 2003).

As institutions garner revenues from a variety of sources, does external funding crowd out other sources? While increases in funding from one source can decrease funding from another, resulting in a zero-sum change, external funding can actually increase the amount of funding from traditional sources dedicated to a recipient (Connolly, 1997). The receipt of external funds can have a multiplier effect on all funding sources dedicated to a program or project. For example, if an institution receives a grant that requires a minimum level of institutional capacity to support the effective accomplishment of the project goals, the institution will commit those extra resources to ensure its success in obtaining and completing the project. This is often perceived as an institutional investment that puts them in a better position to obtain future funding.

For subunits such as divisions, departments, or schools, including those housing sport management programs, the impact on performance is not dissimilar to the concept of "trickle down" economics. Anytime an institution receives external funds, it accumulates amounts beyond the standard state- or tuition-driven revenue stream, which can allow more flexibility in the distribution of funds. These extra funds can be used to support programs and/or individual faculty members in pursuit of their academic objectives. Unrestricted external funds can support research, general administration, or the quest for additional funding. In most circumstances, productive grant recipients retain the most direct benefit, but indirect funds, provided for in most grants, add to the ability of an institution to exert some discretionary control over expenditures.

Indirect funds, also known as facilities and administrative services, are provided in many funded awards to compensate the institution for general institutional supports provided in the execution of an award. For example, a grantor can allow the recipient institution to capture 40 percent of the total awarded amount in order to proactively compensate the institution for sponsored program supports, such as materials and services used to assist the faculty member executing the sponsored research. These funds can be used to support not only the execution of current awards, but the development of new proposals, and in some cases, general institutional operations. Thus, depending on factors such as the level of dependence on collective resources, institutions can attain greater autonomy through external funding strategies (Sanz-Menendez & Cruz-Castro, 2003).

While obtaining external funding is important to institutions, it is also increasingly important to individual units and faculty members as well. For example, a sport management unit obtaining a gift or negotiating a contract to support graduate assistantships can provide new opportunities for students and faculty members. As another example, funding can be obtained to support and expand the pursuit of scholarly interests by supporting research expenses, travel costs, writing time, and so forth for funded faculty members. Funds can also enhance the delivery of sport management content through the recognition and support of effective instruction. Faculty members may enhance course delivery using externally funded technology to better serve students. This would either free up funds to be used for other purposes or directly support programs that would otherwise remain unfunded. Either way, it provides for significant local benefits. External revenue streams can often provide for additional resources for a sport management program, including general support staff, program-specific personnel, and instructional faculty. For example, external revenue obtained in the form of an endowment is often intended to support an additional faculty line. This provides needed resources, but the institution itself is not required to fully fund the position. Therefore, institutional funds can be used for more general program and faculty support (e.g., summer stipends, travel and research support). Clearly, external funds can have significant effects on what a sport management program is able to do and how it can do it.

The influx of external funds at the program level must be aligned with the program mission and objectives to facilitate positive outcomes. Such additional funding can clearly be used to enhance the scope and delivery of sport management programs. And, as the academy places increasing value upon external funding, success in obtaining funds can foster increasing respect for programs and individuals.

The prospective benefits of external funding extend to individual faculty members. Grant awards often support individual faculty research agendas. They can set the stage for the successful progression of a faculty research program. They can support the application of academic expertise to meet existing internal or community needs. External awards enhance individual faculty member's opportunities in research, teaching, and service, assisting faculty members in attaining their own goals. The pursuit of external resources does produce micro-level impacts on individual behavior, influencing the activities upon which faculty members concentrate. Additionally, external awards indirectly impact an individual's capacity and progress toward tenure expectations as discussed later in this essay (Liefner, 2003). In addition to grants, contracts and development relationships can lead to individual consulting opportunities and even endowed positions.

Beyond the institutional and individual benefits, funds can be directed toward broader societal impacts. Often, funding sources target awards and/or contracts to address "big picture" issues such as childhood obesity, at-risk youth, community development, violence prevention, equity issues, or diplomatic interests. If external funding supports, or in some cases stimulates, advancements in critical areas of societal need, it is serving not simply the individual and institutions directly funded, but also the whole of society itself. In turn, if external funds support advancements that positively influence the conduct of the sport industry, their benefit is multiplied beyond the recipient of the funds.

There is continual discourse on the importance of higher education and the need for access to it among all of its stakeholders. However, particularly in difficult economic times, the funding available to support higher education rarely corresponds to its pronounced importance. Yet, the availability of external funding supplements this general deficiency and strengthens academe in its ability to contribute to greater society. In effect, external funding reduces academe's dependence on traditional revenue streams (e.g., tuition, state funding formulas) and thereby facilitates liberty to pursue knowledge and provide applications without the limitations of those traditional sources. However, external funding is not without its drawbacks.

DRAWBACKS TO EXTERNAL FUNDING

As is often the case when money is at stake, the pursuit of external funding presents some common pitfalls. The foremost concern is that institutions and individuals are sometimes diverted from their own mission or agenda to chase the money. Or, perhaps worse, their goal becomes simply to chase the money without regard for any other purpose. This can have unintended consequences. One such consequence is that undue influence can be exerted on individual and institutional research agendas. In these instances, external sources of revenue controlling the field of play can dictate the focus and purpose of research that is undertaken. In the case of institutions chasing the money, they can distort their academic mission in the process.

If the pursuit of funds becomes preeminent, these external funding sources can also drive where faculty spends their time, potentially including what methods, participants, and research questions are utilized (Liefner, 2003; Platt, 1996). This leads to another unintended consequence in which an individual faculty member who chases the money dilutes the focus of her or his scholarly work. When applying for tangentially related or unrelated funding, an individual may attempt to justify the fit. However, for some pre-tenured faculty, this can hinder their chances for success in the tenure process. This can happen by diverting an established research agenda in pursuit of money. For example, if a faculty member has examined coaches as leaders and teams as organizations, and suddenly drops these interests in order to pursue funding to examine childhood obesity, it does not serve anyone well. Or, if external awards are undervalued in the review process, the time spent developing proposals may detract from those endeavors that are valued, such as publishing in quality journals.

Another pitfall that can trap unsuspecting faculty is the issue of time. Faculty are all taxed with multiple responsibilities in research, teaching, and service. Committing time to locating, writing, and executing grants, or to negotiating and executing external contracts, can yield big rewards, yet there is no guarantee. Given a modest success rate of 15 percent, the investment of time in proposal preparation is significant for each successful award, and the unrewarded time might be better spent on other contributions, such as teaching or other scholarship efforts (Levin, 2011). Yet, the availability of external funds influences faculty activity (Liefner, 2003). Denton and Hunter (1995) find that sustained faculty participation in the process results in greater success in obtaining external funds. The study, however, also indicates that sustained faculty participation results in diminished institutional climate and faculty morale. Perhaps this is due to the extensive time commitment and subsequent minimal success rate, or perhaps it creates a cultural divide between the funded and unfunded or haves and have-nots. Despite these drawbacks, there are many incentives to pursue external funding. Recognizing the fine line between the responsible pursuit of external funding and simply chasing the money is important for both individuals and institutions.

ADDITIONAL CONSIDERATIONS FOR STAKEHOLDERS

Who are the stakeholders in the expanded quest for external funding? We can begin with the institutions of higher education themselves. Every institution, whether privately or publicly funded, is in competition for additional sources of revenue. The line between public and private institutions has become increasing less distinct. When it comes to institutional revenue, whether through tuition, direct government support of students, or state funding formulas, traditional funding models are insufficient for both public and private institutions of higher education. Therefore, regardless of size, public institutions have embraced the pursuit of external funding sources alongside their private compatriots. Clearly, governments, along with the public and private agencies funding higher education, albeit at insufficient rates, are also concerned with the institutional pursuit of available external funds.

On a broad scope, funding of specific research or projects is most often viewed as beneficial to greater society and to the grantor's specific interests and, in the case of sport management, to the individual partner or the sport industry itself. As a result, the collective sport industry is also a stakeholder in external funding. Not only may its constituents be the source of revenue, they may also be the beneficiary of the results such funding yields. For example, industry funded partnerships with higher education might result in the betterment of the conduct of the sport industry through sponsored students, the development and application of advanced technologies through sponsored research, or the ability to generate additional revenue through expanded markets.

Another key stakeholder in external funding is the recipient, or grantee. In most cases, while the funds are received by an institution, the work of individual faculty members enables that process. Faculty are typically responsible for generating the proposals seeking external funding, be it a 200-page proposal in response to a grantor's RFP, or a single page executive summary proposing a specific project with an industry partner. Faculty members are also responsible for carrying out the work stipulated by the agreement, whether it is a grant or contract. Faculty must consider their capacity, and that of their institution, to carry out all aspects of their proposal. All too often, funds are forfeited due to the inability (or in some cases unwillingness) to complete the agreed upon project.

What do stakeholders in the funding process need to consider? Grantors should consider broader agendas in the distribution of funds. Yes, the grantors control the money (and in turn, the agenda); however, operating more in partnership with recipients could increase productivity and efficiency in the process and yield additional unforeseen outcomes. It is important that the external funding sources continue to provide access to revenue. In doing so, it is reasonable and necessary for them to establish criteria for funding. It is possible, however, for these parameters to be more general in cases where funding is approached as a partnership. In so doing, sport management faculty may have opportunities to develop proposals that might otherwise have no source for funding. In this sense, individual faculty would not simply chase the money at the expense of their own interests. They would maintain a clear agenda for their work, and commit resources such as time to the partnership. Purposes for funding could continue to focus on specified research projects, applications of research, or teaching and service activities, but would be developed in agreement with the partners.

All stakeholders in external funding, including grantees, need to be invested in the process. Each stakeholder puts "skin in the game," as the saying is known in venture capital circles, in different forms. Faculty put in time and intellect. Grantors typically put in money. Institutions, as grantees, must put in available resources as well. It is essential that they facilitate the institutional capacity to support sponsored programs. It is through this dynamic that the size of an institution can matter in the opportunity to acquire external funding. Large research intensive institutions often have dedicated offices to support sponsored programs, specifically grants and cooperative agreements. If an institution does not have this type of designated office, then the likelihood of obtaining a significant federal grant is very limited. The old adage "it takes money to make money" applies to institutions intending to acquire external revenue through obtaining large awards. Institutions must be realistic about their own access to external funds. Most funding is awarded based upon input criteria, such as numbers of students and resources, rather than output criteria, such as research performance (French, 2003). If institutions want to be competitive, they must invest. Institutional investment in support systems is an essential component in an attractive proposal for large amounts of outside revenue. Institutional capacity can make or break a faculty member's success in obtaining and executing grants.

If appropriate institutional investments are made to support sponsored programs, then whether an institution is private or public has no impact on the opportunity for success. As noted, while federal support of individual students (e.g., Pell grants) and specific programs (e.g., Title I) comes without bias as to the public or private status of the institution, tuition alone, even in the most expensive private schools, is rarely adequate in funding institutional operations. At many schools, such a high percentage of students receive scholarships that this effectively reduces or eliminates their tuition costs. In the public sector, the funds provided by the government to its respective public institutions are rarely sufficient on which to operate. In an era of economic recession, public institutions have seen not only a substantial reduction in government spending on higher education, but also strategic moves to recoup privately garnered revenue, such as the earned interest on tuition dollars. In some cases, this revenue has been redirected to state general funds or to mandated purchasing systems that ensure the state receives a portion of all money spent by a state-supported institution. These strategies put additional pressure on external revenue needs.

As pressure for external funds increases, additional considerations emerge for institutional stakeholders. Whether motivated by the competitive nature of external funding, the increasing costs of higher education, or the retrenchment of public funding mechanisms, academe is fixated on quantifiable matrices and rankings. (See Essay 4 for a discussion of rankings for sport management programs.) External funding is a criteria commonly utilized in ranking systems in higher education. This common practice would likely apply to sport management as well. The amount of external funding obtained by a sport management unit reflects the perceived quality of a program, as it does with an institution. As a result, rankings can drive both institutional and programmatic strategies. Institutions may see increased external funding as a concrete path to a higher ranking. Therefore, institutions already jump through hoops to attain higher rankings, to increase prestige, or even to ensure their survival. Sport management cannot escape these hoops. We are part of a system wherein external funding will, for the foreseeable future, be of increasing importance in the prestige of our programs and in our professional lives as academics.

Institutions undeniably reap budgetary benefits by supporting various operations with additional outside revenue. If achieving increases in external funding is an institutional strategy to supplement traditional revenue streams, then in order to facilitate success, institutions must be transparent about that fact. For example, if deans or program directors are expected to engage in development activities and support grant opportunities that result in increased local level funding, they must be informed and prepared to do so. After being put in a position to succeed, it is appropriate to evaluate these positions on their success in attracting funds. If units are to absorb cuts in traditional funding, or as in many cases in sport management, support massive program expansion without additional resources, then it must be made clear that the funding responsibilities are being decentralized to the program level. Institutions must be transparent about internal strategies in their quest for external funds (Vincent, 2006). It also becomes incumbent on the institution, through local program units, to prepare faculty to acquire outside funds. Program survival can depend on faculty ability to bring in revenue. In sport management, the opportunity to advance is often similarly dependent on external funds.

If institutions want to increase external funding and encourage faculty engagement in such efforts, how can they incentivize the process? One way is through the distribution of indirect costs to provide direct individual reward to faculty members obtaining external funds. Indirects are usually distributed within the recipient institution via formula. In providing direct benefits to the grantee, if indirect costs are 40 percent of an award, the formula would include a small percentage, say 10 percent of the indirects, to be distributed to the grantee. If the institution is willing to share its revenues, this simple financial policy that redistributes a portion of indirect revenues can provide individuals the incentive to spend the time and energy in pursuit of external funding.

Another academic policy for consideration, where it fits appropriately within the institutional mission, is to identify external funding as a fourth category in the tenure process. Currently at many institutions, external funding is often a square peg pushed into a round research, teaching, or service hole, squeezed in where it best fits; but it is neither fully integrated nor appreciated. If an institution places greater importance on the receipt of external revenue, and as this responsibility "trickles down" to faculty members, the pursuit of external funding warrants consideration as a stand-alone ingredient in the tenure process.

Much of the work of academe is accomplished through faculty efforts. Institutions expecting the faculty to be successful across the myriad responsibilities affiliated with obtaining external funds while simultaneously performing at high levels in their teaching, service, and research responsibilities, must provide additional institutional supports. In combination with the capacity of the institution to support faculty, individuals are crucial in successfully obtaining external funding. Yet, as a result of the intensely competitive process, inexperienced faculty members often have difficulty finding examples and assistance from the successful awardees with whom they are competing. To address this dynamic, and to increase the opportunities for success, institutions increasingly hire academic administrators who, as research-development professionals, assist faculty in obtaining funding (Levin, 2011). These professionals can provide various services to faculty seeking grants. They can provide strategic guidance; assist with conceptualizing, writing, and managing finances; and facilitate collaborative efforts. Because sport management research is often interdisciplinary, and outside funders often value team efforts, integrating this type of support into a sport management program would help increase funding opportunities through new collaborations.

It is commonly held that it is more difficult to get external funding in sport management than many other disciplines. We should not blindly accept this assumption. If we collaborate on projects with individuals or units who bring distinct expertise, we increase our opportunities. For example, if we assemble a team of health, nutrition, education, and sport management experts, we may be positioned to obtain funding to address a variety of aspects of childhood obesity in a single grant-funded study. One could apply the same strategy to violence prevention, community development, or many other large-scale concepts. In such collaborations, each sport management program and individual faculty member possesses distinct characteristics and circumstances that impact their access to funding; therefore, each is uniquely positioned to obtain funding. As faculty continue to think outside the box, access to private industry and government funding will continue to increase. We must each ask ourselves, is there a way my research interests can align with others' interests in a fundable project? While we as sport management faculty must work to position ourselves to obtain funds, including through the assembly of interdisciplinary research teams, institutions must also recognize any actual differences in the availability of external funds based on faculty and program interests.

To increase opportunities, sport management academics seeking funding must be aware of what grantors and funders want. Just as the direction of research may be influenced by the interests of external funders (e.g., funds are available for the examination of childhood obesity), so may the purpose of investigation. Applied research, intended to produce clearly identifiable applications or justifications, will often attract funding (Gulbrandsen & Smeby, 2005). Sport management can answer many questions that funders want answered (e.g., Is our program doing what we intend it to do? Could we be reaching a different market?). That is another strategy to employ in the increasingly competitive world of external funding. I'm not suggesting we conduct only applied research, but rather that sport management should strategically value it. This does reflect the increasing influence of external funding in academe. Yet, sport management's elevated status as a discipline, or perhaps even our self-preservation, is in part reliant upon securing external funds.

While we can argue perspectives on program justification, some institutions maintain that sport management's value is that it puts "butts in seats." However, dependent upon institutional mission, the generation of tuition revenue is no longer unilaterally sufficient to justify a program. As external funding is increasingly valued, sport management must embrace the challenge. Housed in units that often have disciplines traditionally well-situated to obtaining external funds (e.g., exercise physiology, health, business management, economics), sport management must find avenues to obtain outside revenue. Toward that end, sport management programs and faculty should be effective in developing and implementing entrepreneurial opportunities.

Institutional entrepreneurship is on the rise and is a significant factor in higher education (Louis, Blumenthal, Gluck, & Soto, 1989). Embracing the entrepreneurial environment should be a natural fit for sport management, which presents several avenues to achieve this. Individuals can be entrepreneurs as consultants, yet the opportunities for programmatic entrepreneurship are intriguing. Clearly, the pursuit of grant funding has an entrepreneurial element that can provide greater revenue generation and supports for both individuals and programs if undertaken in an innovative way. For example, funds acquired to support administrative costs are often used through a vehicle, such as a research center, to establish support systems to facilitate more faculty entrepreneurship. An additional strategy for academic sport management programs might be to form commercial entities to perform specific functions and generate revenue. For example, the ownership and operation of a small, local sport-related franchise might provide both revenue and experiential opportunities for students. Yet another avenue for creative revenue generation comes through academy–industry partnerships. For example, a large sport firm might seek to provide specialized educational opportunities for its management team in an exclusive arrangement with a specific sport management program. In these instances, sport management is well-positioned to tap in to external funding by developing relationships with the industry.

The sport industry is more than a single entity. The sport-related segments of the economy are consistently diversifying, with an overall value estimated as high as $425 billion per year (Plunkett, 2010). For the long-term health of the sport management discipline, it is imperative that diverse individual industry stakeholders invest in sport management research, service, and educational programs. However, the only way that these investments will occur is if there are demonstrable returns to those industry stakeholders willing to invest. While maintaining balance in our academic pursuits and interests, sport management faculty must consider the development of funding proposals that present a clear purpose with applications tied to interests of industry stakeholders. That is not to say that any one external entity will dictate the future of our research interests or our discipline. It is to say that, as a discipline, we must be responsive to current interests and accept a variety of sources for what they are. Sport management academics should consider ways to add to available federal and foundation-based awards through private industry-generated funding. If we understand the strings that exist in all of these revenue sources, based on the funders' interests, we will avoid being trapped by them. An increased interest and investment in our academic pursuits by the sport industry would advance our discipline. It is time for the sport management academy to develop strong industry relationships in order to proactively engage industry, as partners and sources of external funding in our symbiotic future (see Essay 9).

CONCLUDING THOUGHTS

If this essay has proved informative, challenged convention, and stimulated discussion on an issue of critical importance to stakeholders in sport management, then it has achieved its intended purposes. The opinions and perceptions presented here are those of one person. You do not have to agree with them. Nonetheless, external funding is an issue in higher education, and thereby in sport management, that is here to stay. There is no going back to a time when tuition and/or government funds fully supported our academic programming. How each of us, and our sport management discipline, deals with that is up to us. This collection of essays presents abundant opportunities for us, individually and collectively, to establish our own future. In the area of external funding, we can determine the paradigm through which we embrace that future.

REFERENCES

Bowers, L. (2011). *The physical educator's guide to successful grant writing* (2nd ed.). Reston, VA: National Association for Sport and Physical Education.

BusinessDictionary.com. (n.d.). Retrieved July 27, 2011, from http://www.business dictionary.com.

Connolly, L. (1997). Does external funding of academic research crowd out institutional support? *Journal of Public Economics, 64*(3), 389–406.

Denton, J. J., & Hunter, F. A. (1995). The multiple effects of influencing external funding productivity.

FederalGrants.com. (2011). EDRS Report. Retrieved July 27, 2011, from http://www.federalgrants.com/grant-writers.html.

French, N. J. (2003). *Report on the seminar on external funding and university autonomy.* UK: N & S Consulting Services.

Gulbrandsen, M., & Smeby, J. (2005). Industry funding and university professors' research performance. *Research Policy, 34*(6), 932–950.

Laudel, G. (2005). Is external funding a valid indicator of research performance? *Research Evaluation, 14*(1), 27–34.

Levin, J. (2011, March 27). The emergence of the research-development professional. *Chronicle of Higher Education, 57*(30). Retrieved from http://chronicle.com/article/The-Emergence-of-the/126906/.

Liefner, I. (2003). Funding, resource allocation, and performance in higher education systems. *Higher Education, 46*(4), 469–489.

Louis, K. S., Blumenthal, D., Gluck, M. E., & Soto, M. A. (1989). Entrepreneurs in academe: An exploration of behaviors among life scientists. *Administrative Science Quarterly, 34,* 110–131.

Platt, J. (1996). Has funding made a difference in research methods? *Sociological Research Online, 1*(1), 1–13.

Plunkett, J. W. (2010). *Plunkett's sports industry almanac 2010.* Houston, TX: Plunkett Research.

Sanz-Menendez, L., & Cruz-Castro, L. (2003). Coping with environmental pressures: Public research organizations responses to funding crises. *Research Policy, 32*(6), 1293–1308.

Vincent, F. (2006). NGOs, social movements, external funding and dependency. *Development, 49,* 22–28.

Academia and the Sports Industry

9

AN AUTO-ETHNOGRAPHY, PRACADEMICS, AND A COLLABORATIVE MODEL

*Don't ignore the need to be a pracademic in some shape or form.
The industry needs our talents, and our students benefit greatly from
seeing the application of classroom learning and academic theory
in the real-life laboratory that the sport industry can provide.*

William A. Sutton UNIVERSITY OF CENTRAL FLORIDA

William Sutton holds an Ed.D. from Oklahoma State University. Sutton currently holds an appointment as Professor and Associate Department Head on the faculty of the DeVos Sport Business Management Graduate Program at the University of Central Florida and is the founder and principal of Bill Sutton & Associates. He is a co-author of two textbooks, has authored more than 200 articles, and has given over 250 national and international presentations. Sutton is a past president of NASSM.

Introduction

In 2007 I wrote an article, "Academia, industry benefit when interaction is encouraged," for *Street & Smith's SportsBusiness Journal* (Sutton, 2007). It was based on my own sabbatical experience working for Commissioner Stern at the National Basketball Association, a position that evolved into a stint as Vice President for Team Marketing and Business Operations.* It was also influenced by an editorial I had read some years before in *USA Today* by Amitai Etzioni, a longtime sociology professor at Columbia University, in which Etzioni (2002) called for the academic community to become public intellectuals. Etzioni defined *public intellectuals* as those faculty dedicated to teaching and research who also incorporate into their mission an industry-based interaction beyond the physical campus boundaries. In my article for *SportsBusiness Journal,* I used the term *pracademic* to describe how I perceive my role in the world of sport business. I defined a *pracademic* as an academic working with the sport industry and its practitioners to improve the products and services of the industry and increase and retain its consumer base (Sutton, 2007). Rethinking my original definition at this time, I would amend the definition of a *pracademic* to be someone who develops relationships and seeks to integrate his/her teaching, research, and service into a meaningful curriculum and research agenda by working cooperatively with practitioners to identify issues and solve problems in the sport industry.

Over the course of my academic life, which spans 23 years and includes appointments at Robert Morris University, The Ohio State University, the University of Massachusetts, and now the DeVos Sport Business Program at the University of Central Florida, I have always viewed myself as a public intellectual. My work has been characterized by working with practitioners or working as a practitioner. I have utilized those experiences and relationships to influence my students (in and out of the classroom), the sport industry, and in several cases academia through my role as a founding member of both the *Sport Marketing Quarterly* and the Sport Marketing Association. In addition, my co-authorship of the first Sport Marketing text, *Sport Marketing,* and of the first text dealing with sales in sport, *Sport Promotion and Sales Management,* are drawn as much from industry practice as theory. The examples and perspectives contained in each text are often provided and written by practitioners wanting to share their experiences with students aspiring to be future industry practitioners. My body of work also includes a consulting practice (www.billsuttonandassociates.com) focusing on marketing, sales, and revenue enhancement in professional sport; creation of a sport sales training program (www.sportsalescombine.com) for aspiring sport sales professionals developed with Dr. Richard Irwin of the University of Memphis; and authorship of a featured monthly column ("Sutton Impact") in the sport industry trade journal, *Street & Smith's SportsBusiness Journal.*

My professional service record also mimics my pracademic approach as I sit on several editorial boards and have served or currently serve as president of the Sport Marketing Association, on various college and university committees, as a board member of the Orlando Magic Youth Fund and the Central Florida Sports Commission, and on the Steering Committee for the National Sports Forum, one of two academics to hold such an appointment.

---

* My NBA sabbatical experience led to four years of full-time and two years of part-time employment as Vice President for Team Marketing and Business Operations and continued for four additional years as a consultant working with various WNBA and NBA Developmental League Teams.

The following covers my experiences and theories about what I have learned in my pracademic life, how that knowledge has benefitted me and my students, and a road map outlining hazards and considerations to watch out for as you consider how much of a pracademic life you should seek. Any decision results in both intended and unintended consequences that may result in detours to your chosen career path. Thus, I share my ideas and it is up to the reader to choose what, if anything, he or she would like to embrace as part of a lifestyle, be it academic or pracademic.

WHAT WE HAVE TO OFFER AS ACADEMICS AND WHAT THE INDUSTRY WANTS: PROVIDING VALUE AND RECOGNIZING OPPORTUNITY

In the early days of my tenure with the NBA, I was speaking about research and mentioned that I had done statistical analyses to confirm what I was proposing. Needless to say, I saw the eye rolls that sometimes accompany an exchange between academics and industry professionals. Since that point in 2000, statistical analyses, now commonly referred to as *analytics* in the sport industry, has found an important place in the boardroom through the development of variable and dynamic pricing models, demand models, and targeting and scoring sales leads based upon the probability to purchase. Analytics has also found a place in the office of the general manager or the coach; in other words, it is valuable on the sport side as well as the business side of the industry. Starting with Bill James, one of the originators of sabermetrics, and Billy Beane, General Manager of the Oakland A's, who incorporated this statistical approach in his scouting and player evaluation techniques, statistical analysis was greatly advanced by author Michael Lewis in his bestselling work *Moneyball* (2003).

Statistical analyses of trends, predictive modeling, and probability on the sport side have become commonplace (Lewis, 2003). How commonplace? Virtually every NBA team employs an analytics team, which usually comprises a database manager and an analyst. This duo, assisted by one or more interns, is aided either by a market researcher also employed by the team or by contracted outside research firms, such as Turnkey Sports, that conduct customized research jointly designed with the sport franchise. The area of sports analytics has become so popular that the Massachusetts Institute of Technology (MIT), due in large part to the success of one its graduates, Daryl Morey, the GM of the Houston Rockets, developed the Sloan Sports Analytics Conference. The conference attracts virtually all of the progressive professional teams and leagues and regularly sells out. Prior to his position with the Rockets, Morey was with the Celtics. Basketball operations were a key part of his responsibilities, including the development of analytical methods and technology to enhance basketball decisions related to the draft, trades, free agency, and advance scouting of opponents for the coaching staff. His hiring at Houston followed the recent *Moneyball* trend of adding more advanced statistical-based analysis to the traditional use of qualitative scouting and basic statistics (Feschuk, 2008).

So when looking for fertile ground for class projects as a way to connect the academics, the students, and the industry, my advice is to consider projects focused on sports business analytics, market research, predictive modeling, market analyses, and of course any sales-related topics. Such projects would be welcomed enthusiastically by any sport organization eager to improve its performance. The commonality of these projects is that each one has a defined deliverable—the organization knows what it will receive and that the project will have value to them. Value to the organization is the key to building a bridge from the academic community to the business community. I often ask students when they are working on a project or examining a promotional offer that contains a message, "Is the offer about the seller or the receiver?" The more it is about the receiver—the buyer—the higher the likelihood that it will be readily accepted.

Faculty members have more training in research methods and statistics than most practitioners working in the sport industry. Wouldn't it be a valuable developmental tool for faculty members to examine their research agendas to see how that expertise applies to real-world situations? Taking it a step further, would that value be even more enhanced if it were utilized to illustrate to students the value of research and statistics and how those tools can be utilized to make decisions and shape policy in the sport industry?

As a case in point, one of my sport marketing class consulting projects (I will address the concept of class consulting projects later) involved analyzing attendance patterns for the Cleveland Indians baseball team and the impact of promotional activities (events and giveaways) on attendance. The goal of the assignment was to produce a predictive model that would show Indians' leadership the projected attendance for each game the following season, thus identifying games in which they could use promotions to achieve sellout attendance. The project also involved pinpointing reasons for low attendance and determining how to raise attendance through promotional activities. The results? The Indians were highly satisfied and the two team captains for the projects secured employment as business analysts with the NHL Florida Panthers and the Tampa Bay Lightning.

An excellent case of faculty aligning their research agendas to match a critical need in the sport industry is that of Baylor University's Sport Sales Program, headed by Darryl Lehnus and Kirk Wakefield. According to the program's website, "the Baylor Sports Sponsorship & Sales (S3) major is the only one of its kind in the United States to provide a complete major in sports sales. We place all students in internships at the highest level of professional sports for students interested in ticket sales, customer relationship management, or sports media/corporate sales" (www.baylor.edu). According to Lehnus and the website, "Experience = Jobs. Each student will serve two internships in Sales & Promotion before graduating with a degree in Sports Sponsorship & Sales. To get a job in pro sports, you have to have experience. By the time students complete the major, they will have sold ticket packages for the Texas Rangers, interned with a professional team or major media company, and learned how to manage a call center" ("Sport sponsorship," n.d.). I have always viewed the hard sciences as the model for research in academia: identify and solve a problem confronting humanity. As Wakefield demonstrates, the same approach can hold true for academic research in the field of sport business.

If these benefits are not enough, the Baylor University program, along with Ohio University, the University of Massachusetts, the University of Memphis, and the University of Central Florida, annually host recruiters from team sport franchises interested in finding quality sales people. Having recruiters come to campus for sport management majors is not a common occurrence, but this type of industry connection, along with the perceived value and established relationships, shows that merging research, teaching, and service can truly yield opportunities.

Finally, a faculty sabbatical is an opportunity to create a unique learning experience. As discussed earlier, I elected to spend my sabbatical year working at the NBA in New York City. My initial assignment was in the sports communication area. I was asked to conduct an assessment of every NBA team to determine what types of research they were doing, investigate if that research should also be undertaken at the league level, and decide if there should be a more coordinated approach led by the league for the benefit of the teams.

Following personnel changes at the league, I began reporting directly to Commissioner Stern to work on special assignments and was located in an office outside his. My initial assignment for Stern was to create the program for the annual league marketing meetings. This task was followed by my most significant assignment, reviewing the operations of the Team Services Department. The assignment resulted in the creation of the highly successful and imitated Team Marketing and Business Operations Department (now commonly referred to as TMBO), which I also helped to staff. After returning to UMass for my obligatory year after the sabbatical, I was granted an unpaid leave from UMass and accepted a position as Vice President of the department I had helped to build. In short, it was a fantastic learning experience and a life-changing one as well.

My good friend Dr. Irwin at the University of Memphis had a sabbatical in 2010 working with the Memphis Grizzlies. I am not sure, however, if anyone else has considered this nontraditional approach to the sabbatical. It should also be pointed out that not every college or university would approve of such sabbatical activity, as each institution has its own guidelines regarding faculty workload and compensation as they pertain to sabbaticals. Furthermore, this type of experience might not be right for every faculty member, given the breadth of research agendas and interests among academics. However, if an individual is interested in the types of class consulting projects discussed later in this essay, the exposure, networking opportunities, and industry-wide credibility to be gained from such a sabbatical will go a long way in helping to develop and secure the relationships essential to achieving successful projects and meaningful learning outcomes.

Summarizing what the industry wants from us, I offer the following list:

- Incorporate the problems and issues facing the sports industry in our teaching and research.
- Prepare students through coursework (projects and research) and internships to address these problems.
- Engage with industry professionals at the local level and utilize that engagement to offer assistance.

- Publish in academic journals as well as trade journals (translate research into shorter, nontechnical pieces that offer advice and assistance to the industry).

- Stay connected to the industry and continually update our class content to stay current with what is going on in the industry and to incorporate their best practices into our course content.

- Attend industry meetings such as the National Sports Forum that are available to us.

- Invite industry professionals into our classrooms to present.

- Assist in solving industry problems and improving current practices, especially in the areas of market research and business analytics.

- Commit to a partnership and be willing to learn from each other.

THE YIN AND THE YANG: TAKING ADVANTAGE OR BEING TAKEN ADVANTAGE OF?

Traveling down a new path always includes an element of risk. The path is unknown, you meet new people, and you may be proposing to do new things. The aspect of risk that can be of most concern, particularly to young untenured faculty, is whether the endeavor is worth one's time and effort. Unfortunately, there is no one correct answer; it is very likely to be situational.

I have worked in the industry, currently run a consulting practice, write a monthly column in a national trade publication, and am cited from time to time in the media. In addition, I have established class consulting projects over the past five years, so what we offer and what I do are both fairly well-known commodities. Therefore, I am often approached on the business side with opportunities I may not be interested in but that might be appropriate for my class. Similarly, people approach me seeking free services from a class project, because I am the professor and will ultimately be involved in the quality of the final product. I don't want to make a poor decision that will result in a poor learning experience for my students, nor do I want to place them in a project that is beyond their capabilities. Thus, the decision of whether or not to accept a class consulting project is based upon a number of variables. The following list of considerations includes the factors that I use when soliciting organizations or receiving solicitations from them for class consulting projects:

- Is the organization able and willing to pay the fee for the consulting project?

- Is the organization willing to travel to Orlando for the presentation of the final product and the deliverables?

- Is the organization willing to participate in the grading and evaluation of the final projects?

- Will the organization assign specific individuals with the knowledge and patience to work with students over the course of a four-to-six month project?

- Does the subject matter challenge students' academic abilities and their worldview?

- Is there a research and analysis piece that will develop skills in those areas and provide an application opportunity for students?
- Is there an opportunity for the students to develop a creative solution to the problem or situation proposed in the project scope?
- Is there an opportunity to learn new technologies, software, or other programs?
- Am I familiar enough with the organization and the practitioners involved to feel this is a safe and structured learning experience that can be relied upon to have a finishing point?
- Is there an opportunity to develop internships, job opportunities, or future class consulting projects?
- Is there the potential for students to visit the organization and see the issues for themselves? (This is desirable but not required.)

If the list is acceptable to the potential program partner, it is clearly a situation where we will have a positive relationship that is advantageous to both parties, the traditional win-win. If the proposed partner is clearly looking for just a work product and is not willing to address the areas that take it from a work product to a learning experience, then I feel my students and I might be taken advantage of and we politely decline the opportunity.

You are most likely wondering about the types of organizations and projects that we take on as class consulting assignments and how these projects are structured. First, we do two types of projects each fall as part of an MBA-level Sport and Entertainment Marketing class. The first type of project is a group project, or the class consulting type. One semester with 29 students, we accepted six class consulting projects so there would be a maximum number of five people per project. The small number ensures that everyone will have significant responsibilities and obtain a good learning experience. Past project partners have included Coca-Cola, Checkers Restaurants, UCF Athletics, TCU Athletics, Chicago White Sox, the Arnold Palmer Bay Hill Classic, Annika Academy, Nutmeg Sports Marketing, the WNBA, the NBA Development League, Minnesota Vikings, Tampa Bay Buccaneers, and the Tampa Bay Rays.

The second type of project is a pairs project that also serves as the final exam in the class. This project is an exercise in sponsorship activation and is designed to integrate all aspects of what students have learned in the class. It is presented in a capstone approach. I determine the pairings, using what I have observed throughout the semester. One of the lessons I try to teach students is that in the real world, they will have little voice in selecting whom they will be working with on an assignment, especially in an entry-level position. Thus I select the pairings. I sometimes put the poorest performers together, and I sometimes select the best students to work together. I have also paired two of the most quiet students to work together, as well as the two biggest extroverts—all in an attempt to challenge them to cooperate with each other. Students' motivation to work together is also aided by the fact that practitioners from the organizations will be on campus for the presentation and involved in the grading process. In the past, the Cleveland Indians, Pittsburgh Pirates, Seattle Storm, Minnesota Timberwolves, Atlanta Hawks/Thrashers, Orlando Magic, Phoenix Suns, and

Chicago Fire have been part of these projects. The projects require students to create five activation platforms for a particular corporate partner category for the franchise. The five platforms are: (1) in-venue, (2) internet/web, (3) marketing place of business, or (4) cause and (5) ethnic marketing.

Based on the list of project partners, you are probably curious about the geographic range of these projects and how that works for everyone involved. I have already mentioned the importance of knowing the party with whom you will be working. Through my NBA experience and also my consulting practice I have identified the majority of these clients; others have solicited me through the program, and still others have come from student contacts or relationships that they have suggested and the class agreed upon.

You might also ask about the issue of willingness to pay and compensation. I ask for the sponsoring organizations to pay for two reasons. First, people tend not to respect "free" on a variety of fronts, because they are merely offering an assignment and not making an investment. When fees and costs are involved, everyone is more diligent about the project and the results are often as good as if the organization had hired a professional agency. Secondly, the funds generated from the projects are utilized to cover field trips, pay for speakers to come to Orlando, and, most notably, to fund the annual September trip for my second-year MBA students during their last semester of their coursework at UCF. For example, one September we went to Chicago and visited the offices and met with representatives of the Chicago Fire, Chicago White Sox, Octagon Sports Marketing, and Northwestern University. In addition, we hosted a career development panel breakfast with area sport professionals as well as a networking dinner attended by more than 15 professionals working in the sports industry in Chicago. The students were also able to attend a game at Wrigley Field. The class projects fees covered all of the airfare, hotels, ground transportation, and meals for the 29 students and 5 faculty members.

As you might imagine, this approach is a recruiting advantage when it comes to our graduating class each spring. While I think charging a fee is important, I started this project approach years ago while at The Ohio State University. At that time I received a faculty research grant and conducted research studies utilizing my class at no cost for the Indiana Pacers and Cleveland Cavaliers. One year later, we conducted similar studies for the Cleveland Indians, Detroit Tigers, and Pittsburgh Pirates for which we were paid. So the starting point for compensation, in my opinion, rests upon the perceived value the project is bringing to the organization, the content of the project itself, and the fact that the content has been determined to be in the best interests of the buyer.

CAN AN ACADEMIC BE A PRACADEMIC?

While this seems an easy question on the surface, upon further examination it becomes a bit more complex. Are there tradeoffs or sacrifices to be considered? What are the rewards and opportunities? Is recognition a good thing, a bad thing, or both? What are the perils of being more unconventional and nontraditional in an academic role?

These are all legitimate questions, and as mentioned before, the answers depend on who you are and where you are on the tenure track, what your institution values, and, for some, geographic proximity to opportunities. Looking at my own situation, I have utilized the same approach at every institution where I have worked. While I was accepted at each, I probably would not have been the right fit for an institution like Ohio State in the long term. I helped position Robert Morris as a national program, because I sought out opportunities wherever they might be. I utilized this same approach at Ohio State in large part because of the dominance of Ohio University. At UMass I looked to Boston and New York to create more opportunities to add to the alumni network, and at UCF I took advantage of everything in Florida but emphasized the national approach in putting the program on the map quickly. The biggest variation in my approach came between my time at UMass and UCF. While at UMass we took clients from as far away as Cincinnati and Cleveland and did work for the NBA on All Star weekends—all of these projects necessitated traveling to those sites. At UCF I actually broadened the geographic scope but moved away from the on-site data collection projects and more toward strategic and analytical programs that did not involve extensive travel. The tradeoffs, as you can imagine, are time away from home and many more student contact hours than traditional courses. The benefits? Recognition, networking, some funding, and increased opportunities for internships and jobs.

If an institution values funding, the ROI on these projects is not high. Between the projects and related donations and support I generate from various organizations, my best year was about $100,000. Usually I average between $65,000 and $75,000 annually. But as stated earlier, funding for the students and the related publicity on local, regional, and national levels has been warmly received by UCF and has aided our recruitment of students as well.

This brings us to an interesting paradox; namely, that publicity in academia can be both good and bad. Some believe that I am not a true scholar because of what I write and where I choose to publish. While I don't necessarily agree, I would acknowledge that there are far better researchers in our discipline than I. In turn, I argue that I am a top sport marketer and have utilized all of the tools and opportunities at my disposal, many of which are outside the traditional academic standards and criteria for tenure and promotion. As I stated throughout this article, many of the decisions that I have made and that others following me will make are situational and depend on many factors. Every action has consequences, and in many cases the consequences are unintended. For many of us success depends on how we anticipate the unintended consequences and how we deal with them once they occur.

CONCLUDING THOUGHTS

Find the pracademic within you and determine how much of your time you can afford or would choose to dedicate to this aspect of your position. Do the time and demands outweigh the opportunities and benefits or vice versa? Much of life is built on balance and once you have identified your proper balance, it will all come together. In any case, don't ignore the need to be a pracademic in some shape or form. The industry needs our talents, and our students benefit greatly from seeing the application of classroom learning and academic theory in the real-life laboratory that the sport industry can provide.

REFERENCES

Etzioni, A. (2002, January 14). Professors Balance Duty to Students, Public Lives. *USA Today,* p. 13A.

Feschuk, D. (2008, March 13). "Morey's Moneyball approach paying off." *Toronto Star.* Retrieved August 3, 2011 from http://www.thestar.com/article/345327.

Lewis, M. (2003). *Moneyball.* New York: Norton.

Sport sponsorship and sales major. (n.d.). Baylor University website. Retrieved August 3, 2011 from http://www.baylor.edu/business/marketing/index.php?id=23770.

Sutton, W. A. (2007, January 15). Academia, industry benefit when interaction is encouraged. *Street & Smith's SportsBusiness Journal, 9*(36), 14.

The Power of One for the Good of Many

essay

10

ETHICAL AND MORAL CONSIDERATIONS FOR THE SPORT MANAGER

> *Kretchmar (1994) cautions us to recognize the symptoms of "moral callousness," or the lack of caring, in sport. Cheating or unfair play is often justified by statements such as, "everyone is doing it so how could it be wrong?"*

The author introduces the essay

Joy T. DeSensi THE UNIVERSITY OF TENNESSEE, KNOXVILLE

Joy DeSensi earned her Ph.D. at the University of North Carolina at Greensboro. She is currently Associate Dean of the Graduate School and Professor in the Department of Kinesiology, Recreation, and Sport Studies at The University of Tennessee, Knoxville. She was named a Chancellor's Professor, which is the highest honor awarded to faculty at UT. She is a Founding Member of NASSM and received the Earle F. Zeigler Lecture Award in 2003.

Introduction

The interdisciplinary nature of sport management is evident in its title and has been recognized since the development of the initial curricula defining it as a viable area of study. Sport studies is itself inclusive of history, cultural studies, sociology, psychology, political science, economics, and philosophy of sport, for example. These disciplines are as deeply interconnected as management and business studies, both of which are so closely intertwined they define a truly unique phenomenon requiring a broad knowledge and understanding. Knowledge in sport management is more than merely applying management principles to sport, but rather seeing how the context of sport is defined and understood according to multi-disciplinary, cross-disciplinary and inter-disciplinary study. The sport management curricula has evolved into a multitude of academic programs. As a result, various applied courses in athletics management, intercollegiate sports, sport governance, sport marketing, athletic leadership, and sport communications, to name a just a few, have reigned supreme. These courses have proven to be valuable, especially regarding the "how to" in sport management. When academicians challenge students with "how ought we to" or "what is the right thing to do," however, the lessons become more thought-provoking. These questions are directly related to sociocultural and philosophical understandings that can serve as a basis for the applied courses. All too often I am confronted by those who scoff at the thought of combining the words *ethics* and *sport* because the terms are usually thought of as oxymoronic.

This essay reflects the impact that the discipline of philosophy, specifically ethics and morality, can have on the study of sport management and what it means for the sport manager. I believe that focusing on the philosophy of ethics and morality in sport, so that future sport managers integrate ethical decision making and moral responsibility in their jobs, will help them become ethical sport leaders who choose to do what is right, perhaps even over winning. This, however, cannot be accomplished by focusing on the study of ethics and morality alone. It must be intertwined with the other courses and topics that define a true interdisciplinary area of study. Understanding the various "cultures" of sport, its historical and social contexts, political impact, economic structures, and worldviews is crucial to learning about and applying ethical principles to the new challenges sport managers face. With this premise in mind, the following discussion is directed toward the importance of ethics and morality in sport and sport management. I mourn the loss of so many sport philosophy courses and the lack of scholars giving attention to this area not only on behalf of current students majoring in sport disciplines, but also for those working in sport management. I hope for a revival through establishing the importance of ethics and morality in sport management and demonstrating the need for specific required courses at the undergraduate and graduate levels on such topics.

Sport as a cultural practice plays a significant role in our lives and holds varying degrees of meaning and value for each of us. Its importance is relative depending on what is at stake at a particular time in our lives. Be it achieving a personal best in a tee ball game, a national championship, a high school rivalry, or an intramural contest; winning the Olympic or Paralympic gold; or merely attending as a fan or watching via an array of media outlets, the meaning and value of sport is different in each case. This meaning is significant given our choices and opportunities (or lack of opportunities) for engagement in the social phenomenon of sport. The value of competitive sport in society faces daily scrutiny and opposition. As a practice, sport management is laden with philosophical questions related to the definitions of sport and competition; the value of sport in society; and the concepts of fair play, cheating, sportsmanship, and ethical decision making.

It is important to note my position before I address the importance of ethics and morality for the sport manager, so that the framework for this personal approach is understood. As a pre–Title IX intercollegiate athlete, an international competitor, and coach of a number of different college women's sports during the early days of Title IX, foremost in my mind were questions regarding the value of sport. Perhaps these questions were only in my mind and did not concern others. Nonetheless, I knew what the value of sport was for me in the past. That meaning was influenced by my knowledge and understanding of the privilege and access I had that others may not have had; the mutuality that existed between me and my opponents; the presentness, directness, and intensity of the competition; and my inability to explain the relationships established as a result of the competition. Today, my appreciation and concern for sport is different in that it comes much more from the spectator's and teaching professor's points of view. My observations are mixed, and I want to acknowledge all that is good about sport. Yet as I look through a critical lens from my perspective in a different place and time, my observations, while not all that positive, are hopeful. I marvel at the physical excellence, courage, and determination of all elite competitors, whether they be at the Olympic or Special/Paralympic levels. However, I am most disheartened when I observe the moral callousness, the lack of moral respect for competitors and rules, intercollegiate recruitment violations, use of performance-enhancing drugs, human rights violations, and wariness engendered by the pursuit of winning, no matter the cost. These actions occur on the part of many associated with sport, including players, coaches, referees, sport administrators, parents of youth participants, fans, and sport marketers to name a few. I cannot help but question the value and purpose of sport in our society and the meanings it holds for individuals of all ages. But most of all, I am concerned about future sport managers and how they will address such situations.

THE NEED FOR ETHICS AND MORALITY IN SPORT

Espousing that sports are morally objectionable is not popular. Yet when coaches teach their players how to cheat and not get caught, or tell players to take an opponent "out of the game" by intentionally injuring them, such practices are indeed morally objectionable. Furthermore, bribing referees or acting violently against players or officials complicates the moral environment of sport competitions.

Kretchmar (1994) offers an explanation for why individuals associated with sport seem to be caught in a quagmire when faced with ethical decisions. He cautions us to recognize the symptoms of "moral callousness," or the lack of caring, in sport. Cheating or unfair play is often justified by statements such as, "everyone is doing it so how could it be wrong?" The inability to distinguish between what is and is not part of the game also contributes to moral callousness. For example, if there are no penalties in the rulebook for a certain behavior, then it must be a part of the game. Another symptom of moral callousness is difficulty in telling morally sound strategy from win-at-all-costs trickery. We even hear media commentators praise blatant rule-breaking as shrewd strategy or even convey the sense that if one is not caught, nothing wrong happened. Such examples prove the need for the study of ethics and morality. While not all those in sport exhibit moral callousness, sport managers need to recognize these immoral and unethical actions and develop the courage to do the right thing. This will require personal and professional study so that future sport leaders will be prepared to act responsibly both morally and socially. To embed ethical and moral elements into the educational foundation of the theory and practice of sport management, a culture change of sorts is required.

I believe that the positive and moral values of sport are worth pursuing. The development of good character can be a derivative of competitive sport, and the balance between the bottom line and ethical behavior can indeed occur in the sport setting. I do not believe that sport is inherently bad, but much like the concept of power, its worth is judged by how those in control use it. Simon (2010) points out that "reflection on the value of competition in athletics and the emphasis on winning in much of organized sports may shed light on the ethics of competition in other areas, such as the marketplace" (p. 2). I do believe that sport can be a mutual quest for physical as well as moral excellence.

If my beliefs regarding sport are naïve, or worse yet, idealistic, I offer no apology. The moral bottom line in competitive sport is the mutual quest, the place where the value is realized and where knowledge (the lesson) is revealed in the struggle of overcoming the honest challenges of a worthy opponent. Can we measure the true success in sport by excellent play on the part of both teams as the standard for winning? If so, then each team is producing the best cooperative situation, and they create a mutually acceptable quest for excellence through challenge (Simon, 2010, p. 27). This is part of the social contract that exists within sport. That is, the opponents have an obligation to provide an honest challenge for each other within the bounds of the constitutive, proscriptive rules of sportsmanship and fair play (DeSensi & Rosenberg, 2010; Simon, 2010).

I have been engaging students in the topics of ethics and morality in sport and sport management for well over a decade. Yet I am still searching for and experimenting with approaches, techniques, methodologies, theories, and class activities that will make an immediate as well as lasting impact on students to support the argument for moral excellence in sport. It has been no easy task to convince the millennial students of sport management about the need to pursue moral excellence in their careers. In the beginning of this undertaking, my assumptions were, of course, that students of sport management would want to engage in moral practices as they embark on their journey to become leaders of sport teams, athletic directors, sport writers, media personnel, sport marketers, or sport business owners. To my surprise and dismay, even the thought of considering ethics and moral development was not on these students' radar, and they questioned why such a course or dialogue was needed. After all, they told me, the idea of sport is to win, no matter what. My presentation on some of the most egregious incidents of immoral behavior in sport did spark interest, but the bottom line for them was still that the action resulted in a win, therefore it was acceptable.

VALUES-BASED UNDERSTANDING OF ETHICS AND MORALITY

My redress to this situation was to help the sport management students realize their personal moral, non-moral, social, and core values. They were not used to this. At first I listened patiently as they extolled what they were so sure were the character building virtues of sports at all levels, while citing unethical examples and showing video clips of the worst cases of morally bankrupt behavior in sport. Then we engaged in activities to assist them in identifying, examining, and expressing how their values impact their current beliefs regarding sport and how these values may be in concert with or in opposition to the values of the organization in which they may be employed in their future sport management careers.

I limited the discussion to the moral values of honesty, justice, responsibility, and beneficence. The social values of loyalty, sacrifice, dedication, hard work, and privilege, for example, while extremely valuable, are not generally considered ethical values according to Lumpkin, Stoll, and Beller (2003). These authors contend it is the moral principles that serve as the foundation for who we are as ethical individuals. From our moral values we develop principles that determine the written and unwritten rules that guide us to act ethically. This logical progression made sense to my group of students, and I really believed they experienced a moment of illumination in which they envisioned possibilities of ethics in sport management. Looming questions, however, still filled the air: "What if we don't choose to act on our values and principles?" "What if we are challenged by those in authority to do things differently?" It is in these situations where our decisions are the most important. Do we have the courage and conviction to do what is right? Identifying personal values and meeting the challenges that commitment to those values brings are crucial steps in defining ourselves as ethical and moral leaders, managers, and sport participants.

The moral values of honesty, justice, responsibility, and beneficence had never been placed within the context of sport for these students. They more readily identified with the non-moral, material aspects of sport such as winning, performance excellence, the gold medal, the championship, and not losing. When my sport management students considered the depth of meaning associated with the above moral values and realized authentic introspection was a part of the class activity, they became fully engaged. Honesty, justice, responsibility, and beneficence became meaningful in a personal way, whether these values were accepted or not. When honesty was approached with viable examples of those athletes and sport organizations that have overtly and covertly breeched the rules, coupled with the students' own self-admission that they too had done this, the value took on personal meaning.

Likewise, when we examined the moral value of justice, particularly in regard to the concepts of fairness and equity, we closely examined issues related to Title IX. Further discussion included access to sport for individuals who are disabled and other marginalized groups in our society, thereby creating a clearer understanding of justice. Those sport management students who had been denied access as players, coaches, or spectators, for whatever reasons, raised questions, and debate developed on the fairness of such practices and the various ways in which sport policies have been unfairly implemented in some settings. Sport management students expressed deep concern about how those with special needs were accommodated in sport and physical activity in light of the following quote, "justice asks that we treat others equally in the sense that they have the proportionally same contribution to the goodness of their lives in a moral sense" (Lumpkin, Stoll, & Beller, 2003, p. 29). The moral value of justice as applied to sport began to make sense. The students were now developing viable questions about past practices in our society and the injustices that have occurred. Responsibility also took on a more important role as the realization that we must exercise personal accountability for our actions, even our bad decisions in the sports world.

Beneficence is the moral value of civility or doing good. It is the responsibility of every sport manager to do no harm and to prevent harm from occurring. Extending courtesy to our opponents is not something we are used to doing, especially if it means that as a result of this act, our opponent might win the contest. But athletes have been known to do just that. This value met with some resistance from the student group. Helping an opponent is not something usually considered outside of a pick-up game or match. After realizing that they themselves might need some assistance during a contest with equipment or other paraphernalia, they thought this value was indeed important. Fair play is ultimately important in the moral value of beneficence. It was never my intent to choose the moral values for the students, but rather to make them aware of possibilities so they could make their own decisions. For a majority, this was the first time they had considered their moral values and made choices regarding personal moral and social values. Coming to terms with core values or values that are not to be sacrificed was yet another experience for the class. Some students decided they would commit to no core values, so they had an escape when it came to sport explicitly. While these students exhibited a bit of resistance to exploring theoretical perspectives, they did resort to such explanations to support their beliefs. This was an important step for the group as they explored deontological and teleological theories, virtue ethics, and ethics of care. The important approach here was to employ pertinent examples of the theoretical applications, which wasn't difficult given the current moral challenges in sport.

SOCIAL RESPONSIBILITY AND CHARACTER DEVELOPMENT

If we believe that sport plays a significant role in society and in education, we must consider its role in our personal and moral development. Social responsibility entails the moral and legal responsibility for ourselves and others and can certainly be learned and passed on to the next generation when taught in a moral way. This is particularly true within the context of character development (Gough, 1997). Ethical excellence begins with the concept of character—good character. If we believe that participation in sport builds character, we need to know what that means. I assume it means "good" character and how our values are exhibited in building it. Character cannot be defined as what the NCAA promotes as "what we do when no one is looking." What we do when no one is looking is more closely linked to ethical behavior. Good character is working on becoming the moral, ethical person we want to be, and asking the question, "Do I have the courage, the character to do what is right?" This is the bottom line in sport.

Is it too much to expect of sport managers that they become ethically, morally, and socially responsible professionals? My response is no; I believe they should be at the forefront of this issue. As we consider the moral obligations coaches and athletic directors have to athletes and the stated educational objectives of athletic programs, character development becomes the most important responsibility of those associated with athletic programs. In regard to sports, moral education, and social responsibility, Simon (2010) notes that sport raises a number of significant ethical issues:

> At their best, sports are a stimulating challenge to mind and body; at their worst, they can be a joyless endeavor where losing is equated with being a failure as a person and winning becomes just a means to egoistic self-posturing over others. . . . But sports, properly conducted, express, illustrate, and perhaps reinforce values of enduring human significance. . . . Through sports we can develop and express moral virtues and demonstrate the importance of dedication, integrity, fairness, and courage. (p. 214)

While issues of egoism and narcissism have negatively affected contemporary sport in American society, these issues are intricately intertwined with and, according to Morgan (2006), being driven by practices in big-time college and professional sports, the Olympic Games, the media, sponsors, and marketers. As critics offer an explanation for this moral decline, the finger points to those in charge of sport—those managers who turn a blind eye to the massification and commodification of sport.

Whether teaching from a values or theoretical perspective, or more importantly, both, sport management academicians must constantly address the current status of sport from a social and philosophical angle so that ethics and morality will always have a place in sport management. We must initiate and consistently continue such inquiry. While we place blame on sport managers for not following the ethical high road, perhaps as academicians we are to blame for not adequately preparing them to do so.

CONCLUDING THOUGHTS: A VISION FOR THE FUTURE

The concerns expressed in this paper are by no means new to sport management, but our discipline needs a more concerted effort to envision a different approach to what we currently teach in our curriculum; that is, a moral foundation for sport managers based on critical sociological and philosophical perspectives.

The moral climate of sport has always been in need of improvement, and who better than sport managers to assume this responsibility? In their 2008 North American Society for Sport Management Conference presentation, Jennifer Hardes and Melvin Adelman support reconceptualizing sport management through philosophical theory. They state:

> While social theory has been utilized by sport management scholars and is of key importance to the management field, the largely unmediated appearance of sport ethics and

wider moral philosophy ought to be of equal, if not greater concern. While the term "ethics," and to a lesser degree "morality" are thrashed around minimally in scholarly circles of sport management, they have yet to be identified in sport management as central tenets of discussion. . . . Scholarly appeals should be pertained to, not only through sociological theory but also through philosophical theory in order to ensure ethics and morality are identified as key precepts to research in sport management. (p. 45)

The hope for the future is that sport can ultimately be regarded as a respected social practice under the direction of similarly respected ethical and moral sport leaders.

The question we face now is, "How do our academic programs help students answer the ethical and moral questions that arise for sport managers?" It is our responsibility as academicians to be certain the programs and curricula of study in sport management offer social and philosophical study of ethical theory and practical understanding in our field. It is also crucial to encourage that research and theoretical exploration be presented at our international conferences to foster ethical practices in sport and sport management in the future. The title of this paper, "The Power of One for the Good of Many," reflects the impact just one of us can have for the good of sport, our students, our disciplinary study, and ultimately, sport management.

Although sport management students in my class were challenged by questions they did not actually want to face about ethics and morality in sport, they realized the critical importance of such questions as they assumed positions in the field. They stay in contact, sharing ethical issues they face or upon the discovery of yet another article on ethical breeches in sport. This reveals the profound lessons learned and perhaps a way to achieving ethical and moral excellence in sport management in the future. These are the individuals who will have the power and authority to control the future of sport. "Sport managers may be seen as the primary culprits for many of the moral ills in sport, yet at the same time, they are in an optimal position to harness their power, authority, and control to recover and reassert the good in sport" (DeSensi & Rosenberg, 2010, p. 308). In order to do this they must have access to diverse areas of inquiry so they will be able to make informed ethical decisions that will enhance the moral integrity of sport.

REFERENCES

DeSensi, J. T., & Rosenberg, D. (2010). *Ethics and morality in sport management* (3rd ed.). Morgantown, WV: Fitness Information Technology.

Gough, R. W. (1997). *Character is everything: Promoting ethical excellence in sports*. Fort Worth, TX: Harcourt Brace & Co.

Hardes, J., & Adelman, M. (2008). Bridging the dialectic between economics and ethics: Reconceptualizing sport management. *North American Society for Sport Management Conference Abstracts*. Toronto, Ontario, p. 45.

Kretchmar, R. S. (1994). *Practical philosophy of sport*. Champaign, IL: Human Kinetics.

Lumpkin, A., Stoll, S., & Beller, J. (2003). *Sport ethics: Applications for fair play*. New York: McGraw Hill.

Morgan, W. J. (2006). *Why do sports morally matter?* New York: Routledge.

Simon, R. L. (2010). *Fair play, the ethic of sport* (3rd ed.). Philadelphia: Westview Press.

Sport Management

BOTTOM LINES AND HIGHER CALLINGS?

It is imperative that these students, the future sport managers of this century, understand the power they will possess by virtue of working in the sport industry.

The authors introduce the essay

Mary A. Hums UNIVERSITY OF LOUISVILLE

Mary Hums is a Professor at the University of Louisville and holds a Ph.D. in Sport Management from The Ohio State University. Her expertise in policy development focuses on the inclusion of people with disabilities, women, and ethnic minorities in sport management. She received the 2009 Earle F. Zeigler Award. She has published a variety of books and articles. She is an active volunteer for Paralympic Games and sports organizations throughout the country.

Meg Hancock UNIVERSITY OF LOUISVILLE

Meg Hancock is an instructor at the University of Louisville. She is pursuing her Ph.D. in Educational Leadership and Organizational Development with an emphasis in Sport Administration. Her research interests include gender and diversity in the workplace, sport management education, and sport for development. Prior to teaching at the University of Louisville, she worked as an assistant athletic director at Dartmouth College.

Introduction

Marketing and managing events, acquiring sponsorships, selling advertisements, financing, and budgeting—all of these require the essential skill sets sport managers need to possess. Without these business basics, sport organizations cannot successfully fulfill their business plans. Yet these are really twentieth-century "rust belt" skill sets (e.g., organization, strategic planning, facility management, marketing, and promotions). The sport manager of the twenty-first century needs much more than this. According to *New York Times* writer Thomas Friedman (2001), the shape of our world is rapidly changing. Our world is no longer about walls that separate people, but rather about webs that connect people. In this type of business environment, isolationism will soon equal business failure.

WHY WE NEED TO GO BEYOND TRADITIONAL SPORT MANAGEMENT THINKING

Today's business environment is fast-paced and requires multitasking. Decision makers no longer simply affect only their organizations or their local communities. We are linked together now more than ever. As Friedman (2010) writes:

> Today so many more of us are just so much more deeply intertwined with each other and with the natural world. That is why Dov Seidman, the C.E.O. of LRN, which helps companies build ethical cultures, and author of the book *How,* argues that we are now in the "Era of Behavior."
>
> Of course, behavior always mattered. But today, notes Seidman, *how* each of us behaves, consumes, does business, builds or doesn't build trust with others matters more than ever. Because each of us, each of our banks, each of our companies, now has the power to impact, for good or ill, so many more people's lives through so many more channels—from day-trading to mortgage-lending to Twitter to Internet-enabled terrorism.
>
> "As technology has made us more interconnected with others around the world, it has also made us more ethically interdependent with others around the world," argues Seidman. (pp. 5–7)

The actions of sport managers are no different. Their decisions will reverberate not only throughout the global sport community, but throughout the greater global business community as well. Because of sport's global interest, people from outside of sport will observe and discuss the decisions sport managers make.

A number of our recent NASSM Zeigler Lecture Award winners remind us that as sport management educators we need to think more broadly. Chalip (2006, p. 14) writes that "sport can deliver each of the benefits we claim if we manage it appropriately. But to manage it appropriately, we cannot sustain sport's isolation." Inglis (2007, p. 11) poses the question, "What is our role in untangling the issues in which values are interwoven with cultural and political systems that threaten the very basis of human dignity and rights?"

Thibault (2009) points out the "inconvenient truths" related to the globalization of sport include:

> [A] division of labor undertaken on an international scale where transnational companies (TNCs) are drawing on developing countries' work forces to manufacture sportswear and sports equipment; the increasing flow of athletes where country of birth and origin are no longer a limitation on where an athlete plays and competes; the increased involvement of global media conglomerates such as Disney, News Corporation, Time Warner, Vivendi Universal, and Bertelsmann AG in sport; and the impact of sport on the environment. (p. 5)

Finally, Hums (2010) writes:

> [H]ow does a sport management educator prepare students for an industry fraught with rapidly changing issues and treading water in a fragile economy? This complex question has sometimes been referred to as the debate between the Temple (spirit of sport) and the Agora (the marketplace of sport; Martinkova, 2006) or what I call the debate between the conscience and commerce of sport management. As new issues emerge, our graduates will be forced to make decisions which often place the Temple and the Agora—the spirit of sport and the business of sport, the conscience and the commerce of sport management—in opposition to each other. (p. 7)

These combined voices from our academic discipline press us to look beyond the business basics to help our students see sport management's connectedness to greater society, where sport holds a high status. People look to sport and to the leaders in sport to do more than people in many other professions. This is because of the wide-reaching influence sport has in so many settings.

The Societal Influence of the Sport Industry

Never underestimate the power of sport. Nick Keller (2010), the founder of Beyond Sport, an organization that funds and promotes the use of sport for positive social change, suggests that

> Sport has the values and power to do good beyond the confines of the pitch or the court or the track, in short to do good Beyond Sport. Sport's role as a pastime has long been understood. More recently, its growth as an industry has become one of the great business developments of recent decades. But as a force for social change, unlike say music or art, let alone politics, it remains undervalued and underused. And yet sport has the capacity to move, to inspire, and to unite. (p. 4)

Our students will walk into this sphere of influence. It is imperative that these students, the future sport managers of this century, understand the power they will possess by virtue of working in the sport industry. Because of this, they need to be educated on issues that lie beyond the traditional areas of sport management. It is no longer enough to build new state-of-the-art arenas, unless those arenas represent green values. It is no longer enough to have community relations programs that are "one-and-done." Instead, establishing programs that value issues pertaining to local sustainability should be the goal. It is no longer enough to think in terms of using hiring quotas. Rather, sport managers must now think about managing diversity. In other words, it is no longer enough to consider only the economic impact of their decisions. Sport managers need to consider the ethical implications of their decisions as well.

Business Decisions Are Ethical Decisions

One can easily make the case that every business decision is an ethical decision, although the gravity of these types of decisions most certainly varies. For example, after September 11, 2001, sport organizations grappled with whether or not to postpone events scheduled for the following days and weeks. These very public decisions were greatly scrutinized. On the other hand, sport managers also make simple decisions. A stadium operator needs to contract with a company to provide paper towels for restrooms. Does the operator choose recycled products or go with air dryers, which use no paper but require electricity? Business decisions large and small test sport managers to understand that each decision has far-reaching consequences. Simply put, we are challenged to do the right thing.

THE NEW SPORT MARKETPLACE OUR STUDENTS WILL INFLUENCE

As sport management educators, our work will manifest itself in the sport industry through the actions of our students. We influence the skill sets they bring with them to the sport marketplace. Hence, we need to become more aware of the topics and issues they will face as they transition into the working world. This essay challenges us to fold new issues into our lectures, textbooks, and assignments. These issues are:

- sport and human rights
- sport for development and peace
- globalization, migration, and the sport labor force
- sport and the environment
- sport and technology

Of course, other issues will emerge soon after the ink is dry on these pages. The sport industry will need to respond to societal issues we cannot even envisage today. However, the topics in this essay offer a starting point for expanding our curriculum. Twenty years ago, we would not have envisioned a runner with two prosthetic legs on the verge of qualifying for the Olympic Games or athletes tweeting their daily lives to thousands of followers. Fortunately, a good source for new topics of interest will be our students! After all, they will have their finger on the pulse of the next generation of sport managers.

Sport and Human Rights

Sport and human rights takes two forms: (a) sport as a human right, and (b) using sport to promote human rights. The term *human rights* can be daunting for a sport manager. <u>What relevance do human rights have to the everyday operation of a sport organization? How are sport and human rights related at all?</u>

Sport as a human right

The United Nations has indicated sport is a human right through various documents over the years. Each of the following refers to sport and physical activity (Hums, Wolff, & Mahoney, 2008):

- United Nations Educational, Scientific, and Cultural Organization's (UNESCO) Charter on Physical Education and Sport (1978)
- Convention on the Elimination of Discrimination Against Women (1979)
- International Convention Against Apartheid in Sport (1985)
- Convention on the Rights of the Child (1989)
- Convention on the Rights of Persons with Disabilities (2006)

Each of these United Nations documents recognizes sport and physical activity as a human right, but what have sport organizations said about sport and human rights?

From the sport side, the Olympic Charter specifically says, "the practice of sport is a human right" (IOC, 2007, p. 11). The International Olympic Committee's (IOC) Sport for All Commission's mission statement reads, "Sport for All is a movement promoting the Olympic ideal that sport is a human right for all individuals regardless of race, social class and sex" (IOC, 2010, Sport a Human Right for All, section 1).

A number of authors writing about sports have also discussed sport as a human right (DaCosta, Abreu, & Miragaya, 2006; Hums, 2010; Hums, Wolff, & Mahoney, 2008; Kidd & Donnelly, 2000), while others have begun to address the legal aspects of sport and human rights, particularly since the ratification of the Convention on the Rights of Persons with Disabilities in 2006 (Hums, Moorman, & Wolff, 2009; Lakowski, 2009; Lord & Stein, 2009; McArdle, 2009; Roy, 2007). Within the academic discipline of sport management, the concept of sport as a human right is not new, but it remains relatively unexamined and deserves to be explored in greater detail.

Using sport to promote human rights

The other aspect of sport and human rights to consider is using sport to promote human rights. A number of sport figures as well as sport organizations have undertaken activities promoting human rights. Perhaps the most memorable incident occurred at the 1968 Mexico City Olympic Games when John Carlos and Tommie Smith stood on the medal podium with raised, black-gloved fists as a sign of protest against the treatment of African Americans in the United States. Unfortunately, this gesture prompted the IOC to urge the United States Olympic Committee (USOC) to ban the two men from competition (Davis, 2008). The IOC felt the gesture was "a deliberate and violent breach of the fundamental principles of the Olympic spirit" (BBC, 2005). Today, the photo of Carlos and Smith remains an iconic representation of the civil rights movement in the United States.

A more recent example in which sport could have been used to promote human rights involves the International Olympic Committee's decision to award the 2008 Olympic and Paralympic Games to Beijing, despite China's spotty human rights record. The discussion resulting from this decision indicates that international public opinion has raised the bar for sport organizations. Recently, Human Rights Watch, an independent international organization whose purpose is to defend and protect human rights, called on the IOC to more closely monitor human rights in host cities for the Olympic and Paralympic Games (Human Rights Watch, 2009). This discussion brought the relationship of sport and human rights to the public forefront.

Several other major sport organizations have undertaken steps to use their platforms as recognized sport entities to promote human rights. For example, Nike's "Stand Up, Speak Up" anti-racism campaign features famous international football athletes telling spectators to speak out when they hear racist comments in the stands. The campaign also features a set of intertwined black and white wristbands (Football Unites, Racism Divides, n.d.). Similarly, the Federation Internationale de Football Association (FIFA) has been a driving force behind the movement Football for Hope. One of its campaigns, "20 Centres for 2010," was the official campaign of the 2010 World Cup held in South Africa. According to FIFA (2009), "The Football for Hope Centres will provide a platform for communities to address social issues such as children's rights, education, health, HIV/AIDS prevention, social integration and environment protection. They will leave a legacy for Africa that will last long after the final whistle of the 2010 FIFA World Cup has been blown." The nonprofit Grassroot Soccer organization, dedicated to prevention of HIV through the power of soccer, contributes to the Football for Hope Centres in various locations in Africa. Tommy Clark, the founder of Grassroot Soccer, lived in Zimbabwe as a teenager and returned to the country after college to play soccer and teach English. Upon his return to Zimbabwe, he was devastated to witness the impact HIV/AIDS had had on the once-vibrant community he remembered. He established Grassroot Soccer in 2002 to combat the growing epidemic of HIV/AIDS in Africa. He designed the program with health officials and members of the community. As a result, Grassroot Soccer "trains African soccer stars, coaches, teachers, and peer educators in the world's most HIV-affected countries to deliver an interactive HIV prevention and life skills curriculum to youth" (Grassroot Soccer, 2010). This example also serves to illustrate the interconnectedness of the topics discussed in this essay. Grassroot Soccer is also a fine example of an organization involved with sport for development and peace.

Sport for Development and Peace

In many countries, sport has a somewhat dubious reputation. It has been notorious for seeming to promote or tolerate racism, nationalism, discrimination, corruption, drug abuse, and violence (Chalip, 2006; Green, 2008; Sugden, 1995). However, in recent decades, sport scholars and organizations (e.g., the

IOC), humanitarian institutions (e.g., the United Nations), and governmental organizations have identified sport as a tool to facilitate positive social change (Davis-Delano & Crossett, 2008; Green, 2008; Jarvie, 2007; Kidd, 2008; Levermore, 2008; Meier, 2005; Rookwood, 2008; Sherry, 2010; Sugden, 1995; United Nations, 2002, 2003).

The United Nations (UN) Inter-Agency Task Force on Sport for Development and Peace suggested that sport has a unique ability to foster social integration, teach coping mechanisms, increase knowledge and contribute to education, and create social relationships by building connections and improving communication between individuals and groups (United Nations, 2003). Specifically, sport—when combined with educational initiatives—has the potential to help individuals and groups resolve social problems, including deficiencies in education; the spread of disease, poverty, and inter-ethnic conflict; human rights violations; and social inequities due to race, gender, religion, disability, or economic background. Moreover, "sport has been increasingly recognized and used as a low-cost and high-impact tool in humanitarian, development, and peace-building efforts" (United Nations, 2010). Finally, the United Nations (2010) recommended that sport for development and peace programs should: (a) engage communities and program participants in the design and delivery of activities; (b) create and maintain transparency and accountability to build local capacity and community support; and (c) pursue sustainability through collaboration, partnerships, and coordinated action.

In short, sport for development and peace programs employ sport to connect, engage, and educate communities working to resolve social problems. As sport educators and practitioners, our duty is to understand the impact of sport in a global context. But what about our students? How can we help them become more aware of the impact and opportunities of sport for development and peace programs not only around the world, but also in local communities? How can we help our students understand that sport for development and peace programs are not undertaken "someplace else, by someone else" (Hums, 2010, p. 5)?

To help students fully grasp the utility of sport as an agent of positive social change, perhaps the most effective method of instruction involves the use of case studies. Case studies promote critical thinking, self-reflection, and decision making (Heitzman, 2008; Skinner & Gilbert, 2007)—essential skills for the future sport manager. Presenting students with real-life examples of sport for development in action will convince them of sport's power to address social issues. Two good examples of sport for development programs are Street Soccer USA and Fight for Peace.

Street Soccer USA (www.streetsoccerusa.org) aims to end homelessness by providing homeless men, women, and youth the opportunity to participate in soccer and other physical activities. Participation in the program also includes access to community support services, including personal counseling (for drug/alcohol abuse or mental health issues, for example), educational programming, housing, and job training. Currently, Street Soccer USA supports teams in 15 U.S. cities and has identified the need for programs in 24 additional locations across the country. Individuals or groups interested in starting a Street Soccer USA team can contact the organization for tips on how to identify a homeless service provider, attract participants, fundraise, and form a program. The organization also provides start-up equipment from Nike and other corporate sponsors. Fight for Peace (www.fightforpeace.net) is a diversion program founded by amateur boxer Luke Dowdney to "confront the problem of child and youth participation in crime, gangs, and gun violence in disadvantaged communities" (Fight for Peace, 2010). Participation in Fight for Peace affords young men and women the opportunity to train and compete in boxing and martial arts. The program also provides participants access to youth support services, job training, and education. Fight for Peace academies exist in Rio de Janeiro, Brazil and London, England and are funded by individual donations, private foundations, international corporations, and governmental agencies. The organization is also heavily involved in scientific research and program evaluation projects to identify program outcomes for participants and the local community. Fight for Peace uses this information to cultivate relationships with new and existing community partners. It is also useful in obtaining additional funding from community and international sources.

Globalization, Migration, and the Sport Labor Force

Globalization has received significant attention from academics, policy makers, and practitioners in sport (Harvey & Houle, 2001; Harvey, Horne, & Safai, 2009; Harvey, Rail, & Thibault, 1996; Maguire, 1999; Miloch, 2002; Thibault, 2009; see also Essay 12). According to Wong and Trumper (2002), "globalization fundamentally transforms the relationship between 'place' of habitation and cultural practices, experiences, and identities" (p. 171). Falcous and Maguire (2005) also note that the "movement of people, sporting migrants included, across frontiers is symptomatic of the growing mobility that characterizes globalization" (p. 138). Sporting migrants include athletes, coaches, club/team owners, and sport managers. This section will focus primarily on athletes.

Athletes have been migrating to other countries to play for teams and clubs since the early 1900s (Taylor, 2006). However, the movement of athletes and the sport labor force has only started receiving significant attention from sport scholars in the last few decades (Maguire, 1999; Maguire & Pearton, 2000; Poli, 2006; Taylor, 2006; Wong & Trumper, 2002). For example, research on the migration of soccer players reveals an outflow of talent from African countries (Maguire & Pearton, 2000; Poli, 2006). Many African players seek opportunities in Western European countries, including England, France, and Italy. Similarly, the Eastern European countries of Romania and Hungary also experienced "talent drain," as many footballers left their home countries in pursuit of the greater economic incentives of the global stage as represented by the Union of European Football Associations (UEFA) (Maguire & Pearton, 2000; Poli, 2006; Wong & Trumper, 2002). The UEFA offers the world's most competitive soccer teams as well as the most lucrative contracts. For example, in 2000, nearly 20 percent of Italy's 500 wealthiest people were soccer players (Wong & Trumper, 2002). As a result, not only do players from Africa and Eastern Europe seek to play in the professional leagues of Western Europe, so do players from North and South America. Soccer is one of the most prominent examples of athlete and sport labor force migration. However, the trend is also prevalent in other sports and in other countries.

For example, nearly 30 percent of players in Major League Baseball are foreign-born, the majority of whom hail from the Dominican Republic (Sanchez, 2007). The 2009–2010 NBA season began with 83 international players from 33 countries and territories (NBA, 2009). Hockey players from Scandinavia, Germany, and Russia seek opportunities to play in Canada and with teams in the National Hockey League (Wong & Trumper, 2002). Similarly, many North American hockey players look to compete overseas.

While many athletes benefit from moving to a new country to pursue an athletic career, their home countries often suffer. According to Maguire and Pearton (2000), the migration of talented athletes to a new "home" country has deleterious effects for the native-born athletes in that country. They no longer have the opportunity to compete for spots on a club or national team because more talented migrant athletes take the roster slots. National talent remains underdeveloped. As a result, "sport labor unions have sought to protect indigenous players by arguing for quotas and qualification thresholds to be applied to potential migrants" (Maguire & Pearton, 2000, p. 180).

Club and team owners resist this approach because the migration of talent provides great economic benefit to teams, owners, and communities. In fact, in an effort to increase migrant talent, many UEFA football clubs have created academies in Africa. The intention is to develop young athletes and entice them to play in UEFA leagues with lucrative contracts and opportunities to play around the world (Darby, Akindes, & Kirwin, 2007). Similarly, 28 teams in Major League Baseball have developed baseball academies and built multimillion dollar facilities to cultivate talent in the Dominican Republic (Meyer & Kuhn, 2009). Unfortunately, the Dominican Republic and many African countries remain among the poorest in the world. The investment made by major sport organizations to create academies in these poor countries does little to support and sustain economic growth.

The migration of athletes and the sport labor force is an important trend for future research as globalization and the commodification of sport increase. While academy development and migration of talent may benefit a few, it is critical to consider the larger social, cultural, and political impacts of such movement. There are consequences for the new host countries, indigenous athletes, and countries experiencing the drain of talent and potential economic resources. Sport management faculty must help our students understand sport beyond its economic incentives.

These first three topics—sport and human rights; sport for development and peace; and globalization, migration, and the sport labor force—are somewhat inter-related. Other issues are equally important but categorically different from these first three. Two such areas are sport and the environment and sport and technology.

Sport and the Environment

Sport and the environment has two facets: (a) the impact of the environment on sport and (b) the impact of sport on the environment. The former deals with the influence of meteorological conditions such as rain, wind, and even altitude on sporting events. These are beyond the sport manager's control. Another element here is pollution, which although beyond the sport manager's control and artificially created by human activity, is still an influence on sport. This section focuses on conditions sport managers can in fact control, which is the impact of sport on the environment.

Sport organization responses

Think about a sporting event you attended recently. Most likely after driving to the event, you enjoyed some sort of food or beverage, used the restroom, and watched a game under the lights. Think about the carbon footprint (i.e., the ecological impact of your activities in terms of fuel use, energy consumption, and waste produced) you left on the environment. Now multiply that by the number of fans in attendance. Remember looking around the stands as you exited and seeing the debris left behind by the fans? Whether you are thinking about a high school football game or an NFL football game, the result is same, although the scope may be different.

So what can sport organizations do to minimize their carbon footprint? This is best illustrated by some examples. Sustainability was a key theme for the 2010 Vancouver Olympic and Paralympic Games. One legacy of those games was how green they were. The organizing committee for the Vancouver Games (VANOC) touted 12 principles of sustainability built into the games, including a sustainable purchasing and ethical sourcing program called Buy Smart, as well as incorporating Leadership in Energy and Environmental Design (LEED) standards into venue construction (Vancouver2010, 2010). LEED is a certification system designed to help building owners and managers construct and maintain environmentally friendly and sustainable facilities (U.S. Green Building Council, 2010). "LEED promotes a whole-building approach to sustainability by recognizing performance in five key areas of human and environmental health: sustainable site development, water savings, energy efficiency, materials selection and indoor environmental quality" (U.S. Green Building Council, 2010, What is LEED section). LEED certification should now be on the minds of sport managers as they build new facilities or renovate existing ones.

Major sport organizations are not the only ones using sport to promote environmental awareness. GreenLaces is a small not-for-profit organization that enlists Olympic and professional athletes from all over the world in making promises to the planet and then wearing green shoelaces to symbolize their commitment to those promises. One hundred athletes from five countries were part of Team GreenLaces at the Vancouver 2010 Winter Olympic Games (GreenLaces, 2009). However, it is not only famous athletes who can join in the green effort. Project GreenHands in India uses sport activities such as volleyball to initiate community involvement in tree-planting activities (Project GreenHands, n.d.). The organization has planted millions of trees over the past few years in the Tamil Nadu region of India, and sport played an integral role in engaging local residents in the project. Specifically, "Project GreenHands uses sport as the primary entry level activity to reach these communities: organising and coaching volleyball and handball teams, implementing yoga programmes, facilitating tournaments, and hosting the "Rural Olympics." These sports activities serve as a means to unite community members, whilst providing an opportunity to raise awareness about the issue of environmental degradation; conveying its urgency and willing people to act" (Beyond Sport, 2011). In short, Project Greenhands introduces sport and recreation as a mechanism to teach people how to take care of themselves and their community.

Sport industry in the post–Gulf of Mexico oil spill era

Corporate responses to environmental issues are in the news more than ever since the Deepwater Horizon oil spill in the Gulf of Mexico in the spring and summer of 2010. According to *Science Daily* (2010), a recent study reported that "60% of business executives consider sustainability to be very or extremely important in their overall business strategy." The Gulf of Mexico oil spill will have far-reaching consequences for executives everywhere, including sport managers. More than ever, sport executives will need to make sustainability and environmental responsibility priorities in their business strategies. For example, according to a 2010 survey of professional sport franchises in North America, "60% of teams say their sustainability initiatives are a 'high or 'very high' priority; over 90% of teams say their executive management have a positive perspective on developing a green business strategy; 80% of teams have formed or are actively considering forming an internal green team; [and] 80% of teams expect the emphasis on environmental programs to be increasing in the future" (ProGreenSports, 2010a).

Similarly, in intercollegiate athletics, 52 percent of athletic departments are making green initiatives a "high" or "very high" priority; nearly 80 percent of key decision makers in athletic departments have a positive perspective on environmental issues; 38 percent of athletic departments have formed or are firmly planning to form an internal green team; and 83 percent of athletic departments expect the emphasis on environmental programs to increase in the future (ProGreenSports, 2010b). These numbers clearly indicate that sport managers are in line with the greater corporate emphasis on thinking about environmental issues from a strategic management perspective.

Sport and Technology

Remember when the Intel 80286 computer was so fast we could not imagine a computer that could operate any faster? Remember when the Sony Walkman was the gold standard for portable music? Remember when only the military used GPS devices? And remember when the first Indy car broke the 200 mph (320 km/h) mark? Whether you remember these things or not, the point is that technological advances permeate all aspects of society, and the sport industry is no exception. A generation ago, could we ever have envisioned the influence of the Internet, much less the connectivity of social networks?

Sport incorporates technology in many ways. New training techniques push athletes past limits never thought attainable. High-tech materials are incorporated into equipment. The big issue here, however, is the responsible use of such technology. For example, just because a scientist can design a highly technical piece of equipment, does that mean it should be allowed for use in competition? According to Hums and MacLean (2008), "while examining the impact of technology, one must ask three questions: (1) is the technology safe? (2) Is the technology fair? and (3) Is the technology accessible for all?" (p. 352). New equipment requires testing for safety. The National Operating Committee on Standards for Athletic Equipment (NOCSAE) oversees testing of equipment such as football, hockey, and lacrosse helmets, as well as baseball and softball batting helmets and catcher's gear. This is especially important with the recent heightened concern about concussion injuries in sport. As athletes get bigger, faster, and stronger, their collisions become more violent, increasing the chance for injury.

Next is the issue of fairness, which rose to the forefront in 2008 as people followed Oscar Pistorius, a sprinter whose legs are amputated below the knee, in his quest to qualify for the 2008 Olympic Games. Pistorius used Cheetah prosthetics and questions arose about whether not the devices gave him an unfair advantage (Zettler, 2009).

The final issue is that of accessibility, which is closely related to the issue of cost and is particularly evident in the Paralympic Games, where the newest sit-skis for downhill skiers can cost upwards of $20,000 (T. Fay, personal communication, March 17, 2010). A Cheetah prosthetic can cost $18,000 (Tucker & Dugas, 2007). However, able-bodied sport also provides examples of highly priced new technologies. A new LZR Racer Elite Jammer competition suit from Speedo costs $260 (Speedo, 2010), and an Easton Stealth Speed Comp Fast Pitch softball bat costs $300 (Easton Stealth Speed, n.d.)

When sporting goods and equipment cost so much, who will be able to afford them? The high costs involved with some sports present barriers to entry for people with low incomes, schools in poor districts, or people living in developing countries. This definitely places those athletes at a competitive disadvantage, which is inherently unfair.

Aside from equipment, communication is another aspect of technology that impacts sport. The Internet and social networks such as Facebook and Twitter have reinvented the way we think about communicating information about ourselves and our organizations. Athletes use Twitter to market themselves and their teams (Hambrick, Simmons, Greenhalgh, & Greenwell, 2011). Fans demand instantaneous access to live games, interviews, and "inside information." Sport managers need to harness these new communication technologies to maximize their reach.

CONCLUDING THOUGHTS

This essay has attempted to stretch our understanding of the impact of sport on a global scale. The topics addressed, which reach beyond the traditional academic topics in sport management, need to be included in our curricula. As the world "shrinks," communities become more connected economically, politically, technologically, socially, and culturally (Maguire, 1999). Our world is rapidly changing; people by the millions migrate by choice or are displaced by conflict or natural disasters. The sport industry is more diverse than ever as men and women, people with disabilities and able-bodied people,

people from developed as well as developing countries, and people of all different religious backgrounds mix together. This is our reality as we move forward. This will be the reality that our students, and the people they train and mentor, will face in the sport marketplace.

REFERENCES

BBC. (2005, October 17). 1968: Black athletes make silent protest. *BBC*. Retrieved August 3, 2011 from http://news.bbc.co.uk/onthisday/hi/dates/stories/october/17/newsid_3535000/3535348.stm.

Beyond Sport. (2011). Project Greenhands. Retrieved from http://www.beyondsport.org/the-awards/entries/view.php?Id=474.

Chalip, L. (2006). Toward a distinctive sport management discipline. *Journal of Sport Management, 20,* 1–21.

DaCosta, L., Abreu, N., & Miragaya, A. (2006). Multiculturalism and universal proclaimed values in the Olympic movement: An approach to human rights and sport development? *ICSSPE Bulletin, 48.* Retrieved August 3, 2011 from http://www.icsspe.org/bulletin/drucken_a4b0b689.php.html.

Darby, P., Akindes, G., & Kirwin, M. (2007). Football academies and the migration of African football labor to Europe. *Journal of Sport and Social Issues, 31*(2), 143–161.

Davis, D. (2008, July 8). Once united, now divided. *Los Angeles Times.* Retrieved August 3, 2011 from http://articles.latimes.com/2008/jul/08/sports/sp-forty8.

Davis-Delano, L., & Crossett, T. (2008). Using social movement theory to study outcomes in sport-related social movements. *International Review for the Sociology of Sport, 43,* 115–134.

Easton Stealth Speed Comp Fast Pitch softball bats (n.d.). Retrieved August 3, 2011 from http://www.google.com/products/catalog?q=louisville+slugger+softball+bat+cost&cid=7838199420202039724#checkout=1.

Falcous, M., & Maguire, J. (2005). Globetrotters and local heroes? Labor migration, basketball, and local identities. *Sociology of Sport Journal, 22,* 137–157.

FIFA. (2009, August 7). Football for Hope helping women to live free of HIV. Retrieved from http://www.fifa.com/aboutfifa/worldwideprograms/releases/newsid=1087995.html.

Fight for Peace. (2010). About us. Retrieved August 3, 2011 from http://www.fightforpeace.net/default.asp?contentID=2&lang=1.

Football Unites, Racism Divides. (n.d.). Nike "Stand Up, Speak Up" campaign. Retrieved August 3, 2011 from http://www.furd.org/default.asp?intPageID=275.

Friedman, T. (2001). *Longitudes and attitudes: The world in the age of terrorism.* New York: Anchor Books.

Friedman, T. (2010, May 15). A question from Lydia. *New York Times.* Retrieved August 3, 2011 from http://www.nytimes.com/2010/05/16/opinion/16friedman.html?hp.

Grassroot Soccer. (2010). Who we are. Retrieved August 3, 2011 from Grassrootsoccer.org.

Green, B. C. (2008). Sport as an agent for social and personal change. In V. Girginov (Ed.) *Management of sports development* (pp. 129–145). Burlington, MA: Butterworth-Heinemann.

GreenLaces. (2009). Team GreenLaces Vancouver 2010. Retrieved August 3, 2011 from http://www.greenlaces.org/promise/Team_GreenLaces.html.

Hambrick, M. E., Simmons, J. M., Greenhalgh, G. P., & Greenwell, T. C. (2010). Twitter in sport: A content analysis of professional athlete tweets. *International Journal of Sport Communication, 3,* 454–471.

Harvey, J., & Houle, F. (2001). Sport, world economy, global culture, and new social movements. In A. Yiannakis, & M. Melnick (Eds.), *Contemporary issues in sociology of sport* (pp. 447–459). Champaign, IL: Human Kinetics.

Harvey, J., Horne, J. & Safai, P. (2009). Alterglobalization, global social movements, and the possibility of political transformation through sport. *Sociology of Sport Journal, 26*, 383–403.

Harvey, J., Rail, G., & Thibault, L. (1996). Globalization and sport: Sketching a theoretical model for empirical analyses. *Journal of Sport and Social Issues, 23*, 258–277.

Heitzman, R. (2008). Case study instruction in teacher education: Opportunity to develop students' critical thinking, school smarts, and decision making. *Education, 128*(4), 523–542.

Human Rights Watch. (2009, February 23). Human Rights Watch submission to the 2009 Olympic Congress. Retrieved August 3, 2011 from http://www.hrw.org/en/news/2009/02/23/human-rights-watch-submission-2009-olympic-congress.

Hums, M. A. (2010). The conscience and commerce of sport management: One teacher's perspective. *Journal of Sport Management, 24*(1), 1–9.

Hums, M. A., & MacLean, J. C. (2008). *Governance and policy in sport organizations.* (2nd ed.). Scottsdale, AZ: Holcomb Hathaway.

Hums, M. A., Moorman, A. M., & Wolff, E. (2009). Emerging disability rights in sport: Sport as a human right for persons with disabilities and the 2006 UN Convention on the Rights of Persons with Disabilities. *Cambrian Law Review, 40*, 36–48.

Hums, M. A., Wolff, E. A., & Mahoney, M. (2008). Sport and human rights. In J. Borms (Ed.) *Directory of Sport Science* (pp. 467–478). ICSSPE: Berlin, Germany.

Inglis, S. (2007). Creative tensions and conversations in the academy. *Journal of Sport Management, 21*(1), 1–14.

IOC. (2007). *Olympic charter.* International Olympic Committee: Lausanne, Switzerland.

IOC. (2010). The Sport for All Commission. Retrieved August 3, 2011 from http://www.olympic.org/en/content/The-IOC/Commissions/Sport-for-All/.

Jarvie, G. (2007). Sport, social change, and the public intellectual. *International Review for the Sociology of Sport, 42*, 411–424.

Keller, N. (2010). *Welcome to beyond sport.* Speech given at the Beyond Sport Summit 2010, Chicago, IL. Retrieved August 3, 2011 from www.beyondsport.org.

Kidd, B. (2008). A new social movement; Sport for peace and development. *Sport in Society, 11*(4), 370–380.

Kidd, B., & Donnelly, P. (2000). Human rights in sports. *International Review for the Sociology of Sport, 35*(2), 131–148.

Lakowski, T. (2009). Athletes with disabilities in school sports: A critical assessment of the state of sports opportunities for students with disabilities. *Boston University International Law Journal, 27*(2), 283–316.

Levermore, R. (2008). Sport: A new engine of development? *Progress in Development Studies, 8*(2), 183–190.

Lord, J. E., & Stein, M. A. (2009). Social rights and the relational value of rights to participate in sport, recreation, and play. *Boston University International Law Journal, 27*(2), 249–282.

Maguire, J. (1999). *Global sport: Identities, society, civilizations.* Malden, MA: Blackwell Publishers.

Maguire, J., & Pearton, R. (2000). Global sport and the migration patterns of France '98 World Cup Finals players: Some preliminary observations. *Soccer & Society, 1*(1), 175–189.

Martinkova, I. (2006). *The ethics of human performances.* Lecture at the 2006 International Olympic Academy Educators Session, Olympia, Greece.

McArdle, D. (2009). Elite athletes and disability discrimination. *Cambrian Law Review, 40*, 49–62.

Meier, M. (2005). *Gender equity, sport and development* (Working paper). Biel/Bienne, Switzerland: Swiss Academy for Development.

Meyer, C., & Kuhn, S. (2009). Effects of Major League Baseball on economic development in the Dominican Republic. Unpublished manuscript. Retrieved August 3, 2011 from http://mason.gmu.edu/~cmeyer/Meyer-MLB%26DR.pdf.

Miloch, K. S. (2002). Coming to America: Immigration and the professional athlete. *Journal of Legal Aspects of Sport, 13*(1), 55–78.

NBA. (2009). Season opens with record-tying 83 international players. Retrieved from http://www.nba.com/2009/news/10/27/international.players/index.html.

Poli, R. (2006). Africans' status in the European football players' labour market. *Soccer & Society*, 7(2–3), 278–291.

ProGreenSports. (2010a). 2009 pro team survey report. Retrieved August 3, 2011 from http://progreensports.com/wordpress/?page_id=173.

ProGreenSports. (2010b). 2010 college athletic department sustainability survey results. Retrieved August 3, 2011 from http://progreensports.com/wordpress/?page_id=406.

Project GreenHands. (n.d.). Community mobilization. Retrieved August 3, 2011 from http://www.projectgreenhands.org/our-work/community-mobilization.

Rookwood, J. (2008). Sport for peace and social development. *Peace Review: A Journal of Social Justice*, 20, 471–479.

Roy, E. C. (2007). Aiming for inclusive sport: The legal and practical implications of the United Nation's Disability Convention for Sport, Recreation and Leisure for People with Disabilities. *Entertainment and Sport Law Journal*, 5(1). Retrieved August 3, 2011 from www2.warwick.ac.uk/fac/soc/law/elj/eslj/issues/volume5/number1/roy.

Sanchez, J. (2007, September 18). Creating complete, healthy players. MLB.com, Retrieved August 3, 2011 from http://mlb.mlb.com/news/article.jsp?ymd=20070918&content_id=2215646&vkey=news_mlb&fext=.jsp&c_id=mlb.

ScienceDaily. (2010, June 16). Consumer responses to gulf oil spill reflect Americans' changing corporate expectations. Retrieved August 3, 2011 from http://www.sciencedaily.com/releases/2010/06/100616122132.htm.

Sherry, E. (2010). (Re)engaging marginalized groups through sport: The Homeless World Cup. *International Review for the Sociology of Sport*, 45(1), 59–71.

Skinner, J., & Gilbert, K. (2007). Sport management education: Teaching and learning for the future. *Sport Management Review*, 10, 125–131.

Speedo. (2010). LZR racer elite. Retrieved from http://www.speedousa.com/family/index.jsp?cp=3124322.3124332&categoryId=3124355.

Street Soccer USA. (2010). About: Mission. Retrieved August 3, 2011 from Streetsoccerusa.org.

Sugden, J. (1995). *Sport, sectarianism, and society in a divided Ireland.* London: Leicester University Press.

Taylor, M. (2006). Global players? Football, migration, and globalization, c. 1930–2000. *Historical Social Research*, 31(1), 7–30.

Thibault, L. (2009). Globalization of sport: An inconvenient truth. *Journal of Sport Management*, 23(1), 1–20.

Tucker, R., & Dugas, J. (2007). Oscar Pistorius: Science and engineering vs. training. An evaluation of ALL the evidence. Retrieved August 3, 2011 from http://www.sportsscientists.com/2007/07/oscar-pistorius-science-and-engineering.html.

United Nations. (2002). Resolution adopted by the General Assembly: A world fit for children. Retrieved August 3, 2011 from http://www.unicef.org/specialsession/docs_new/documents/A-RES-S27-2E.pdf.

United Nations. (2003). Sport for development and peace: Towards achieving the millennium development goals. Report from the United Nations Inter-Agency Task Force on Sport for Development and Peace. Retrieved from http://www.un.org/themes/sport/reportE.pdf.

United Nations. (2010). Why sport? Retrieved August 3, 2011 from http://www.un.org/themes/sport.

U.S. Green Building Council. (2010). What LEED is. Retrieved August 3, 2011 from http://www.usgbc.org/DisplayPage.aspx?CMSPageID=1988.

Vancouver2010. (2010, December 20). VANOC releases final sustainability report. Retrieved August 3, 2011 from http://www.olympic.org/vancouver-2010-winter-olympics?articleid=110042.

Wong, L. L., & Trumper, R. (2002). Global celebrity athletes and nationalism: Futbol, hockey, and the representation of nation. *Journal of Sport and Social Issues*, 26(2), 168–194.

Zettler, P. J. (2009). Is it cheating to use Cheetahs? The implications of technologically innovative prostheses for sports values and rules. *Boston University International Law Journal*, 27(2), 367–409.

The Internationalization of Sport Management Academia

essay 12

RISING TO THE CHALLENGE

It is important that our students be prepared to participate in societies that are no longer defined by nations and geographical borders—and our sport management students are no exception.

The author introduces the essay

Karen Danylchuk THE UNIVERSITY OF WESTERN ONTARIO

Karen Danylchuk is an Associate Professor at The University of Western Ontario in London, Canada. Prior to that, she taught at Hong Kong International School and served in administrative capacities at the World University Games. She is a former President of NASSM and currently serves as its international representative. She is a NASSM Research Fellow and recipient of the Earle F. Zeigler Lecture Award (2010) and the Garth Paton Distinguished Service Award (2007).

Introduction

We cannot refute the fact that we live in a global era—an era no longer defined by nations and borders. In fact, the phrase "the world is getting smaller" has become a cliché suggesting that globalization has affected every dimension of life, including sport.

As noted by Merryfield, Lo, Po, and Kasai (2008):

> The acceleration of knowledge creation, the dynamics of electronic communication and the resulting availability of global perspectives are changing the nature of public dis-

course and action. As more and more people gain access to information and interact with individuals and communities across the planet, they acquire new worldminded ways of learning, debating, and creating which in turn expand the scope of civic consciousness and responsibilities beyond national borders. (p. 6)

This concept of "worldmindedness" is not new. In fact, the term was used as early as the 1950s to suggest that individuals should value the viewpoints, experiences, and worldviews of others, especially those quite different from themselves. Merryfield et al. (2008) further noted a differing perspective:

Many people across societies wear blinders of ethnocentrism (we are the best, we don't need to learn about anyone else). In some communities, xenophobia is pervasive, and young people may grow up learning that anything foreign is bad, bizarre, dangerous, or evil. Lack of interest in other cultures or just ignorance about how the world works may serve as blinders for action when people who are faced with seemingly local issues do not understand the possible global connections. (p. 7)

Today's citizens need to use their global knowledge and intercultural skills to make informed decisions in our interconnected world (Mudimbi-Boyi, 2002). In turn, it is important that our students be prepared to participate in societies that are no longer defined by nations and geographical borders—and our sport management students are no exception. Consequently, institutions of higher education have in recent years realized the need to prepare graduates to live and participate as global citizens through the internationalization of their campuses.

This essay, therefore, will address a variety of questions: How can institutions of higher education adequately prepare graduates to live and participate as global citizens and professionals? Why is it important? Whose responsibility is it? How can academicians prepare themselves to assist students? How is sport management as an academic discipline affected? What are our sport management academicians and professional associations doing in this regard? What are the issues and challenges we face? Where do we go in the future?

THE GLOBALIZATION AND INTERNATIONALIZATION INTERFACE

irst it is important to distinguish between the terms *globalization* and *internationalization*. The concept of *globalization* is not to be confused with the term *internationalization*, even though they are dynamically linked concepts (Knight, 1999). Whereas globalization refers to an ongoing process by which regional economies, societies, and cultures have become integrated through a globe-spanning network of communication and trade, internationalization may be viewed as a reaction or response to globalization, and in the case of higher education, in the university and college environment (Knight, 1999). In other words, "globalization can be seen as the catalyst whereas internationalization is the response, albeit the response in a positive way" (Knight, 1999, p. 14). Internationalization professes to promote recognition and respect between countries, whereas globalization has been suggested to promote de-nationalization and homogenization (Gacel-Avila, 2005) and is often characterized by unequal power relations (O'Shea, 1997). As noted by Westerbeek and Smith (2003), there are seven driving forces of globalization: (1) economy, (2) technology, (3) social science, resources, and natural environment, (4) demography, (5) governance, (6) conflict and war, and (7) religion and cultural identity.

Knight (2003) provides one of the most widely recognized definitions of internationalization in the context of higher education as "the process of integrating an international or global dimension into the purpose, functions or delivery of post-secondary education" (p. 2). This definition is broadly accepted by other bodies, such as the United Nations Educational, Scientific and Cultural Organization (UNESCO), the Organization for Economic Development and Cooperation (OECD), the International Association for Universities (IAE), the Association of International Educators in the United States, and the Association of Universities and Colleges of Canada (AUCC). International educators advocate systemic international infusion by weaving international perspectives into every discipline, faculty hiring decision, and mission statement for universities. Activities related to internationalization fall into two categories—those that occur on the home campus (e.g., international course content) and those that happen abroad or across borders (e.g., study abroad and exchanges) (Knight, 2004).

THE IMPETUS FOR INTERNATIONALIZATION IN HIGHER EDUCATION

Internationalization is a very relevant topic on university campuses around the world and has become an organizational priority. It has even attracted the attention of governments and groups such as the United Nations Educational, Scientific and Cultural Organization (UNESCO, 2005). Many universities have demonstrated their commitment to internationalization through their university mission statement or strategic plan. For example, a recent survey of Canadian universities revealed that 95 percent explicitly refer to the international dimension in their strategic plans, and more than three-quarters cite internationalization as one of their top five priorities (Tamburri, 2007). As Tamburri notes (2007), "over the years, universities have grown increasingly aware of the benefits of diversifying their student body and providing students with an international perspective that will allow them to succeed in an increasingly globalized world" (p. 8).

Dramatic demographic changes in the cultural and linguistic diversity of people are occurring in many nations throughout the world. This is evidenced by the fact that worldwide migration has climbed to unprecedented levels and more people live outside their country of birth than in any other period of human history (Esses, 2009). The changing faces of our communities resulting from migration and increasing diversity have challenged higher education institutions to modify their curricula and instructional strategies to meet the needs of diverse learners and to prepare all graduates to have the awareness, knowledge, and skills to be effective in a diverse society (Morey, 2000). Moreover, universities in some countries have undergone a major shift to recruit international students.

The education of international students is considered a major industry and a significant benefit to the economy of the host country. For example, international students spent an estimated $6.5 billion on education in Canada in 2008—more than the revenue generated by exporting softwood lumber and coal (Stewart, 2010). In addition, 83,000 jobs were created from international student activities (Stewart, 2010). Similar examples may be found in other countries, such as Australia, where international students and the travel prompted by their family and friends contributed $12.6 billion to the economy in 2007 and 2008 (Access Economics, 2009). In that same year, international student expenditure was estimated to have generated just over 122,000 full-time employment positions, 33,482 of them in the education sector (Access Economics, 2009).

Increasing wealth in Asia and other places around the world translates into a rapidly growing supply of international students. In fact, 2.8 million students from around the world studied abroad in 2006 (Access Economics, 2009). The United States used to account for more than 40 percent of the total number of international students in the world. However, after the 9/11 terrorist attacks, many prospective international students chose to study abroad in Australia and the United Kingdom, because the U.S. government tightened its immigration policy toward international students and other countries increased their global recruiting campaigns (Ota, n.d.). According to 2006 figures, the United States and the United Kingdom accounted for the largest proportion of higher education international students—21.2 and 12 percent, respectively (Access Economics, 2009). For a relatively small country population-wise, Australia hosts a large proportion (7.5 percent) of the world's international students (Access Economics, 2009). While Canadian universities lag behind their Australian and U.K. counterparts, in part due to Canada's rather late entry into the field of active recruitment, visa students now represent 7 percent of that country's full-time undergraduates and almost 20 percent of graduate students. This percentage is slightly lower in the United States—2 percent of undergraduates and 22 percent of graduates at four-year institutions are international students. At four-year private institutions, the numbers are 4 percent and 15 percent respectively (AUCC, 2007). In Canada, these students have come from more than 200 countries, with China in the lead, followed by the United States, France, India, and other Asian countries (AUCC, 2007). The focus on internationalization at universities around the globe continues. Consider, for example, that the government of Ontario, Canada, recently committed to a 50 percent increase in international enrollment.

THE EFFECTS OF GLOBALIZATION ON THE SPORT INDUSTRY

It is certainly no revelation that the sport industry is a global phenomenon. Countless examples abound to support this notion: the continual commercialization of the Olympic Games and other major international sporting events such as the FIFA World Cup, Le Tour de France, and the Ryder Cup; the export and import of international talent at all competitive levels; the expansion of multinational sport product and service corporations; cross-marketing and promotional agreements between partners in different countries; advances in on-demand information technologies resulting in virtual fans; the shift in the balance of power in international sport; and the increased role of sport in the world economy are just a few examples of this phenomenon (Fay & Snyder, 2007). The evidence of global brands is pervasive and no longer defined by nations and geographical borders. Sport is big business, charging full-speed ahead with new opportunities for the participant and fan alike. Advanced technology and the elimination of trade barriers have had a profound effect on the globalization of the sport industry, further enhancing the development of international sport.

INTERNATIONAL SPORT

The internationalization of sport has been accurately described by Fairley, Lizandra, and Gladden (2009) as being reflected in many spheres. It may merely involve the introduction of a sport into new countries where the sport has not been traditionally played. From a team and/or league perspective, internationalization may entail countries competing against each other in international competition; the expansion of established national leagues to include teams that are based in different countries; teams touring foreign countries to generate interest and awareness of their sport or league; individuals competing alongside players from different countries in organized leagues; and even travel to sport events in different countries as a spectator, official, or volunteer. From another perspective, it may involve the international reporting of sport competition and events through various online, broadcast, and print media. And finally, internationalization may encompass the availability of licensed merchandise outside of the home country of the team or player; global companies sponsoring international sport events; and the use of sport as a social and political tool. Fay and Snyder (2007) further noted two factors that determine whether a sport is international: (1) the degree to which, or the regularity with which, action by an organization, company, event, or individual focuses primarily on international activity, and (2) the context in which an individual, an organization, or an event operates within the international sport environment.

While the Olympic Games may be viewed as the original international sport product, sport began to spread across international borders through colonization efforts by countries such as Great Britain. Consider, for example, the British introduction of cricket to their Far East colonies. Over the years, professional sport leagues created demand for their products in international markets. The globalization of sport has resulted in the involvement of corporations, product manufacturers, sponsors, media, and sport tourism managers, to name but a few.

Consequently, these trends require us to prepare our students to operate in the sphere of international sport. As suggested by Fay (2011), the "emergence of international business and management as a field of study within the broader confines of academic programs in business and management predicts the potential of international sport for being a new sub-discipline of study within sport management." This is not surprising given that sport has become a powerful vehicle in the international exchange process by delivering lasting economic, social, and health benefits. Furthermore, "the global sports industry is increasingly reflecting the trends in the world economy, with a growing shift towards emerging markets" (Wilson, 2009). Given these trends, it is important that sport managers understand the international environment in which they operate. Therefore, "sport professionals must be aware of the opportunities that are available on a global scale, as well as the challenges that arise from conducting business in this new, global market" (Apostolopoulou & Papadimitriou, 2005).

It is not the purpose of this essay, however, to focus on international sport per se, as this area is covered in other sport management resources, but rather to address how we may prepare ourselves (academicians and students alike) to become global citizens through internationalizing our teaching and learning curriculum, our research, and our service. After all, given the globalization trends in the world of sport, career opportunities in international sport are increasing. We must ensure, therefore, that we adopt a global strategy by teaching, researching, and advocating from an international perspective.

INTERNATIONALIZATION OF SPORT MANAGEMENT AS AN ACADEMIC DISCIPLINE

As previously noted, globalization has served as the catalyst for internationalization in higher education. Sport is a global phenomenon, and as such, sport management is an academic discipline ideally positioned to incorporate internationalization into the body of knowledge, its delivery, and the preparation of its students. The following section will outline methods for internationalizing the curriculum, research, and service components, first from a generic perspective, and then from a sport management perspective. An evaluation of our efforts in this regard from both a disciplinary and professional association perspective will be provided.

Internationalizing our Teaching and Learning Curriculum

The most common way to internationalize a teaching and learning curriculum is to incorporate international content into courses, be it through international resources, such as readings, textbooks, films, videos, case studies, and guest lecturers, or to devote a session to an international topic. However, these are considered "add-on approaches" and may be criticized for failing to present a rethinking of the course from international perspectives. Therefore, a more in-depth approach might entail the addition of an international course within the program itself. Another related approach is to require students to take an internationally oriented course from another faculty (e.g., international relations/affairs and global studies, European studies, Asian studies, international business, and international development studies), or even a foreign language.

Many sport management academicians already employ many of these strategies, such as the use of international content. In addition, international sport management courses and the preparation for careers in international sport have gained momentum in many, but not all, university sport management programs.

Some programs have lagged in this effort due to a variety of factors, some of which are beyond the control of the current program managers (e.g., faculty workload, finances). The content of these courses, however, varies among universities, because there is no one agreed upon definition of "international sport," nor of what should constitute the course's curriculum. For some, it may be merely focusing on international sport bodies and international hallmark events, whereas for others, it may be delivering an internationally oriented course with international partners. Given the convenience and advancement of technology nowadays, the latter type of courses may be delivered through electronic means, such as Blackboard/WebCT. Consider, for example, the International Sport Management course originated by Victoria University in Melbourne, Australia, involving university partners from around the world. It is currently hosted and delivered via Blackboard/WebCT by The University of Western Ontario in London, Canada. This online course is directed at senior undergraduate sport management students, and offers students and professors an opportunity to engage in discussions about specific internationally oriented case studies. Another example is a course conducted by LaTrobe University in Melbourne, Australia, that involves interaction between partner universities using video as the medium. While these are only two examples, they demonstrate that the creativity in delivering programs has most certainly evolved over time. Attend a sport management conference these days and you will undoubtedly notice presentations of innovative and creative teaching and learning techniques throughout the academic program, along with topics addressing transnational and cross-cultural issues.

Despite efforts to internationalize our sport management curricula, however, there are no international curriculum standards in place. Sport management professors who wish to incorporate an international component use a variety of their own methods. At the graduate level, there appears to be no requirement at many of our universities for students to take an international course. This is particularly problematic at the doctoral level. Given that some doctoral programs are so research-focused, with very little emphasis on teaching, many of our doctoral students do not take any international courses during their degree study. Consequently, the next generation of faculty members will have difficulty in introducing any international content into the courses they teach if they do not have any background (Nehrt, 1987). This prompts the question: Should we be recommending that doctoral students engage in some sort of international course throughout their term of study?

Teaching resources

There has also been a slow but gradual increase in the number of books devoted to international and global sport management, but there is much room for growth in this regard. In addition, many introductory textbooks now include a chapter on international sport, and others have incorporated more of an international focus throughout. Hopefully, the introductory textbooks will continue to substantially emphasize this component in their updated editions. But once again, the point is the varying perspective on *what* should constitute the international sport body of knowledge.

There has also been a dramatic growth in the number of sport management-related journals that contain contributions from international authors and may be used in the classroom. Finally, other journals and trade publications, such as *Street & Smith's SportsBusiness Journal* and *SportBusiness International,* focus on international sport issues.

Despite the variety of sport management resources, however, challenges remain. These resources, for the most part, are only available in English, which may pose a challenge for some academicians and students in non–English-speaking countries. Furthermore, there are financial barriers to accessing many of these resources. New technologies, such as e-format, however, have made the process of sharing our information internationally easier than ever and will hopefully assist in addressing this challenge, but change may be slow in this regard.

Knowledge export

Knowledge export, which is the delivery of knowledge products and services overseas, has become yet another integral aspect of many universities in their efforts toward internationalization. Delivery modes include distance education, offshore campuses, twinning programs, joint degrees, and even franchised courses and programs. These approaches hold huge potential in sport management, given the proliferation of programs around the globe. With the existence of sport management associations in most regions of the globe, namely NASSM, the European Association for Sport Management (EASM), the Sport Management Association of Australia and New Zealand (SMAANZ), the Asian Association for Sport Management (AASM), the Asociacion Latinoamericana de Gestion Deportiva in Latin America (ALGeDe), and the African Sport Management Association (ASMA), opportunities for establishing connections are greater than ever. Committed leadership and resources, however, are important.

Faculty opportunities

Opportunities for faculty members to internationalize themselves entail exchanges, visiting scholars' programs, study abroad programs, and attendance at international conferences, to name but a few. Some universities have taken a less common approach by hiring faculty members from other countries to provide a truly international perspective.

Again, we can implement these approaches within our academic discipline, given the growth in the number of sport management programs and the existence of regional sport management associations around the world. The opportunity to attend international conferences, for example, is greater than ever. But human and financial capital, differences in institutional commitment, and language barriers pose a few challenges for some countries in this regard.

Student opportunities

Finally, from the perspective of students, opportunities for international experience may be achieved by studying abroad in exchanges, co-op programs, internships, and service learning. Interest in and support for these methods have increased dramatically in recent years. Although the percentage is still small in Canada (2.2% of full-time students studied abroad in 2006), the absolute numbers have skyrocketed (AUCC, 2007). In fact, the number of U.S. students studying abroad in 2007–08 increased by 8.5 percent from the previous year to 262,416 (Open Doors, 2009).

While study abroad programs are not new to sport management, the number of programs has increased, as has the emergence of companies to service this growing aspect of the international market. For example, GlobaLinks Study Abroad, a Colorado-based company, has worked for over 20 years in the field of international education. They provide a wide variety of opportunities for North American students and advisors to study abroad in Australia, New Zealand, Fiji, Asia, and Europe. By partnering with universities in other countries, they offer a wide variety of programs. The classes are taught in English due to the range of countries, and no prior language experience is required to participate. The participating universities also provide opportunities for the students to study the native language of the host country. This is just one example demonstrating the inroads made in recent years to overcome some of the inherent barriers of study abroad, such as language. A number of sport management university programs in Canada and the United States have created opportunities to visit another country (e.g., England, Australia, New Zealand, Cuba) during the summer semester or student study break. In many instances, these excursions target countries where English is a common language.

Finally, internships are an important and popular aspect of our sport management programs. There is much room to internationalize these experiences for our students by developing relationships with international partners. Our sport management colleagues need to coordinate efforts to lessen the challenges of culture and language. From an international student recruitment perspective, the strong interest from students around the world in studying in North America is clear. The same may be said for other countries as well.

Internationalizing Our Research

Research is by nature a collaborative activity, and "historically, this collaboration has always included a robust international dimension, which has influenced the research enterprise itself and enriched the internationalization of our campuses" (AUCC, 2009). Promoting an international dimension in research is important to ensure a country's economic, scientific, and technological competitiveness. Recent trends to increase institutional engagement in international research collaboration have included international research networks, tech transfer agreements, joint research projects, the sharing of research facilities and major infrastructure, the linking of research centers and virtual networks, faculty and student exchanges and sabbaticals, and the co-supervision of Ph.D. students from other countries, to name a few.

The growth in the number of sport management related journals demonstrates that our research is being circulated around the world. While some valuable research collaboration is ongoing within our field, there remains a great deal of opportunity in this regard. In my study concerning research collaboration within the *Journal of Sport Management* from 1987 to the present (Danylchuk, 2010), I found the number of collaborative pieces ranged from 7 percent in 1987 to 23 percent in 2009, with an average of 14 percent. Of the 60 collaborative articles over this time period, 38 percent involved American researchers paired with Canadian researchers, 23 percent were American and/or Canadian with Australian and/or New Zealander collaborators, 15 percent entailed American and/or Canadian with Asian collaborators, 12 percent were American and/or Canadian with European collaborators, and 12 percent involved collaborators who were not from the United States or Canada. While limited to only one journal, these findings demonstrate the ongoing collaboration between North American researchers and researchers from other countries, but there is certainly room for expansion.

Internationalizing Our Service

Professors can internationalize themselves through the service component by participating in community committees and organizations that have an inter-national flavor and by attending international events held in our communities. For students, opportunities for service learning projects outside the classroom that may operate locally or in another country are increasing. Some campuses offer International Development and Education Weeks, student-sponsored in-ternational seminars, and buddy programs that pair domestic and international students. Sport management is an ideal discipline in which to experience these opportunities. This may be achieved through involvement in hosting interna-tional sport events, and working with community sport councils, recreation departments, fitness clubs, sport clubs, and schools, with a particular focus on the international and/or ethnically diverse cohort.

Internationalization Within Our Regional Sport Management Associations

As previously noted, we now have regional/continental associations around the world—NASSM, EASM, SMAANZ, AASM, ALGeDe, and ASMA. There are also sport management associations in countries such as Japan, Korea, Thai-land, and Malaysia. The International Sport Management Alliance, an informal organization comprised of NASSM, EASM, and SMAANZ, was established in 1999 but existed largely to give each of the regional associations a turn hosting the International Alliance Conference every few years. With the recent establish-ment of regional associations in Asia (AASM), Latin America (ALGeDe), and Africa (ASMA), a dialogue is currently underway among the regional association presidents to explore a World Association for Sport Management. This body, however, is not without its challenges, such as establishing the most effective and inclusive governance structure, ensuring the protection of the development of the regional associations, and addressing the challenges of regional associations operating in third world countries.

The regional associations themselves have made efforts to encourage the internationalization of our field. NASSM, for example, has for many years demonstrated both a commitment to and willingness to be involved in internationalization. This has been achieved in a variety of ways, such as encouraging international presenters at its annual conference, publishing international papers in its journals, appointing an international delegate (and most recently, establishing an International Initiatives ad hoc committee), and promoting study abroad and internship opportunities in the NASSM newsletter. EASM has for many years encouraged sport management students around the world to become involved in various initiatives, such as their pre-conference student seminar. As well, they organized EASM Summer Schools in Germany during 2010 and 2011 directed at senior undergraduate students, with one of the goals being the provision of international perspectives and experience.

BARRIERS TO INTERNATIONALIZATION

Notwithstanding these seemingly universal methods, there are some very realistic barriers to a university's internationalization. As noted by Green (2003), "barriers can be institutional, such as scarce resources, disciplinary paradigms, and structures, or the absence of incentives. They also can be individual in nature, including lack of faculty expertise, lack of interest, negative attitudes, or the unwillingness or inability of faculty to integrate international learning into their disciplinary perspectives" (p. 1).

Interestingly, in 2003, the International Association of Universities, a UNESCO-based, international, non-governmental organization founded in 1950 to facilitate international cooperation in higher education, conducted the first-ever global survey of its 621 members in 66 countries related to the practices and priorities of internationalization at their institutions (Danylchuk, 2010). Lack of financial support at the institutional level was identified as the most important obstacle to internationalization. While two-thirds of the institutions had an internationalization policy/strategy in place, only about half of these institutions had budgets and a monitoring framework to support its implementation. Therefore, the presence of such a policy in the strategic plan is one thing, but the institution must make a commitment to it, provide visionary leadership, and devote the human and financial resources necessary to support it.

Despite these challenges, a number of strategies may be utilized to address these obstacles, namely providing a supportive and highly committed leadership; outlining a coherent, institution-wide (or unit-wide) strategy; enumerating clearly defined goals; obtaining faculty engagement; sharing leadership responsibilities; aligning resources and removing barriers; and persisting over time. We, as leaders in the field of sport management, must ensure that we teach, research, and advocate from an international perspective. The inherent challenges, such as differences in language, culture, institutional commitment, human and financial capital, and lack of standardized curricula, must be overcome.

CONCLUDING THOUGHTS: FACING THE CHALLENGES OF INTERNATIONALIZATION IN SPORT MANAGEMENT ACADEMIA

Given the impact of globalization on the sport industry, this essay has attempted to address the importance of internationalizing our academicians and students through their teaching and learning curriculum, research, and service. Careers in the international sport environment abound, be they through corporate sport, professional sport leagues, sport marketing companies, or international sport governing bodies. In order to prepare for careers in the international setting, it is imperative to garner a cultural awareness and sensitivity that may be attained through study abroad or exchange programs, courses in international studies, and foreign language training. Only through efforts to internationalize ourselves will we, our programs, and our students be successful in the international marketplace.

REFERENCES

Access Economics. (2009). *The Australian education sector and the economic contribution of international students.* East Melbourne, Victoria, Australia: Australian Council for Private Education and Training.

Apostolopoulou, A., & Papdimitriou, D. (2005). Global sport industry. In A. Gillentine & B. B. Crow (Eds.), *Foundations of Sport Management* (pp. 169–183). Morgantown, WV: Fitness Information Technology.

Association of Universities and Colleges of Canada (AUCC). (2007). *Internationalizing Canadian campuses: Main themes emerging from the 2007 Scotiabank–AUCC workshop on excellence in internationalization at Canadian universities.* Ottawa, ON: AUCC.

Association of Universities and Colleges of Canada (AUCC). (2009). *International research collaboration.* Ottawa, ON: AUCC.

Danylchuk, K. (2010, June 5). *Internationalizing ourselves: Realities, challenges, and opportunities.* Earle F. Zeigler Lecture Award Address, North American Society for Sport Management Conference, Tampa, Florida.

Esses, V. (2009). Migration and ethnic relations: Study at UWO. *Your city.* London, ON: London.

Fairley, S., Lizandra, M., & Gladden, J. M. (2009). International sport. In L. P. Masteralexis, C. A. Barr, & M. A. Hums (Eds.), *Principles and practice of sport management* (3rd ed.). (pp. 170–201). Sudbury, MA: Jones and Bartlett.

Fay, T. G. (2011). Preface. In M. Li, E. McIntosh, & G. Bravo (Eds.), *International sport management.* Champaign, IL: Human Kinetics.

Fay, T. G., & Snyder, D. (2007). A North American perspective on international sport. In J. B. Parks, J. Quarterman, & L. Thibault (Eds.), *Contemporary sport management* (3rd ed.). (pp. 164–188). Champaign, IL: Human Kinetics.

Gacel-Avila, J. (2005). The internationalization of higher education: A paradigm for global citizenry. *Journal of Studies in International Education, 9,* 121–136.

Green, M. F. (2003). *The challenge of internationalizing undergraduate education: Global learning for all.* Global Challenges and US Higher Education Conference, Duke University, 1–30.

Knight, J. (1999). Internationalization of higher education. In J. Knight & H. de Wit (Eds.), *Quality and Internationalization in Higher Education.* Paris: Organization for Economic Cooperation and Development.

Knight, J. (2003). Updated internationalization definition. *International Higher Education, 33,* 2–3.

Knight, J. (2004). Internationalization remodeled: Definition, approaches, and rationale. *Journal of Studies in International Education, 8*, 5–31.

Merryfield, M., Lo, T. Y., Po, S. C., & Kasai, M. (2008). Worldmindedness: Taking off the blinders. *Journal of Curriculum and Instruction, 2*(1), 6–20.

Morey, A. I. (2000). Changing higher education curricula for a global and multicultural world. *Higher Education in Europe, 25*(1), 25–39.

Mudimbi-Boyi, E. (2002). *Beyond dichotomies: Histories, identities, cultures and the challenges of globalization.* Albany, NY: SUNY Press.

Nehrt, L. (1987). The internationalization of the curriculum. *Journal of International Business Studies, 18*(1), 83–90.

Open Doors. (2009). *Open doors report.* Washington, DC: Institute of International Education.

O'Shea, B. (1997). Internationalization: Opportunities and challenges for occupational therapy. *Canadian Journal of Occupational Therapy, 64*, 236–239.

Ota, H. (n.d.). Differences in the context of internationalization by region: North America. Retrieved August 3, 2011 from http://hdl.handle.net/10086/14559.

Stewart, P. (2010, June). Academic values v. commercial values. *CAUT Bulletin, 58*(6). Retrieved 8/1/11 from http://www.cautbulletin.ca/en_article.asp?articleid=3026.

Tamburri, R. (2007, November). A helping hand in a strange land. *University Affairs*, 8–11.

UNESCO. (2005). *Toward knowledge societies.* Paris: United Nations Educational, Scientific and Cultural Organization.

Westerbeek, H., & Smith, A. (2003). *Sport business in the global marketplace.* New York: Palgrave Macmillan.

Wilson, B. (2009, October 27). Ghana looks to build sports industry. *BBC News.* Retrieved August 3, 2011 from http://news.bbc.co.uk/2/hi/8320342.stm.

Internships

INDENTURED SERVITUDE OR RIGOROUS EXPERIENTIAL LEARNING?

In an ideal world, the internship experience mutually satisfies the needs of both the student and the host site. However, we do not live in an ideal world and the use of internships in the sport industry has not been without controversy and problems.

The author introduces the essay

William F. Stier, Jr. THE COLLEGE AT BROCKPORT, STATE UNIVERSITY OF NEW YORK

William Stier, Jr. holds the highest academic rank within the SUNY system, Distinguished Service Professor. He directs the undergraduate sport management program at the College at Brockport, State University of New York, where he also serves as graduate director in athletic administration. He has authored 376 articles in 99 different scholarly publications and has written 25 books. He serves as editor of two journals: *The Physical Educator* and the *International Journal of Sport Management*.

Introduction

The history of internships in preparing future employees in many fields and professions is long and successful (Moorman, 2004). Internships (field experiences) have played an integral part in the professional preparation of both graduate and undergraduate students in sport management ever since such programs came into existence (Cuneen, 2004; NASPE, 1987; Ross & Beggs, 2007). Today, even midcareer, established professionals in a wide range of occupations are finding it worthwhile and/or necessary to intern with no pay in the hope that such involvement will eventually result in a paid position (Tahmincioglu, 2010).

One can view internships as serving as the bridge between *theory* (learning in the typical college classroom) and *practice* (learning in the real world). As such, the internship has become a "lynchpin element in the training and education of future workers within the sport management profession" (Stier, 2001, p. 5). Among today's leaders in the world of sport and sport management, the culminating internship is considered "probably the most rewarding, educationally significant, and career enhancing venture that any future sport manager can experience" (Stier, 2002, p. 9).

An internship can be a supervised field experience, a practical learning experience in which the individual student is involved in real-life (actual) work experiences within the sport business world, under the supervision and direction of an experienced, qualified, on-site professional. The truly meaningful sport management internship or field experience is one in which the student *learns by doing,* demonstrating competency and professionalism by assuming important responsibilities and completing meaningful tasks for the organization.

An essential element of any internship is the on-site supervisor's periodic assessment or evaluation of the intern. Typically, such an evaluation is sent to the college supervisor on a prearranged schedule. This written report details how the intern is performing within a wide range of areas. These areas could include personal qualities, professional qualities, and technical preparation. The use of both checklists and narrative comments can be part of this assessment form (see Exhibit 13.1). The reports from the on-sight supervisor serve as important means of keeping the college supervisor and other faculty up to date relative to the intern's progress. If necessary, the college supervisor or other faculty member may visit the site if the supervisor requests such a meeting.

The major advantages of any internship, from the perspective of the student intern, are threefold. First, the internship allows the student to have numerous and meaningful opportunities to broaden one's work experience within the sport management arena. "Educators are increasingly realizing that the integration of study and practice is a more powerful way to learn" (Aoun, 2010, p. 1). Second, the hands-on experience helps the student to develop and further refine skills, competencies, and abilities (including networking) that will put the student in a position to be a valued employee within the world of sport (Bell & Countiss, 1993; Kelley, 2004; Stratta, 2004). And third, the internship enables the student to demonstrate experience, skills, and competencies by completing tasks and responsibilities associated with the field experience (Stier, 2006). In short, the internship is an excellent learning opportunity that allows students to demonstrate and apply their abilities, skills, and competencies in an effort to impress professionals in the field and convey their capacity for growth, their ability to learn, and their overall potential (Stier, 2008).

Many professionals see the culminating internship as the pinnacle of their professional preparation. That is, they consider the internship completed just prior to graduation to be most important in that it may (but not necessarily) lead to actual employment at the site where the student has interned, if there is an opening at that time. It is this exercise of linking traditional classroom theory to real-world work that warrants the academic credit to be earned by the student intern (Young & Baker, 2004).

EXHIBIT 13.1

Sport management internship evaluation form.

SPORT MANAGEMENT INTERNSHIP EVALUATION

ASSESSMENT WEEK #   Date:

Name of Intern:

Name of On-Site Supervisor:

Description of Intern's Duties:

Directions: Please evaluate the athletic administration intern at the conclusion of each week of the internship experience. The following code is used for uniform evaluation. Thank you.

  5 excellent;   4 very good;   3 acceptable;   2 needs improvement;   1 unacceptable;
  NA = not applicable

I. PERSONAL QUALITIES

  Shows Initiative

  Exhibits Self-confidence

  Communicates Effectively

  Uses Voice Effectively

  Shows Sensitivity to and Respect for Colleagues

  OVERALL IMPRESSION IN THIS CATEGORY

II. PROFESSIONAL QUALITIES

  Is Punctual

  Demonstrates Dependability

  Willingness to Change—Flexible

  Makes Efforts to Improve

  Interacts with Colleagues

  Accepts Criticism

  Has a Professional Appearance

  OVERALL IMPRESSION IN THIS CATEGORY

(continued)

EXHIBIT 13.1

Sport management internship evaluation form, *continued.*

Name of Intern: _____   Date: _____

5 excellent;   4 very good;   3 acceptable;   2 needs improvement;   1 unacceptable;
NA = not applicable

III. TECHNICAL PREPARATION

Utilizes Problem Solving Skills   _____

Shows Knowledge of the Sport Operation   _____

Demonstrates Basic Accounting Knowledge   _____

Demonstrates Selling Ability   _____

Demonstrates Knowledge of Marketing Sport Products and Services _____

Shows Understanding About Financing Sport Operation   _____

Shows Ability to Organize Efforts   _____

Demonstrates Good Writing Skills   _____

OVERALL IMPRESSION IN THIS CATEGORY   _____

COMMENTS (please list strengths and weaknesses and steps taken for possible improvement):

_____

_____

_____

_____

OVERALL EVALUATION AT THIS POINT IN TIME: _____

_____

_____

Is a consultation with the college supervisor desirable at this point in time?

_____ Yes   _____ No

Site Supervisor's Signature: _____   Date: _____

Please send this form (both pages) when completed to via e-mail to: [college sponsor]

ASSESSING SUITABLE INTERNSHIP SITES

To determine the appropriateness of an internship site, the would-be intern is encouraged to ask the following questions (Stier, 2009):

1. Will the site provide meaningful work experiences for the intern in the areas or functions that are of interest to the student?

2. Will there be adequate supervision and direction of the intern by qualified and experienced staff at the site?

3. Has the site utilized interns appropriately in the past, or have interns been used inappropriately as substitutes for paid employees?

4. Has the site previously hired interns when openings are available?

5. Will the site assist the intern in subsequent job hunting endeavors (assuming the student is successful as an intern)?

6. Does the site view the internship as an indentured servitude situation or as a rigorous learning opportunity?

INTERNSHIPS: CONCERNS AND CONTROVERSIES

In an ideal world, the internship experience mutually satisfies the needs of both the student and the host site. However, we do not live in an ideal world and the use of internships in the sport industry has not been without controversy and problems. Four major concerns plague the world of sport management in regard to internships. All four concern the proper use and treatment of the student in the internship or field experience magnified by the student intern's fear of exportation.

Duties and Responsibilities Assigned to Interns

The first of these concerns revolves around the tasks that the would-be intern is expected to perform on a consistent basis. The intern needs to be given meaningful tasks and responsibility for significant and important areas within the organization. While no intern is too good to perform menial chores in a pinch, assigning monotonous and meaningless tasks to the intern on a consistent basis is unacceptable. For example, an intern at a fitness club should not be assigned to work in the site's child care center. Additionally, allowing an intern to do no more than watch and observe is similarly unacceptable.

The tasks and responsibilities assigned to the intern should be commensurate with his or her experience, skills, and motivation. The intern should be given *real jobs* to complete—tasks that cannot be successfully performed by an untrained, uneducated, and inexperienced individual. The ideal internship experience strikes a balance between having the intern *continue to learn* while actually *providing appropriate, significant, and timely contributions* for the host site, its personnel, and customers/constituencies.

The on-site supervisor is responsible for providing a true learning experience for the intern. This meaningful learning experience should take place throughout the total internship experience rather than sporadically. Ideally, the experience should be varied and in-depth. The student, investigating possible internships, is responsible for uncovering the tasks and opportunities he or she might encounter while working with the site before accepting an internship offer. Additionally, the student must stay in contact with the college supervisor or contact person regarding the caliber of the daily tasks assigned to him or her. Finally, the college supervisor is responsible for keeping abreast on a continual basis of the caliber of activities assigned to the student intern.

Increased Competition for Limited Internship Sites

The second area of concern deals with the increased competition for limited opportunities for meaningful internships or field experiences. One of the reasons why sport management professional preparation programs have problems with the culminating internship is because of the great number of both undergraduate and graduate students seeking internships. If one combines the undergraduate and master's sport management programs together, there are 331 such professional preparation programs, most of which are sending out soon-to-graduate students seeking meaningful internships. If each of these 331 programs produces only 30 students in the year 2012, *then some 9,930 students are looking for internships in that year alone.* From 2012 to 2016, a total of 49,650 men and women will seek internships and, ultimately, entry-level, full-time positions following graduation. What are the chances for these students to obtain appropriate internships as well as full-time positions in the profession?

The intense competition for professional and suitable internships is very real indeed. It partially explains the existence of many poorly organized and implemented internship experiences. It also partially explains why there are so few paid internship sites available. Interns must prepare themselves for the tough competition for meaningful internship experiences. This is the responsibility of the college faculty as well as the interns themselves. In light of such intense competition, students must possess an excellent academic record together with a wide variety of meaningful experiences related to the world of sport and/or management, both pre-internship experiences as well as volunteer and/or work experiences.

There is not only intense competition for internships and jobs from other would-be college sport management interns but also from other individuals who are not part of any college professional preparation programs. These are individuals of varying ages, competencies, and experiences who are willing to serve as volunteers in any number of sport organizations and businesses. They have been laid off or are otherwise unemployed/underemployed, and view volunteering as a means of proving themselves in the hope of obtaining an eventual full-time job. The fact that many of these volunteers possess college degrees and years of experience and previous full-time employment, makes the search for such sport management internship or volunteer opportunities, not to mention full-time employment, much more difficult and competitive for all concerned (Bryant, 2010).

Using Interns as Unpaid Substitutes for Paid Employees

The third controversy centers on the possibility that some sites use interns as a ready supply of free labor, thus enabling those organizations to avoid hiring either part-time or full-time paid employees (Cunningham & Sagas, 2004). <u>The question is whether the culminating internship is truly an educational opportunity—a rigorous experimental learning occurrence—or merely an example of indentured servitude, free labor provided by a student who is being taken advantage of by the sport site.</u> Federal law, contrary to popular belief, does not prevent all entities from using unpaid interns as substitutes for paid employees.

The Fair Labor Standards Act (FLSA) was created at the federal level in 1938 to establish a wage floor and deal with abusive labor practices. Although the FLSA affects both public and private employees, the manner in which the law is written enables many companies and organizations to be deemed exempt, including many seasonal and recreational establishments. However, professional sport organizations and franchises, as well as schools, colleges, and universities, and all government agencies, are generally considered to fall under the FLSA (U.S. Department of Labor, n.d.; Gargone, 2008; Unpaid Interns, 1996).

In recent years there have been discussions about the need to update and strengthen federal laws dealing with unfair labor practices and abuses with cheap or unpaid labor vis-à-vis internships and field experiences. However, Joseph E. Aoun, President of Northeastern University, issues a warning against going too far in an attempt to curb perceived abuses, pointing out that "just the threat of increased regulation could have a chilling effect on the willingness of the employers to offer internships—paid or unpaid. With experiential learning on the rise, through co-ops, internships and other approaches, the country cannot afford to create disincentives for employers to play a valuable role in the educational enterprise" (2010, p. 1).

It remains up to the student, the educational institution, and the host site to see that the internship is a worthwhile learning experience and a capstone educational opportunity that will help the student develop greater competencies and marketability and provide meaningful contributions to the internship site.

Actual Possibilities for Meaningful Full-Time Employment in Sport

The fourth area of concern is whether the intern has the opportunity to gain full-time employment at the conclusion of the experience. Is the possibility of a full-time job or employment at the internship site or elsewhere possible, likely, unlikely, or impossible?

A very real concern in some quarters is that some sites and organizations take advantage of young people seeking internships because they have no intention of hiring anyone at the end of the internship. The supply of interns becomes a revolving door where interns come and go but are infrequently—if ever—hired.

Of course, internship sites cannot be assumed to take advantage of student interns as a source of cheap or free labor or as substitutes for hired personnel simply because employment is not subsequently offered. In many instances, sites simply have no vacancies to offer the former interns. Again, potential interns need to be made aware of this possibility and keep their options open. Interns need to do all they can to make themselves marketable to a wide range of potential employers.

The ultimate objective of every sport management student is "securing a meaningful and productive professional position in sport management, in the real world" (Stier, 1997, p. 56). Would-be interns would do well to assess each potential internship site in terms of possible employment at the site itself or the likelihood of employment elsewhere with help and guidance from the internship site's personnel.

CONCLUDING THOUGHTS

The internship is such an important, indispensible part of the total educational experience for sport management students that it behooves both faculty in professional preparation programs as well as those individuals representing businesses and organizations to "insure that meaningful field experiences remain at the forefront of the educational experiences of our future leaders in the sport industry" (Stier, 2006).

In fact, volunteer, practica, co-ops, pre-internship, and mini-internship experiences have also become very important for the sport management student due to the increased competition for capstone internships and for subsequent employment. Such pre-internship and volunteer experiences can go a long way in helping one secure the all-important capstone internship. And it is this culminating internship that paves the way for that all-important entry level position within the world of sport.

Through close cooperation between the college/university faculty and administration and the on-site supervisor(s), potential worrisome, problematic and controversial situations can be avoided or greatly minimized. Advance planning and appropriate supervision, coupled with adequate and timely communication, will go a long way to insure that the intern is not exploited and that the experience can be a positive one for all involved.

REFERENCES

Aoun, J. E. (2010, July 13). Protect unpaid internships. *Inside Higher Ed*. Retrieved August 3, 2011 from http://www.insidehighered.com/views/2010/07/13/aoun.

Bell, J. A., & Countiss, J. R. (1993). Professional service through sport management internships. *Journal of Physical Education, Recreation & Dance, 64*(7), 45–48.

Bryant, E. (2010, November 21). Volunteering could lead to permanent employment. *Democrat and Chronicle*, p. 3E.

Cuneen, J. (2004). Adding rigor to the sport management internship: Introduction. *Journal of Physical Education, Recreation & Dance, 75*(1), 20–27.

Cunningham, G., & Sagas, M. (2004). Work experiences, occupational commitment, and intent to enter the sport management profession. *The Physical Educator, 61*(3), 146–156.

Gargone, D. (2008). Sport management field experiences: The impact of the Federal Labor Standards Act on internships. *Sport Journal, 11*(2). Retrieved August 3, 2011 from http://www.thesportjournal.org/article/sport-management-field-experiences-impact-federal-labor-standards-act-internships.

Kelley, D. R. (2004). Quality control in the administration of sport management internships. (Adding rigor to the sport management internship). *Journal of Physical Education, Recreation & Dance, 75*(1), 28–30.

Moorman, A. M. (2004). Legal issues and the supervised internship relationship: Who is responsible for what? *Journal of Physical Education, Recreation & Dance, 75*(2), 19–34.

NASPE. (1987). *Guidelines for undergraduate and graduate programs in sport management: Membership report*. Reston, VA: National Association for Sport and Physical Education.

Ross, C., & Beggs, B. (2007). Campus recreational sports internships: A comparison of student and employer perspectives. *Recreational Sports Journal, 31*(1), 3–13.

Stratta, T. M. (2004). The needs and concerns of students during the sport management internship experience; analysis of students' experiences in a sport management internship reveals a typology of their concerns. *Journal of Physical Education, Recreation & Dance, 75*(2), 25–34.

Stier, W. F., Jr. (1997). *Sport management: Career planning and professional preparation.* Boston: American Press.

Stier, W. F., Jr. (2001). Sport management internships—A double edged sword. *The Clipboard, 21*(3), 5.

Stier, W. F., Jr. (2002). Sport management internships—From theory to practice. *Strategies, 15*(4), 7–9.

Stier, W. F., Jr. (2006). Sport management field experiences as experimental learning: Ensuring beneficial outcomes and preventing exploitation. *Sport Management and Related Topics Journal, 2*(2), 36–43.

Stier, W. F., Jr. (2008). *Sport management: The business of sport.* Boston: American Press.

Stier, W. F., Jr. (2009, March 19). *The trials, tribulations and future of an emerging profession/ discipline: Sport management.* Paper presented at the Distinguished Speakers Series, University of Florida: Gainesville, Florida.

Tahmincioglu, E. (2010, April 12). Working for free: The boom in adult interns. *Time, 175*(14), 63–64. Retrieved August 3, 2011 from http://www.time.com/time/magazine/article/0,9171, 1977130,00.html.

Unpaid interns: Cheap, effective and often illegal. (1996, August 26). *Dominion Post*, p. 4D.

U.S. Department of Labor. (n.d.). FLSA Overview. Retrieved August 3, 2011 from http://www. dol.gov/whd/flsa/index.htm.

Young, D. S., & Baker, R. E. (2004). Linking classroom theory to professional practice: The internship as a practical learning experience worthy of academic credit. *Journal of Physical Education, Recreation & Dance, 75*(1), 22–25.

Preparing the Next *essay* Generation of Doctoral Students

14

TEN CONSIDERATIONS TO HEIGHTEN EFFECTIVENESS AND IMPACT

We need to do some serious navel gazing in our field of sport management to ensure that we are teaching the right students the right things in the right place and at the right time.

The author introduces the essay

W. James Weese THE UNIVERSITY OF WESTERN ONTARIO

W. James Weese is the Dean of the Faculty of Health Sciences at The University of Western Ontario in London, Canada. He is a graduate of The Ohio State University (Ph.D., 1991) and the Harvard University Best Leadership Practices Program (2010). He is a former President of NASSM, a NASSM Research Fellow, and recipient of the Earle F. Zeigler Lecture Award (2001). He was awarded the Queen's Jubilee Medal by the Government of Canada in 2002.

Introduction

What a pleasure it has been to prepare this essay. Graduate education has been a career passion of mine as a student, graduate advisor, and over the past 13 years, as an administrator. I appreciate the invitation to reflect on my experiences, pore over the literature, and capture some of my personal thoughts on doctoral education in sport management.

I paid close attention to the instructions given me as I prepared this essay. The editors asked me to push the envelope, be provocative, challenge the status quo, question

The author wishes to acknowledge the contributions of Mr. Wesley Moir, who served as a research assistant on this essay.

conventional thinking, and stimulate reflection and debate. I hope my approach does all of the above and more.

As I reflected on how to approach this essay, I quickly concluded that we have some excellent sport management graduate programs, especially at the doctoral level. Our leaders have worked long and hard to position their programs within their university frameworks, secure the resources necessary to launch and deliver their programs, and set the stage for generations of colleagues to follow. We have a solid platform from which we can build. But build we must.

We know that resources are tight, especially following the economic downturn of the late 2000s and early 2010s. Many of us have been asked to do more with less. This seems to be the case with contemporary university life. The fact that we need more doctoral students to meet the demand for faculty positions is not a hotly contested point. Most administrators attempting to secure new faculty would unquestionably agree that the task is an onerous one. The more difficult points that I challenge my colleagues to consider pertain to the design and delivery of our programs. I will ask tough questions about what we are doing in these programs. I hope that readers will conclude that, in many cases, we are not meeting the needs of graduates and/or the ever-changing needs of society. In making this claim I am reminded of the blunt assessment of Mintzberg (2004), who has been on a long-standing campaign to reform graduate education in the management field. He has stated, on many occasions and often at high volume, that MBA programs of the day teach the *wrong stuff* to the *wrong people* in the *wrong place* and at the *wrong time*. Otherwise, I suspect, he feels that the programs are doing just fine!

In the following pages I will outline what I think is wrong with the way we typically prepare doctoral students in sport management (e.g., the far too frequent pattern of one student, one mentor, one project), and offer alternative approaches that, in my opinion, are in closer harmony with the current and future needs of both graduates and society.

While I will be forever grateful for the experiences I have had with my graduate advisors, professors, mentors, colleagues, and graduate students, I believe graduate education should change. Consequently, I offer this essay as "food for thought" for current and future members of the academy with the hope that they too will reflect on their practices and programs, consider some of the suggestions offered, and make the necessary changes to ensure that their programs prepare doctoral graduates to meet the needs of a changing world.

ARE WE PREPARING ENOUGH SPORT MANAGEMENT DOCTORAL STUDENTS?

In short, no.

Countries looking to compete in the knowledge economy know the value of a highly educated citizenry. Not surprisingly, governments in North America have been pressuring our institutions of higher learning to expand graduate programs to fill positions that will require advanced educational credentials (Council of Graduate Schools, 2008; Council of Ontario Universities, 2009). The demographic realities of an aging workforce whose members will soon retire only compound the problematic supply and demand equation. For example, the Association of Universities and Colleges of Canada (2009) called on Canadian universities to significantly increase graduate enrollments to avert the anticipated shortage in the workforce of employees with advanced degrees. A similar situation was reported in the United States (Mangan, 2001) and in Australia (Hugo, 2004).

While fields such as business and nursing are often held up as exhibits A and B in our institutions of higher learning, the situation in sport management is also troubling from a human resource planning perspective. I pointed to the collision course that our field was on in my 2002 Zeigler address. I emphatically stated that doctoral program production had not kept pace with the explosive growth of sport management programs in our institutions of higher learning. I also stated that the supply and demand equation for professors was seriously out of balance and that more and/or expanded doctoral programs were required to meet the current and excepted future demand for graduates. Unfortunately, my predictions proved to be true.

Danylchuk and Boucher (2003) confirmed the explosive growth of the field by noting that the 20 post-secondary programs that existed in the United States in 1980 grew to over 200 by 2003. As I predicted (Weese, 2002), the corresponding low number of doctoral programs (confirmed as 30 around the world by Danylchuk and Boucher in 2003) has led to an acute shortage of sport management professors to meet the demand for teaching positions. Mahony, Mondello, Hums, and Judd (2004) substantiated the situation by noting that there were five sport management professorial positions for every sport management doctoral graduate coming out of a university. The situation becomes more acute when one realizes that not all doctoral-prepared students wish to pursue careers in higher education upon graduation (Nicolas, 2008). Issues such as work–life balance, delayed job security, and comparatively low salary levels add to professorial defection of many (Austin & Barnes, 2005). Nerad (2005), in a study examining doctoral students 10 years after the completion of their degrees, found that job satisfaction was higher for those employed outside of the academy. One wonders if we spend enough time with our graduate students discussing the realities of the career. <u>Are students given the opportunities to develop appropriate coping strategies that will help them stay and be successful in careers in higher education? Do we discuss these possibilities with our graduate students, and are we preparing them effectively for the demands of a contemporary faculty position?</u>

It may be comforting for sport management academicians to know that they are in good company in dealing with these issues. In fact, the issues facing sport management administrators pale in comparison to the challenges faced by administrators of nursing and business programs when they search for doctoral-prepared candidates to assume faculty positions. *The Chronicle of Higher Education* seems to include features on this challenge in every issue. Further evidence of the prevailing concern for the management field was on display at the

2010 Academy of Management conference. Speaker after speaker at this meeting addressed this issue. However, another popular theme emerged. Many of the speakers addressed the question of program preparation and relevancy. Others questioned some of the tried and presumed true practices of the past. Many called for new approaches to structuring and delivering doctoral programs. It made me reflect on our field. All this transpired as I was writing this essay. I confirmed my feeling that we need to do some serious navel gazing in our field of sport management to ensure that we are teaching the *right students* the *right things* in the *right place* and at the *right time*.

TEN CONSIDERATIONS TO HEIGHTEN EFFECTIVENESS AND IMPACT IN SPORT MANAGEMENT DOCTORAL PROGRAMS

Mintzberg (2004) and other leading theoreticians continue to ask some pointed questions of their field that, upon reflection, have significant relevance to the field of sport management. Are we attracting the right students? Do they bring the right backgrounds and levels of preparation to the program? Are we preparing graduates for the current and anticipated demands of the field? Should we consider new perspectives in filling, structuring, and delivering our doctoral programs? I believe that it would be prudent, if not essential, to consider the 10 common problems that I believe often exist in our programs, and consider some of the suggestions outlined in the following pages.

1. Insist Our Students Have Some Work Experience Prior to Admission

Many writers suggest that students with work experience bring maturity, insight, and informed perspectives to the classroom that those without such experience cannot offer. Learning environments are enriched when students have, and are willing to share, relevant experiences and perspectives. Miller, Vick, and Furlong (2010) bluntly assert how critical it is that new candidates have worked full-time prior to enrolling in a doctorate program. Students who are mature, experienced, and can bring case study examples to the discussion make for a better learning environment for all. Mintzberg (2004) believes that all MBA students should be managers before becoming graduate students. He notes that students with relevant experience add a needed dimension and perspective to classroom discussions. By extension, doctoral students in sport management should have some pre-admission experience (e.g., in higher education if pursuing a career in the area, in sport management if pursuing a professional career in the field). Professors can take advantage of this experience by structuring highly participative learning groups and dialogue sessions where students can reflect, test, and validate theoretical concepts based on their past experiences. Think about the students we typically admit to our doctoral programs. Too many of them enter these programs immediately after completing their master's degrees (which they have typically received immediately following their undergraduate degrees). Now consider the enriched learning experiences that professors could structure if all their students brought a wealth of career-related experiences to the classroom. The contrast is stark and significant. We need to add relevant employment experience to the list of prerequisites for doctoral program admission.

2. Consider the Economic Realities and Synergistic Opportunities that Exist for Program Design and Delivery

The saying "necessity is the mother of invention" could have been coined about the higher education environment. This is exactly the situation that many leaders in institutions of higher learning are currently facing. We are in tough financial times, and we need to be creative in structuring and delivering our programs. Considerable good can come from deeper conceptual and greater creative thinking, and I believe we can make our programs more effective and efficient.

It is often human nature to do this type of conceptual housecleaning only in times of crisis. A prominent business leader once told me that crisis can be good because it forces us to tighten our belts, remove extraneous items that creep into operations, and force leaders to carefully scrutinize every expenditure. We don't typically do this to the same degree in times of plenty, but we should. The current economy has forced us to make better use of our existing resource base, necessitating that we tap into courses that exist in other sectors of our campus, and perhaps, more actively share resources with other institutions.

Our course offerings need to be rationalized to ensure the experiences are relevant and necessary. Often courses that align with a professor's academic interest (sometimes called "vanity courses" in the field) work their way into programs as required courses. These courses are offered year after year, without consideration of their true value to the program. In some cases, the course should be offered every year. In other cases, however, the course could and should be rotated, or it may not be necessary at all. Each and every course should be evaluated with a mission-critical lens.

Furthermore, we need to take greater advantage of the existing expertise and resources that exist on our respective campuses. At the same time, we also need to make our own courses available to students from other programs. This cross-pollination of learning is healthy for all parties. As my former colleague at the University of Windsor, Gordon Olafson, used to say, "a community of scholars" exists on our campus and we're foolish not to tap into it. How true! As Bennis (2010) reinforced in his recent memoir, we need to broaden our horizons, not narrow them. Professors and their doctoral students often focus too narrowly and become trapped in disciplinary silos. We need to break the silos down.

Broadening students' skills and expertise beyond their specific discipline has emerged as a desired feature of contemporary graduate programs (Nyquist & Woodford, 2000; Walker, Golde, Jones, et al., 2008). While students are required to become experts in their field, their ability to disseminate findings and apply their expertise across boundaries has become an essential skill, not only for those in going into industry, but also for future academicians.

A notable program that puts interdisciplinary themes into practice is IGERT (Interactive Graduate Education and Research Traineeship). This National

Science Foundation fellowship program promotes collaborative research and multidisciplinary learning in the sciences and engineering. Some of the concepts could be adapted and implemented in the preparation of doctoral students in sport management. The program utilizes the team approach and facilitates inquiry and understanding in several areas surrounding students' research, including ethics, policy, and social and business issues. The ultimate goal is to produce researchers who are experts in a particular field but are also able to communicate their research in a variety of contexts, thereby increasing the application of their work and expertise. We need interdisciplinary orientations in our doctoral sport management programs.

Nicolas (2008) outlined a project undertaken at the Universitè de Sherbrooke involving doctoral students from engineering, science, medicine, and health sciences that promotes interdisciplinary collaboration and skill development in hopes of better preparing students for a variety of careers. The workshops actively involve students in communicating all aspects of their research through several avenues and analyzing its associated ethical issues with others from a variety of fields and perspectives. Students are taught to broaden their viewpoints and deepen their understanding through dialogue and feedback from colleagues in other disciplines. Graduates leave their programs with more diverse research application skills and greater comprehension of how individuals in other fields do their work.

The economic times might force us to do what we should be doing anyway—make better use of the resources in the academy. Technological developments can support alternative and blended delivery models, which can only benefit our students. We can use distance education to greater effect, exposing our students to the top minds in our field. Online discussion groups can facilitate more frequent interaction and heightened understanding and learning. We can engage our alumni more actively as mentors and partners in the educational process (and keep them current and engaged in lifelong learning as well). We should be sharing professors between institutions through the creation of Summer Sport Management Institutes, where all students travel to a campus for a term and world experts are brought in to teach intensive courses. We must also be more creative in the use of Visiting Scholars and Scholars-in-Residence programs that are popular in other fields, but have been less popular, if not virtually absent, in sport management to date. We could be more creative!

3. Encourage and Value Collaboration and a Learning Culture as Much as Independence and a Performance Culture

Many graduate student advisors talk to their students about the need to "pursue an independent line of inquiry" in their research program, despite the fact that they will need to operate as part of a research team if they assume an academic appointment (or work as a team member if they enter the profession). We live in a collaborative world where teamwork is valued and encouraged. We should have a greater team orientation in our doctoral programs, encouraging students to partake in team research projects, group assignments and discussions, even group composite examinations and dissertations. Senior students should be taught to practice effective leadership by serving as mentors for new students, orienting them to graduate education in the same way that they will be asked to mentor new colleagues in employment situations. As noted above, this would all mirror the experiences most, if not all, of our doctoral graduates will have upon graduation.

Critics of doctoral preparation also state that there is too much pressure on doctoral students to perform—to publish and secure grants in order to be competitive for new faculty positions in our institutions of higher learning (see Essays 7 and 8). Some (Mitchell, 2010) feel that this mindset is often counter to the deep learning required in doctoral education. We should be encouraging our doctoral students to read more, immerse themselves in systematic reviews, reflect, synthesize, and seek to understand concepts more fully. Advisors and program leaders should reinforce a learning culture, not performance culture (i.e., measured by grants received and research published). To do so, graduate students need "white space" in their schedules to sufficiently do the reading and reflecting required in a learning culture. Do we emphasize a performance culture over a learning culture? This question certainly warrants some reflection on our part, and perhaps a change in our orientation.

4. Refrain from Preparing Our Doctoral Students in Ways Similar to Our Own Graduate Student Experience

It is a fact of academic life and a natural tendency for professors to prepare students in ways similar to their own experience as graduate students (Kamler & Threadgold, 1996). Do we hold our practices up against the research findings in pedagogy? Do we consider the current needs of the field as we are preparing our course outlines for both content and process? I am not convinced that we do to the levels necessary.

Speakers at the 2000 *Re-envisioning the PhD* conference addressed the usefulness of the widely practiced apprenticeship model, arguing that it is outdated and irrelevant (Magner, 2000). Kehm (2009) discovered higher drop-out rates and longer time-to-completion periods in programs employing the traditional apprenticeship model. The relative lack of structure and the preeminent focus on research projects may not provide doctoral students with an end-point and facilitate timely completion of their degrees. Kendall (2002) suggests that the apprenticeship model does not sufficiently assist doctoral students who intend to enter industry rather than take an academic appointment. Nyquist and Woodford (2000) note that many students believe that the current mentoring practices they experience are inadequate and believe that having multiple mentors would provide a better experience. Walker et al. (2008) called for greater collaboration between faculty and students as opposed to apprenticeship-type relationships. Such issues, however, touch upon program structures of the doctorate degree, including the overarching model employed and the rules and requirements that follow. Program advisors and leaders will need to break away from traditional thinking, and it will require a seismic shift.

I suggest that we think hard about the experience we need our doctoral students to have and the learning process required to deliver this experience. We also need to consider some alternative forms of preparation and consider models of blended learning, such as webinars, distance learning, scholar-in-residence programs, intensives, summer institutes, etc.

New formats for doctoral education could broaden the marketplace and increase interest in the degree. They may also appeal to the experienced students we seek to attract to our programs. Professional doctorate programs and executive education programs are popular and should also be considered for our field. Officials in Australia witnessed the number of professional doctoral programs increase from one in 1990 to 131 in 2001 (McWilliam, Taylor, Thomson, et al., 2002). The key factor in advancing change is getting stakeholders to break away from the status quo (Kotter, 1996). Shulman (2010) underscored this point for doctoral educators, suggesting that they break with tradition, try new and innovative teaching and learning strategies, and most of all, avoid the ever-present tendency to replicate their own graduate experience with their students. The landscape is changing for our graduates. We need to embrace it. We were taught to be curious, and we need to apply this mindset to the way we educate our graduate students.

5. Better Prepare Graduates for Teaching and Service Roles in Higher Education

Some of our graduates in sport management will seek or find positions in Tier 1 research institutions. Even if they do, however, they will still be expected to teach (usually 40% of their appointment). Others of our doctoral-prepared graduates will gravitate to positions in institutions that place a high premium on undergraduate teaching. Given this reality, we must ask if we are preparing graduates for the type of appointment they will likely hold upon graduation. Many would suggest that we are not (Mitchell, 2007; Utecht & Tullous, 2009). An honest assessment of our graduate programs would undoubtedly reveal that we are focused on developing research competence in our graduates. Preparation and development in the area of teaching is given minimal attention, if any at all. Thus, students are being prepared for positions in which they have received little formal preparation to perform. Can you imagine graduating as a doctor, dentist, or nurse with little or no training in at least 40 percent of your job?

Not surprisingly, many administrators feel new hires are unprepared for the challenges they face as incoming professors (Murray, 2000). This criticism is also shared by the doctoral students themselves who report that they lack the requisite teaching skills to be an effective faculty member (Magner, 2000). Golde (2007) notes that while the doctoral degree is first and foremost a research degree, an important component lies in one's ability to communicate one's findings effectively, not simply through publications and small lectures. The neglect in instruction for this facet of doctoral education is a significant concern as it impacts negatively on graduates' ability to meet the demands of the marketplace.

Mitchell (2010) convincingly addressed this point in his Lifetime Achievement Award speech at the 2010 Academy of Management conference. He provocatively stated that doctoral students are often inadequately prepared for careers in higher education. He called for greater attention to preparing graduates for their teaching roles. While research competence is always important and needs to be cultivated, he suggested that graduates also be provided with education and experiences to develop both teaching effectiveness and service. He insists that his first-year doctoral students take a class on teaching as part of their program.

Some universities have begun offering a variety of pedagogical training in their graduate programs (Gale & Golde, 2004). Utecht and Tullous (2009) explored one such program in the form of a summer seminar for doctoral students in business at the University of Texas at San Antonio. The Doctoral Teaching Seminar focused on active learning techniques to improve students' teaching skills and ability to engage their audiences. Additionally, a significant amount of reading was assigned to encourage students to understand their personal philosophies on teaching and learning. This seminar emphasized five critical driving forces for creating an effective teaching and learning environment in classrooms: (1) connection, (2) concern, (3) competence, (4) clarity of impact, and (5) conducting class fairly. A major component of the course required students to present their course syllabus and conduct a scheduled lesson from the syllabus at random, as selected by the instructor. Feedback from former students indicated that this was the most beneficial element of the course in preparing them for their first teaching experience in the fall term. I believe that this would be a valuable experience for sport management students.

Gale and Golde (2004) also support the need for graduate programs to engage their students in departmental concerns aimed at improving various educational outputs. This involvement would allow students to gain practical experience in addressing common faculty issues. Students should also be given greater guidance in both understanding and adapting to academe values, which would assist them in discovering their compatibility with an academic profession (Nyquist, Manning, Wulff, et al., 1999). While our students generally have a disposition to get involved, they should be continually encouraged and recognized for assuming service roles. As professors, they will most likely be asked to carry a minimum of a 20 percent service role. They will be asked to serve on committees and councils and lead initiatives that advance their school, department, and/or faculty. They must know the importance of serving their university, their profession, and their community. We should strive to produce graduates who see service as admission to an amazing profession. Why not guide our doctoral students in this area during their programs of study and teach them about the types, amounts, and levels of engagement that will serve them and their units well once they enter the academic career? The graduate student experience must adapt to the rapidly changing landscape of doctoral education in order to better prepare future faculty members (Austin & Wulff, 2002). We tend to focus on one component exclusively (research), and at the expense of the other two areas of a professorial role (teaching and service). This marginalizes these roles and does not prepare our graduates for the true demands of the profession.

6. Respond to the Need for Greater Interdisciplinary Teaching and Learning

Our increasingly interdisciplinary and collaborative world has also brought forward new perspectives on the doctoral program curriculum, which has traditionally been narrow and disciplinary in scope. As stated previously, students are often instructed to pursue an independent line in a research field. As a result, they run the risk of becoming too specialized, lacking the breadth of understanding needed to address problems in more interdisciplinary ways. Re-envisioning the Ph.D., a large-scale research project composed of various industry experts and researchers and funded by the Pew Charitable Trusts, served to address the pressing need for doctoral education to adapt to current realities of the new century. Among these issues was a shared consensus that interdisciplinary training and study be incorporated into graduate curricula. The justification behind this was threefold: (1) industries require graduates of doctoral programs to collaborate with others in various contexts, (2) teaching institutions require faculty trained in a variety of disciples in order to teach in broader contexts to wider audiences, and (3) research-intensive institutions require both faculty and students to use several modes of thought and ideologies to approach research questions (Nyquist & Woodford, 2000). The ever-changing landscape of collaboration in higher education has produced a number of partnerships to bring together individuals from diverse backgrounds, integrate their ideas, and participate in new developments in both theory and practice. Implementing interdisciplinary approaches in doctoral education would enable students to apply their expertise in a number of areas and develop team-oriented learning abilities, skills that industries desire in graduates of doctoral programs (Greene, Hardy, & Smith, 1995).

Based on their findings from a national survey examining over 4,000 doctoral students in numerous disciplines, Golde and Dore (2001) note that many students are keen to partake in such practices, yet are given limited opportunities to do so under their current program structures. They contend that, "Coursework outside of the department can give students additional breadth, which is helpful both for advancing their disciplinary research and scholarship, and for providing them with skills to expand their careers in diverse directions. Doctoral students want to reach beyond the confines of their disciplines and understand, at least in hindsight, the value of curricular breadth" (p. 13).

Thus, students recognize the importance of engaging in experiences beyond their specialization, in addition to enhancing their research and analytical skills through alternative ventures and challenges. As Walker et al. (2008) note, "much of the most important, path-breaking intellectual work going on today occurs in the borderlands between fields, blurring boundaries and challenging traditional disciplinary definitions" (p. 2).

I believe that this is a shortcoming of most doctoral programs in sport management. We have our students take our sport management courses. We likely sprinkle in one research course or more, and perhaps a couple of cognate courses. It begs the question: Are we giving our students a broad enough, interdisciplinary-based education to help prepare them for a complex, interrelated world? We need to cross-pollinate our students with those from other disciplines. We need to attract students from other fields of study into our courses more frequently. We need to arrange seminars filled with students and professors from other disciplines to ensure that issues and research questions are viewed through an interdisciplinary lens. In short, we need to broaden our students' horizons and get them in the habit of considering interdisciplinary approaches to preparing themselves, addressing their research questions, and influencing their students upon graduation.

7. Provide More International Study Experiences

The importance of graduate programs' ability to prepare students for research and practice in a global world has become more pressing than ever (see also Essay 12). Nerad (2005) argues that the effects of globalization have created a need for doctoral programs to educate students beyond traditional means, not simply to prepare them for a variety of careers on the global stage, but also to instill the morals and ethics such work will require. One method of influencing a greater understanding and appreciation for global issues is through the creation of international study experiences for students. Sport is played on an international stage; sport management doctoral programs must have a similar orientation. Redd (2007) highlights the recent proliferation of collaborative partnerships that exist between institutions to facilitate international student and faculty exchange programs, research exchanges, and greater institutional reach and branding in new countries. The benefits of a robust international program are significant. Students recognize the benefits and enrichments of adding an international experience to their preparation. It may be a tipping point when the best prospective students seek such a program to complete their doctoral studies. Sport management programs and their institutions can also benefit from the reputational gain of partnering with respected international institutions.

European education leaders recognize the benefits as do policy makers, as evidenced in the Bologna process (European University Association, 2004) that trumpets international initiatives for their role in improving student experiences and preparation (Tauch & Rauhvargers, 2002). The same can be stated for the United States, where the results of a Council of Graduate Schools survey reveal that roughly 24 percent of graduate schools planned to implement international collaborative degree networks with non-U.S. institutions (Redd, 2007). A follow-up survey indicates significant increases in available dual/double degree programs with international components in both small and large enrollment schools throughout the country (Redd, 2008). With the improvement of web-based tools and communications technology, Redd (2007) notes that faculty members now have several options in facilitating program delivery beyond the physical classroom, thus increasing their programs' outreach.

Sport management doctoral programs could benefit from robust student exchange and dual degree programs. Technological advancements and student/professor mobility make these attractive options for our field of study. In addition to exposing our students to international enrichment experiences and new professors with different expertise and perspectives, this approach can be a cost-effective measure (e.g., universities pool and share teaching resources/expertise using lecture simulcasts). It makes both programmatic and fiscal sense. We need to act on these options more aggressively.

8. Provide More Support for Our Students

Governments in many countries, including Canada and the United States, continue to encourage universities to broaden post-secondary access as they transition to a knowledge-based economy. Government leaders believe that citizens with advanced degrees are integral to driving innovation and increasing global competitiveness. However, higher education comes at a cost, and governments must provide greater financial support for students, even in difficult economic times. Katz (2001) illustrates that graduate departments face several challenges due to cutbacks in student funding, because lack of funding ultimately affects students' abilities to immerse themselves in all elements of their programs, including attending conferences and finding time to publish their work. An example of this situation is provided by the Province of Ontario. Since 1990–1991, the Ontario universities' inflation-adjusted tuition has risen 28 percent in comparison to 7 percent in other Canadian Provinces (Ontario Confederation of University Faculty Associations, 2009). As a result, we had the highest average graduate tuition in the country for the 2009–2010 academic year, approximately $2,700 greater than the national average (Statistics Canada, 2009). It is crucial that institutions do all they can to increase support for society's future researchers in order to reduce debt loads and enhance their graduate student experience.

We need to find donors in sport management so we can provide higher levels of support for our doctoral students. We also need to make scholarships and grants high priority items in our annual fund-raising campaigns. We need to make our programs affordable so qualified students are not turned away on the basis of financial means. We also need to find funds to support assistantship programs that provide students with career-related work experience (e.g., 10 hours per week) and financial support at the same time. As in other fields, our professors need to secure research grants that support doctoral students and get them to the conferences and workshops necessary to refine their skill sets and expand their networks. Most of all, we need to ensure that our doctoral students have the financial support to invest their time and energies into the learning experience I advocated for earlier in this essay. They cannot maximize their learning if they are working part-time as well as studying.

9. Rationalize the Required Courses, Rules, and Routes

Programs must clearly rationalize the required courses and overarching rules and ensure that each course and rule in the program is truly required. In other words, a program must find the "essence" of its program delivery and ensure this carries forward in practice in order to streamline its focus and reduce rising time-to-degree rates (Nyquist & Woodford, 2000). Golde and Dore (2001) suggest that this should include publishing clear and understandable program requirements, establishing time-to-completion policies, and publicizing financial support policies. Such initiatives would clarify the essential aspects of a student's degree program and help guide him or her through what is largely an autonomous undertaking. Di Pierro (2007) argues that greater tracking of student progress is needed to lower time-to-degree periods.

Doctorate education can also benefit from incorporating themes normally associated with professional degree programs into different aspects of program delivery (Shulman, 2010; Pearson, 1999; Smart & Hagedorn, 1994). Shulman (2010), while speaking as the president of the Carnegie Foundation for the Advancement of Teaching, argued that doctoral curriculums in the humanities and sciences should be shortened in order to reduce burgeoning time-to-completion rates. Shulman (2010) states that the open-ended nature of doctoral education is one of its deepest flaws. He suggested, metaphorically, that students often wander aimlessly for interminable periods once their course work ends, which is normally only two or three years into their program of study. He calls for more structure in the early years of the program and advocates for a more systematic design of the curriculum of practice, with a willingness to build on some of academy's best ideas (e.g., rotations and rounds in hospitals; the case-method approach in business schools, the use of role-playing in clinical and legal education) to better prepare students for the practices of research, teaching, and service. Shulman also says that such practices would enable community-based learning—especially in the latter half of one's program—and allow students to collaborate with others and participate in team-based approaches to projects.

Sport management is an applied field. We need to be sure that our programs are conceptually tight. Advisors and program leaders should be able to articulate the goal of the program and then explain how each course and experience contributes toward meeting that goal. I believe that too many sport management doctoral programs suffer from a conceptual malaise. Students are instructed to take certain courses because they exist, not because they are needed or contribute to the preparation needs of the student. We could benefit from an on-going conceptual belt-tightening.

10. Prepare Graduates for Alternative Careers

Graduate program officials and student advisors must realize professorships are not the only road graduates of doctoral programs can take, and support and guidance must be in place to accommodate alternate directions (Miller Vick & Furlong, 2010). We understand that this only aggravates the faculty shortage, but we have an obligation to educate our students in ways that allow them to make an impact on the field. Demers & Desai (2002) note that faculty members must continually assess their programs' career preparation and actively disseminate changes.

Members of the Committee on Science, Engineering, and Public Policy (COSEPUP) argued in 1995 that curricula must be reformed at the department level to better serve doctoral students who aspire to careers in industry, and that department faculty have an obligation to enhance the educational experience by providing accurate career guidance and curricular options. This sentiment was expressed by doctoral students in a recent *University Affairs* article on this issue, who note that non-academic career direction and learning opportunities are often reduced to basic seminars that occur infrequently, indicating a need for a cultural shift among graduate programs (Tamburri, 2010). I believe the same scenario is being played out in many of our doctoral sport management programs. One suggestion to combat this practice is to increase participation of alumni who followed non-academic career paths (Greene, Hardy, & Smith, 1995; Miller Vick & Furlong, 2010). This could take the form of career discussions, or better yet, alumni–student mentorships that provide guidance in how students can prepare and market themselves for careers in industry, and how to benefit from networking opportunities (Miller Vick & Furlong, 2010). The more frequent use of consulting projects outside of academia, employing career mentors, and utilizing sport management practitioners in the classroom as guest speakers may all be helpful suggestions that would better prepare graduates pursuing professional careers in sport management after graduation.

In a world characterized by rapid change, industries continue to alter their research and business strategies in light of current market developments and needs, thus increasing the need for graduates who can quickly adapt to these changes (COSEPUP, 1995). This is also true for the field of sport management. The Canadian Association for Graduate Studies (2008) argues that professional development should be implemented as complementary to knowledge learned in the classroom and lists four broad skill areas they feel encompass the most critical aspects of students' development for the workforce. These include communication skills, management skills, teaching and knowledge transfer skills, and ethics. It would be hard to argue that these areas are not important in any graduate sport management program, regardless of a student's career ambition.

CONCLUDING THOUGHTS

Sport management is an exciting and vibrant field of study that has come a long way, especially in the area of doctoral student preparation. Excellent doctoral programs house committed and highly skilled professors and bright and eager students. That said, we need more doctoral programs in our field to meet the current and anticipated demand for professors and professionals holding advanced degrees.

In addition, we need to reflect on the types of programs we offer. We need to be open to content and process questions to ensure that our graduates have the type of preparation they need to excel in their chosen field following graduation. We need to ensure that they are exposed to collaborative and cross/interdisciplinary teaching, learning, and service experiences that model what they will experience in the field upon graduation. We need to ensure that they have access to the campus-wide learning opportunities that exist at our respective institutions. We also need to prepare students for alternative careers and the full spectrum of duties they will assume if they enter the professoriate. Finally, we live in a global society, so our graduates must gain an international perspective and approach through their preparation.

Economic factors and technological advancements may assist us in delivering our programs in ways that meet some of the ends listed above. We need to make the most of the technological developments and synergies afforded to us through the distance and alternative delivery paradigms (i.e., summer institutes, intensives, distance learning, study abroad programs, visiting scholar and scholar-in-residence programs). I personally feel that we can do better in these areas. Let us take a close and honest look at our students, their course experiences, our rules, and enrichment opportunities. We should also look at the career experience of our graduates. We must capitalize on the resources that exist on our campus and around the world to give our students an exceptional level of preparation, so they can make greater contributions in their profession, and do the same for their students should they enter the academy following graduation.

Generations of professors in sport management have given us a wonderful platform on which to build our future doctoral programs. We owe it to them and our current and future graduate students to consider the 10 factors presented in this essay, so we can more effectively prepare the next generations of doctoral students to tackle the current and existing areas and challenges in our field of study.

REFERENCES

Association of Universities and Colleges of Canada. (2009). Building a competitive advantage for Canada. A brief submitted to the House of Commons Standing Committee on Finance. Ottawa: Publications and Communications Division. Retrieved from http://www/aucc.ca/.pdf/english/reports/2009/prebudget_11_18_e.pdf.

Austin, A. E., & Barnes, B. J. (2005). Preparing doctoral students for faculty careers that contribute to the public good. In T. Chambers, A. Kezar, and J. C. Burkhardt (Eds.), *Higher education for the public good: Emerging voices from a national movement* (pp. 272–292). San Francisco: Jossey-Bass.

Austin, A. E., & Wulff, D. H. (2002). The challenge to prepare the next generation of faculty. *Journal of Higher Education, 73*(1), 94–122.

Bennis, W. (2010). *Still surprised: A memoir of a life in leadership.* San Francisco: Jossey-Bass.

Canadian Association for Graduate Studies. (2008). Professional skills development for graduate students. Report of the *Canadian Association for Graduate Studies.*

COSEPUP (Committee on Science, Engineering, and Public Policy). (1995). *Reshaping the graduate education of scientists and engineers: Executive summary.* Washington, DC: National Academy Press.

Council of Graduate Schools. (2008). Ph.D. completion and attrition: Analysis of baseline program data from the Ph.D. completion project. Washington, DC.

Council of Ontario Universities. (2009). Competitive boost from the expansion of graduate studies. Report of the Council of Ontario Universities, Toronto.

Danylchuk, K., & Boucher, R. L. (2003). The future of sport management as an academic discipline. *International Journal of Sport Management, 4*(4), 281–300.

Demers, P., & Desai, R. (2002). Brave new worlds. Graduate education for the 21st century. Report of the Canadian Association for Graduate Studies. Ottawa, Ontario.

Di Pierro, M. (2007). Excellence in doctoral education: Defining best practices. *College Student Journal, 2*, 368–375.

European University Association. (2004). Developing joint masters programmes for Europe: Results of the EUA Joint Masters Project. Brussels, Belgium. Retrieved August 3, 2011 from http://www.eua.be/eua/jsp/en/upload/Joint_Masters_report.1087219975578.pdf.

Gale, R., & Golde, C. M. (2004). Doctoral education and the scholarship of teaching and learning. *Peer Review, 6*(3), 8–12.

Golde, C. M. (2007). Preparing stewards of the discipline. In C. M. Golde & G. E. Walker (Eds.), *Envisioning the future of doctoral education: Preparing stewards of the discipline* (pp. 3–22). San Francisco: Jossey-Bass.

Golde, C. M., & Dore, T. M. (2001). At cross purposes: What the experiences of doctoral students reveal about doctoral education. A Report for The Pew Charitable Trusts. Philadelphia, PA. Retrieved August 3, 2011 from www.phd-survey.org.

Greene, R. G., Hardy, B. J., & Smith, S. J. (1995). Graduate education: Adapting to current realities. *Issues in Science and Technology, 12*, 59–66.

Hugo, G. (2004). The demography of Australia's academic workforce: Patterns, problems and policy implications. Paper presented at the Monash Seminars on Higher Education. Retrieved August 26, 2011 from http:www.gisca.adelaide.edu.au/gisca/flash.html.

Kamler, B., & Threadgold, T. (1996, November). *PhD examiner reports: Discrepant readings, conflicting discourses.* Paper presented at the meeting of the Australian Association for Research in Education Conference, Singapore.

Katz, P. M. (2001). CGE's e-mail survey focuses on challenges in graduate training. *Perspectives, 39*(4), 11–15.

Kehm, B. M. (2009). New forms of doctoral education and training in the European higher education area. In B. M. Kehm, J. Huisman, & B. Stensaker (Eds.), *The European higher education area: Perspectives on a moving target* (pp. 223–244). Rotterdam, NL: Sense.

Kendall, G. (2002). The crisis in doctoral education: A sociological diagnosis. Higher education research and development. *Journal of the Higher Education Research and Development Society of Australia, 21*(2), 131–141.

Kotter, J. P. (1996). *Leading change.* Boston: Harvard Business School Press.

Magner, D. K. (2000, April 28). Critics urge overhaul of Ph.D. training, but disagree sharply on how to do so. *The Chronicle of Higher Education, 46*(34), A19. Retrieved January 19, 2001, from http://chronicle.com/weekly/v46/i34/34a01901.htm.

Mangan, K. S. (2001, May 4). A shortage of business professors leads to 6-figure salaries for new PhD's. *Chronicle of Higher Education.* Retrieved August 3, 2011 from http://chronicle.com/weekly/v47/i34/34a01201.htm.

Mahony, D. F., Mondello, M., Hums, M. A., & Judd, M. R. (2004). Are sport management doctoral programs meeting the needs of the faculty job market? Observations for today and tomorrow. *Journal of Sport Management, 18*(2), 91–110.

McWilliam, E., Taylor, P., Thomson, P., Green, B., Maxwell, T., & Wildy, H. (2002). *Research training in doctoral programs: What can be learned from professional doctorates?* Report of the Department of Education, Science and Training, Evaluation and Investigations Program. Canberra, Australia.

Miller Vick, J., & Furlong, J. S. (2010). Following the nonacademic track. *Chronicle of Higher Education.* Retrieved August 3, 2011 from http://chronicle.com/article/Following-the-Nonacademic/64864/.ehler.

Mintzberg, H. (2004). Managers not MBAs: A hard look at the soft practice of managing and management development. San Francisco: Berrett-Koehler Publishers.

Mitchell, T. R. (2007). The academic life: Realistic changes needed for business school students and faculty. *Academy of Management Learning & Education, 6*, 236–251.

Mitchell, T. R. (2010, August 10). *The academic life: A personal and professional journey.* Paper presented at the 70th Annual Conference of the Academy of Management. Montreal, Quebec, Canada.

Murray, B. (2000). The growth of the new PhD. *Monitor on Psychology, 31*(10), 24–27.

Nerad, M. (2005, February 16). *From doctoral student to world citizen: The chance for innovative doctoral education.* Miegunyah Lecture given at the University of Melbourne, Australia.

Nicolas, J. (2008, January 7). Researchers for tomorrow. *University Affairs.* Retrieved August 3, 2011 from http://www.universityaffairs.ca/researchers-for-tomorrow.aspx.

Nyquist, J., & Woodford, B. (2000). *Re-envisioning the Ph.D.: What concerns do we have?* Report of the Center for Instructional Development and Research. University of Washington. Seattle, Washington. Retrieved from http://depts.washington.edu/envision/resources/Concerns Brief.pdf.

Nyquist, J. D., Manning, L., Wulff, D. H., Austin, A. E., Sprague, J., Fraser, P., Calcagno, C., & Woodford, B. (1999). On the road to becoming a professor: The graduate student experience. *Change, 31*(3), 18–27.

Ontario Confederation of University Faculty Associations. (2009). Comparative student tuition and fee revenue. *Trends in Higher Education.* Retrieved August 3, 2011 from http://notes. ocufa.on.ca/HETrends.nsf/trends_v1n1.pdf?OpenFileResource.

Pearson, M. (1999). The changing environment for doctoral education in Australia: Implications for quality management, improvement and innovation. *Higher Education Research & Development, 18*(3), 269–286.

Redd, K. (2007). Data sources: International dual, joint and other collaborative programs. *Council of Graduate Schools.* Retrieved August 3, 2011 from http://www.cgsnet.org/portals/0/pdf/ DataSources_2007_10.pdf.

Redd, K. (2008). Data sources: International graduate programs—2007 & 2008. *Council of Graduate Schools.* Retrieved August 3, 2011 from http://www.cgsnet.org/portals/0/pdf/Data-Sources_2008_10.pdf.

Shulman, L. (2010). Doctoral education shouldn't be a marathon. *Chronicle Review.* Retrieved August 3, 2011 from http://chronicle.com/article/Doctoral-Education-Isnt-a/64883/.

Smart, J. C., & Hagedorn, L. S. (1994). Enhancing professional competencies in graduate education. *Review of Higher Education, 17,* 241–257.

Statistics Canada. (2009). Average graduate tuition fees for Canadian full-time students, by province. Statistics Canada. Retrieved August 3, 2011 from http://www.statcan.gc.ca/daily-quotidien/091020/t091020b2-eng.htm.

Tamburri, R. (2010). Give us the dirt on jobs: Why universities need to prepare doctoral students for careers outside academe. *University Affairs.* Retrieved August 3, 2011 from http://www. universityaffairs.ca/give-us-the-dirt-on-jobs.aspx.

Tauch, C., & Rauhvargers, A. (2002). Survey on master's degrees and joint degrees in Europe. European Commission Directorate-General for Education and Culture, Brussels. Retrieved September 8, 2011 from http://www.eua.be/eua/jsp/en/upload/Survey_Master_Joint_degrees_ en.1068806054837.pdf.

Utecht, R. L., & Tullous, R. (2009). Are we preparing doctoral students in the art of teaching? *Research in Higher Education Journal, 4.* Retrieved August 3, 2011 from http://www.aabri. com/rhej.html.

Walker, G., Golde, C., Jones, L., Bueschel, A. C., & Hutchings, P. (2008). *The formation of scholars: Rethinking doctoral education for the 21st century.* San Francisco: Jossey Bass.

Weese, W. J. (2002). Opportunities and headaches: Dichotomous perspectives on the current and future hiring realities in the sport management academy. *Journal of Sport Management, 16*(1), 1–17.

Welcome the Millennial Faculty

essay

15

PREPARING FOR NEW PROGRAMMATIC CUSTOMS

The new generation of faculty entering our twenty-first century classrooms will likely be less accepting and more transforming to academe, inducing a state of affairs that will impact themselves as well as faculty already firmly entrenched.

The authors introduce the essay

Jacquelyn Cuneen BOWLING GREEN STATE UNIVERSITY

Jacquelyn Cuneen, Ed.D., is a Professor of Sport Management at Bowling Green State University, where she teaches sport and event promotion and supervises sport management field experience students. Her research foci are sport-related advertising and professional preparation of sport managers. She has authored or co-authored over 50 scholarly and professional articles for numerous journals. She has served in various elected and appointed offices for NASSM, the Sport Marketing Association, and the Ohio Association for HPERD. Prior to her academic career, she was Account Executive, Director of Women's Programming, and Educational Correspondent for two New York State–based ABC radio affiliates.

Heather Lawrence OHIO UNIVERSITY

Heather Lawrence is an Associate Professor of Sports Administration and Director of the Professional Master's in Sports Administration program at Ohio University. She earned her Ph.D. in Higher Education Administration from the University of Florida. She has published a textbook and 18 peer-reviewed articles and has presented both nationally and internationally.

Lawrence's research interests include event and facility management, luxury suite sales in professional sport, intercollegiate athletics, and sport management pedagogy.

Introduction

They are the largest and perhaps most discussed generational cohort since their grandparents, the baby boomers. They are certainly the most analyzed student group in modern time, and all this scrutiny has led to one conclusion: The millennial generation is thoroughly unique. As they enter the workplace, our campuses and environments will change; tradition and customs will evolve to reflect their more individualistic thinking. Is this a breath of fresh air or the loss of convention? Energizing or counterproductive? Good or bad? All new generations leave their own stamp on the campus and the marketplace and often clash with the establishment in the process. The subsequent compromises may result in a stronger work unit or induce temporary dysfunction. This essay addresses critical issues associated with the pending influx of millennial faculty to sport management preparation programs. In order to prepare fully for the introduction of millennials into the university faculty setting, administrators and current faculty must recognize the differences between millennials and past cohorts of faculty and be aware of how certain aspects of the job should be modified to get the most out of the new cohort. As millennials replace the retiring baby boomers, we might be wise to recall the words of 1960s boomer icon Bob Dylan, *The Times They Are A-Changin'*.

The baby boomers themselves shocked their "greatest generation" parents, also known as the silent generation, by transforming their campuses from idyllic havens into hotbeds of protest. Similarly, when the millennials become faculty, they are apt to change everything about a campus, including the office suites, classrooms, and the time-honored delivery of higher education itself. Kelly (2007) believes that we should start planning early for the millennials' arrival, since it generally takes three to five years to transform campus culture. Their arrival will impact recruitment, retention, professional development, decision-making, and particularly technology. This impact will be felt over the long term for every institution from community colleges to four-year universities.

ACADEME AS WE KNOW IT

Brubacher and Rudy (1976) stressed that even as the American college morphed into the modern university, with enrollments increasing from hundreds to thousands and budgets escalating from thousands to millions, the organizational groundwork dating from colonial times existed well into the twentieth century. It was not until the transformational 1960s that pressure groups prompted large fundamental changes in campus governance and power. Anne Matthews' (1998) exploration of the symbolic college environment portrayed a typical campus that appeared to be serene to the outside world, yet was full of conflict to campus insiders.

While institutions typically reflect the culture that surrounds and sustains them, the reputation of our institutions is established by the reputations of our programs and our scholars (Brubacher & Rudy, 1976). Faculty and program reputations have customarily been built through teaching, research, and service. Faculty have habitually spent long hours originating or preparing courses; designing, implementing, and publishing scholarly inquiries; and making numerous contributions to their programs and profession. These functions have often been fulfilled outside of school hours and may even have been chiefly self-funded. Although many other academic practices have changed over time, generations of professors have acquiesced to the custom of devoting personal time to their professional responsibilities, albeit with frequent discontent. Faculty have flourished together by embracing the routines associated with college and university teaching. However, the new generation of faculty entering our twenty-first century classrooms will likely be less submissive and accepting and more transforming to academe, inducing a state of affairs that will impact themselves as well as faculty already firmly entrenched in their office suites.

DIVERSE GENERATIONS IN ACADEME

Never before has there been such potential for generational diversity among cohorts at work. Scholarly and popular culture literature suggests that four generations have started to intermingle in the marketplace. While various authors (Bennis & Thomas, 2002; Lancaster & Stillman, 2002; Pew Research Center, 2010; Zemke, Raines, & Filipczak, 1999) have affixed different descriptive labels to the generations, they are in agreement that these cohorts are challenged to understand, communicate, and collaborate with each other under established customary ground rules. Each generation (i.e., the silent generation, born from the 1920s to the mid-1940s; the baby boomers, born in the mid-1940s to the mid-1960s; generation X, born in the mid-1960s to 1980; and the millennials, born after 1980) believes itself to be smarter than any previous or subsequent cohort, and each also views itself as unique when compared to the others (Pew Research Center, 2010). For instance, those of the silent generation believe themselves to be honest and to possess high moral values and a strong work ethic. They feel defined by their proximity to World War II and/or the Great Depression. Baby boomers believe themselves to be respectful. Like their parents in the silent generation, they believe they possess high moral values and a strong work ethic, and they define themselves as part of the baby boomer generation. Generation X believes itself to be respectful and possessing of a strong work ethic. They define themselves as conservative, traditional, and technologically sophisticated. Millennials also believe their proficiency with technology makes them unique, yet they also feel liberal, tolerant, and define themselves through their music, pop culture, and clothing styles (Pew Research Center, 2010).

No matter what we call them, even a fleeting acquaintance with each group reveals the differences in era-related values, outlooks, cultural norms, and worldviews. The differences can test our tolerance of each other when engaged in work-related endeavors as well as in social circumstances. Fortunately, college faculty have an advantage in that they are already accustomed to a diverse workplace; campuses have always been a hotbed for a generational mix of students, faculty, and administrators. However, in the approaching years the four generations of college professors teaching in sport management classrooms and working side-by-side in faculty offices may experience frustrations and complications in their interactions with each other. Thus, it is time to focus on the influx of the millennial generation as they replace the existing mix of the silent generation and the boomer faculty about to retire and the gen X'ers who are fast becoming the campus establishment.

WHAT WE KNOW ABOUT MILLENNIALS IN OUR CLASSROOMS

Millennials have been defined in various ways. Many describe them as sheltered, overprotected, entitled, empowered, self-absorbed, and autonomous (Cuneen, Gray, Verner, et al., 2008; Cuneen, Verner, Gray, et al., 2006; Lowery, 2004). They have received awards and recognition for participating in events for which their performance did not warrant a prize. They have lived their entire lives according to a pre-planned schedule of activities arranged for them (Howe & Strauss, 2000, 2007; Pew Research Center, 2010; Walker, 2009). They have been highly praised, expect to be granted do-overs on their work, and are unaccustomed to stark criticism. However, they are used to the company of adults and accustomed to taking advice from them, particularly from their parents. They are team-oriented, confident, self-expressive, collaborative, techno-savvy, open to change, and they embrace diversity (Kelly, 2007). Millennials, more than any previous generation, come from diverse families that often include nontraditional family structures and multiple ethnicities; thus their global view of the world and understanding of the inter-connectivity of the world marketplace differ from those of past generations (Alch, 2000). When they enter academe as our colleagues rather than as our students, millennial faculty will bring new attitudes, behaviors, and expectations to our sport management office suites just as they brought unique nuances to our classrooms (Kelly, 2007).

WHAT WE NEED TO KNOW ABOUT MILLENNIALS AS OUR COLLEAGUES

Cultural differences in the office suite, work style and methodological differences in the classroom, and technological differences on and off campus are areas in which millennials will affect academe with their nontraditional expectations and novel approaches to their sport management academic careers. To what extent should these differences be accommodated? Many of these cultural, pedagogical, and technological shifts will seem exotic to established faculty, yet they will be entirely routine to the millennial faculty and, incidentally, to future incoming students.

Office culture will be as important to millennial faculty as their professional accomplishments (Erwin, 2009; Lawrence et al., 2010). Millennial faculty will seek a fun, comfortable, employee-centered workplace. They will bring informality to the sport management office hallway not only in their appearance, but also in their approach to the work environment. Expect casualness to rule the day. Sport management academe has been traditionally conservative; yet expect new faculty dress codes to be relaxed, their language to be informal, and their office décor to reflect individuality. The highly family-oriented millennials may even have their family members come to school with them. Children, spouses, and even pets may be hallway fixtures. New assistant professors may have visible body art as well as piercings, and they might express their uniqueness through inventive hairstyles.

Millennial faculty may not want to be readily available for informal or even formally scheduled meetings. Instead, they will prefer digital meetings on their own schedule, giving them free time to pursue their own goals in or out of the office. Because millennials' technological communication skills will be sophisticated, their one-on-one and in-person styles may be weak (Walker, 2009), particularly as compared to their silent generation and baby boomer colleagues. They may prefer to communicate through online chat, texting, email, or even by phone (Lawrence et al., 2010), with less face-to-face contact than older colleagues prefer. In other words, many of the existing unofficial rules, traditional role expectations, and the established bureaucracy associated with current office culture will be questioned and perhaps eventually discarded.

The silent generation, baby boomers, and some generation X'ers will note a marked difference in millennials' work styles. Previous generations, especially the boomers, tend to come in early, stay late, and make themselves available on weekends if needed (Klein, 2007). Millennials will expect to have their specific roles and work parameters clearly defined (Kelly, 2007), assume their administrators and colleagues recognize their need for a personal life (Erwin, 2009; Walker, 2009), and want enough latitude to complete their work in a way that makes sense to them even though it may not make sense at all to other faculty and administrators. Still, millennials are highly goal-oriented and want to move quickly up the career and pay ladders (Walker, 2009). They are used to multitasking, and want the flexibility to keep more than one project going at a time (Erwin, 2009). Consequently, they will need encouragement for their risk taking and creativity in teaching, research, and service. This millennial cohort values group work and will look for collaboration in their teaching, perhaps even requesting teaching circles comprised of as many as six to ten faculty members (Kelly, 2007). Furthermore, they may want to do all this work and collaboration from home with technology provided by the sport management department.

Regarding technology, millennials' facility with sophisticated programs and portals will undoubtedly transform campus operations and revolutionize the delivery of sport management's teaching services. They bring with them the potential to improve performances and assist other generations of faculty to better adapt their own pedagogies for contemporary students' styles of learning. Millennials are the first generation to have had computers consistently present in their lives and educational settings (Nikirk, 2009), and they have an overall comfort level with a variety of electronics. Silent generation, boomer, and gen X faculty who may be reticent to embrace the new technologies in and out of their classrooms will find that millennials who are more comfortable with interactive applications (Diaz, Garrett, Kinley, et al., 2009) may have a paperless approach to teaching. For instance, they may have future sport management students submit projects and portfolios online exclusively. Entrenched faculty who are slow to adapt to new forms of teaching and advising will have to keep pace or they are likely to be alienated from their students.

Because they have used technology in their own learning, millennial sport management faculty will expect to have diverse technologies available to them, including discipline-specific tools (Diaz et al., 2009; Walker, 2009). They will be uber-comfortable using them both in the traditional face-to-face classroom setting as well as for virtual teaching on demand around the clock, perhaps with a focus on individualized instruction (Klein, 2007) in their web-based or web-centric courses. Millennials who think in terms of visuals and sound bites will implement assorted technologies in their classes (Diaz et al., 2009). Expect them to use Skype, Elluminate, or similar vehicles for sport management field experience supervision, thus eliminating some or all of the communication and travel expenses for practicum, internship, and other field teaching. They will also likely find numerous imaginative ways to use nonstandard technology from various open-source communities in their pedagogy (Lawrence et al., 2010).

Millennials will no doubt incorporate social media in their pedagogical delivery. They spend at least 16 hours per week on the Internet (not including email). Additionally, 40 percent of millennials create blogs and 80 percent read blogs regularly (Tresser, 2007). They will use Facebook or the next social networking tool, texting, and tweeting to replace or at least augment face-to-face student advising. Additionally, this generation is fixated on mobile devices and technology such as iPads, console games, and instant messaging (Nikirk, 2009). Over 50 percent of millennials rate instant messaging as their preferred method of communication (McCasland, 2005).

By contrast, other generations—the silent generation and boomers in particular—tend to be more attuned to the traditional forms of interaction and pedagogy, and their lack of technological sophistication will tend to make their millennial colleagues impatient (Taylor, 2005). Sport management students used to social media will gravitate toward the newer, more progressive faculty. If the entrenched faculty are not using the same electronic vehicles, they will not be part of the exchange of ideas. Furthermore, if entrenched sport management faculty fail to comprehend or embrace the unique characteristics of their future millennial colleagues, they will have difficulty understanding how to attract the best millennial faculty to their existing programs.

RECRUITING THE MILLENNIAL FACULTY MEMBER

Given the steady proliferation of sport management major programs and the paucity of doctoral programs to supply future faculty to teach in them (Weese, 2002; see also Essay 14), knowing how to attract the best candidates to our institutions and to subsequently help them succeed as academicians is vitally important. Diaz et al. (2009) suggests that institutions and programs would be wise to survey millennial faculty requests rather than assume their specific needs. Millennial faculty candidates will want to know about realistic timelines and goals, and they will want a specific road map to success (Walker, 2009). Therefore, position announcements and particularly information disseminated during campus visits need to focus on a candidate's needs as much or more than the institution's needs and requirements.

For instance, the traditional content of a position announcement usually contains an inventory of the job description, job specifications, required content expertise or possible course assignments, and salary range among other details. In order to attract top-tier twenty-first-century candidates, the inventory might also emphasize such existing campus or program features as sport-management or related learning communities, team teaching opportunities with established faculty, and service learning prospects involving local or regional sport enterprises.

When a millennial-era candidate is invited for an interview, the itinerary may need to be amended from the typical routine of meeting the faculty, students, deans, directors, coordinators, and various campus officials. Considering Kelly's (2007) observation that millennials are team-oriented, techno-savvy, and embrace diversity, a candidate's campus visit should be designed to highlight collaboration and an office environment that encourages brainstorming and idea sharing (Lawrence et al., 2010). Because they are accustomed to seeking and accepting advice, visiting candidates should be assigned an "interview mentor" or actually meet the probable mentor who will assist them as they transition into their new university environment. Knowing the experienced sport management faculty member who will offer guidance and answer their questions will let the candidate know in advance that they will be in a supportive, collaborative setting as they navigate through the orientation and eventually the tenure process.

Showing candidates their potential support network during the visit will prove reassuring, because it will demonstrate how they may achieve a balance between their professional, social, and personal lives. It will also give them an idea of how they will fit within the sport management department and program. While teaching load and research expectations will always be essential elements in academic job planning, job fit will be an important objective for millennials not only because it will expedite their own success, but also because a good fit will sustain them in providing for their colleagues and students (Lawrence et al., 2010).

The monetary aspects of a college professorship have been important in the past, and they are likely to escalate to a whole new level in the future. However, in addition to salary and benefits, millennials will consider other types of resources (e.g., pedagogical supplies, office gear) and funding (e.g., research supplies, data collection devices) to be essential elements in their final decision. Thus, supplemental resources should be highlighted during the visit, due to the fact that salaries and benefits are likely to be unimpressive at the majority of sport management departments. It will be equally important for the prospective mentor to explain the advantages of any available non-monetary compensation (e.g., assigned time for scholarship, campus fitness center memberships, parking privileges, beneficial associations with local sport teams). Such amenities can compensate for an underwhelming salary scale when provided continuously or on a rotating complimentary basis.

Of course, the fundamental attraction that will draw the best of the millennial sport management faculty to our programs, and one of the most important facets to highlight during an interview, is the technology available to them. Their foremost resource requests will likely be for sophisticated, state-of-the-art technologies— hardware and software—with high speed and large storage capacity (Lawrence et al., 2010) to be used in teaching, research, and service. This demand may be the most problematic to meet in that higher education can be infamously outmoded in regard to the latest technology. New technologies as well as course management platforms and portals seem to emerge monthly and the infrastructure of the university is often slow to respond. Millennials do not like delay; they are used to immediacy and quick responses regarding such issues.

Changes in the position announcements, communications, interviews, and follow-up contacts are vital to attract the best candidates to sport management programs. Once they arrive on campus, retention will be paramount because millennial sport management faculty will have many chances to make lateral or upward moves to other programs or to other occupations that offer more appealing conditions.

RETAINING THE MILLENNIAL FACULTY MEMBER

As much as office culture, work conditions, and technology will be principal factors in millennials' decisions to accept a sport management position, an environment where they can thrive will make or break their job performance and career longevity. Because their work is consequential to the current and future success of the entire organization (i.e., institution, department, program), established faculty must understand the millennial mindset as they initiate them into academe and monitor their progress. Recommendations and caveats will change from year to year, but generally, remember that millennials need to know they are an essential part of the professional and social order of the sport management program.

Because millennials seek fulfillment in their jobs, congenial mentoring will be a critical piece of the puzzle in keeping them satisfied in their sport management work environment (Meister & Willyerd, 2010). The idea of mentoring in higher education is nothing new, but traditional mentoring will need some tweaking as millennials enter the sport management faculty ranks. A strategic approach to mentoring can prove beneficial for new sport management professors and more established faculty alike. Both group mentoring and reverse mentoring can be viable alternatives to traditional one-to-one mentoring.

Group mentoring, in which one mentor works with several protégés at once (Scheef & Thielfoldt, 2004), is especially attractive to millennials. Considering their need for interactive relationships (Scheef & Thielfoldt), millennials will enjoy working with others and sharing their growing pains as they adjust to academe. Consider that new professors might be struggling with how to navigate the publishing world; instead of posing their question to just one mentor, group mentoring will permit them access to insights from a variety of colleagues. In addition, group mentoring requires fewer mentors than a one-to-one structure. The concept of group mentoring is explained by Meister & Willyerd (2010), who suggest that group mentoring can even take place online so that one mentor can interact with multiple protégés simultaneously, even if they are dispersed in various locations. As online teaching and learning become more prevalent, group mentoring will be a useful tool for sport management programs where faculty are not place-bound. Whether in person or online, group mentoring can provide the service and support millennials expect without draining human resources.

As an alternative to the group format, reverse mentoring can provide a win–win experience for both the protégé and mentor. In the corporate environment, reverse mentoring occurs when a younger employee teams up with a senior executive in the hopes of fast tracking his or her career. In return, the younger employee educates the established executive about cutting-edge tools that are commonplace for the younger set, such as social networking (Meister & Willyerd, 2010). Academe is a natural fit for reverse mentoring. In a sport management program context, the millennial faculty member teaches the more experienced professor such skills as the use of social networking in teaching, creative use of technology, and other concepts needed to reach the contemporary college student. A by-product of this reverse mentoring relationship is that more experienced professors will undoubtedly find themselves providing guidance on more traditional academic matters related to research, service, and tenure. In fact, millennials may not even realize that they are also being mentored.

As stated previously, millennials are accustomed to special consideration, praise, and "do-overs," and they do not respond well to stark criticism (Howe & Strauss, 2007), even from a respected mentor. Therefore, feedback, especially corrective suggestions, should be interspersed with positive reinforcement as millennials traverse the tenure and promotion process. Meticulous mentoring and time/resource investment in faculty development programs may replace rigid rules, yet millennials, as part of the gaming generation, appreciate crystal clear directions. Standards, especially those related to tenure, promotion, research, and dissemination will need to be well defined.

This is the generation that has embraced collaboration since childhood. Tenured faculty working in partnership with new faculty colleagues from the day they commit to the sport management program should demonstrate awareness and empathy to their new colleagues' aspirations. Taking an interest in their off-campus lives might be the best way for tenured faculty to join the collaborative environment in which their millennial colleagues operate.

Millennials may wish to collaborate with established faculty as well as with faculty from other programs by working with whomever, whenever, and wherever they wish. They will expect the appropriate platforms to be in place to support these collaborations. Established faculty should be empathetic and flexible enough to help them accomplish their goals. The presence of millennial faculty who bring more collaborative approaches to their work may reveal a new order to entrenched sport management faculty and convince them to follow in seeking a balance between their boundaries and freedoms.

Incoming faculty are often the architects of change in academe; they push organizations to adopt new technologies and ways of operating. They bring strengths in social media, networking, and e-literacy, and they find amazing ways to use these technologies beyond their original intents. For instance, a millennial might request to use electronic portfolios and secure portals to file their annual review materials and later to submit their credentials for tenure and promotion reviews in the same manner. Thus, costs for document duplication will be eliminated, the process will be more environmentally friendly, and the materials will be accessible to reviewers around the clock.

Still, many of the venerated rules of academe need to be preserved, and millennials accustomed to autonomy may experience culture shock when navigating the confines of academic bureaucracy. Accordingly, the established faculty will need to show them the ropes in several areas that both generations might find inane. Some examples follow.

Predictions indicate that millennials will spend a great deal of time in pursuit of a personal life, so of the idea of traditional office hours will be met with resistance. No matter how easy technology makes communication between students and colleagues, administrators consider office hours to be sacrosanct and there are times when face-to-face meetings are compulsory.

Millennials will likely be product- not process-oriented. For instance, they may be perfectly comfortable in contacting central-level administrators without considering lines of authority, or they may not quietly follow the required steps in annual or merit reviews. Established faculty may need to enlighten millennials on campus operations and academic protocol and guide them toward the conventional means of completing tasks.

The academy is one of the most politically treacherous environments in the entire workforce. Former U.S. Speaker of the House Tip O'Neill offered the famous credo that all politics is local (Hymel, 1995; O'Neill, 1987). For all new and often for some established faculty, local means the hallway. Faculty of any rank cannot avoid politics; they can only deal with them.

The most zealous battles in the sport management hallway are likely relate to power: Who is in charge of what? Who makes decisions about what? Who is apt to bully others? Who will champion a cause or defend a colleague? Faculty of all ranks deal each day with a myriad of complexities arising from human interactions. Power, as related to new faculty in particular, may stem from knowing the campus governance documents, yet quoting them sparingly so as not to appear to be contrary. The power of newer faculty members is definitely related to their competencies in teaching, research, and service and emanates somewhat from their ability to establish themselves as key players by fitting in quickly and shaking things up later.

Finally, the silent generation, the boomers, the gen X'ers, and millennials each need to be aware of existing as well as emerging program values and they need to embrace them. If new faculty members find that transpiring ideals conflict with their own core values, they are in the wrong place.

CONCLUDING THOUGHTS:
HIGHER EDUCATION IS STILL IN TRANSITION

long time ago the privileged sons of the colonial elite made room for their brothers from the bourgeois class on the nation's fledgling college campuses. Then the middle-class brotherhood made way for their sisters. The sisters paved the way for diversity. Diversity brought globalization in cohorts and curricula. Campuses became extraordinary learning centers offering major programs of study, such as sport management, that most institutional founders could not have imagined. Campuses thrive because academe always demonstrates an inclination to adjust to the prevailing social milieu (Matthews, 1998), operating in what Brubacher and Rudy (1976) call a state of dynamic evolution. Welcome to the contemporary milieu and get ready to go forward at light speed. However, as office culture, work styles, technology, and faculty expectations transform, one overriding interest should remain constant in sport management education no matter what generation is keeping the flame: We may do things differently, but we all need to arrive at the same place. Faculty come and go, generational cohorts emerge, and cultures shift—but the program stays. Take care of the program!

REFERENCES

Alch, M. L. (2000). Get ready for a new type of worker in the workplace: The net generation. *Supervision, 61*(4), 3–7.

Bennis, W. G., & Thomas, R. J. (2002). *Geeks and geezers: How era, values, and defining moments shape leaders.* Boston: Harvard Business School Press.

Brubacher, J. S., & Rudy, W. (1976). *Higher education in transition* (3rd ed.). New York: Harper & Row.

Cuneen, J., Gray, D., Verner, M. E., Baker, R. E., Hoeber, O., & Young, D. Y. (2008, June). *Teaching the millennial student redux: A discussion on connecting with generation me.* Paper presented at the meeting of the North American Society for Sport Management, Toronto, Ontario.

Cuneen, J., Verner, M. E., Gray, D. P., Baker, R., McDonald, M. A., Bell, J., Gillentine, A., Kreutzer, A., & Young, D. (2006, June). *A discussion on "millennials": Teaching the post-modern sport management student.* Paper presented at the annual meeting of the North American Society for Sport Management, Kansas City, Missouri.

Diaz, V., Garrett, P. B., Kinley, E. R., Moore, J. F., Schwartz, C. M., & Kohrman, P. (2009). Faculty development for the 21st century. *EDUCASE Review, 44*(3), 46–55.

Erwin, A. (2009, May). Millennials at work: How to implement the millennial work style. *Campus Activities Programming,* 10–13.

Howe, N., & Strauss, W. (2000). *Millennials rising: The next great generation.* New York: Random House.

Howe, N., & Strauss, W. (2007). *Millennials go to college* (2nd ed.). Great Falls, VA: LifeCourse Associates.

Hymel, G. (1995). *All politics is local: And other rules of the game.* Avon, MA: Adams Media Corporation.

Kelly, R. (2007, February). Now is the time to prepare for millennial faculty. *Academic Leader, 23*(2), 1, 6.

Klein, K. E. (2007). Managing across the generation gap. *Business Week Online*. Retrieved August 3, 2011, from http://www.businessweek.com/smallbiz/content/feb2007/sb20070212_399060.htm.

Lancaster, L. C., & Stillman, D. (2002). *When generations collide*. New York: Harper Business.

Lawrence, H. J., Cuneen, J., Baker, R., Gillentine, A., Gray, D. P., & Simmons, J. (2010, June). *Millennial faculty: Space invaders "invade" higher education*. Paper presented at the annual meeting of the North American Society for Sport Management, Tampa, Florida.

Lowrey, J. W. (2004). Student affairs for a new generation. *New Direction for Student Services, 106*, 87–99.

Matthews, A. (1998). *Bright college years*. Chicago: University of Chicago Press.

McCasland, M. (2005). Mobile marketing to millennials. *Young Consumers, 2*, 8–15.

Meister, J. C., & Willyerd, K. (2010). Mentoring millennials. *Harvard Business Review*, Retrieved August 3, 2011, from http://hbr.org/2010/05/mentoring-millennials/ar/1.

Nikirk, M. (2009, May 1). Today's millennial generation: A look ahead to the future they create. *Techniques, 84*(5), 20–23.

O'Neill, T. P. (1987). *Man of the house: The life and political memoirs of Speaker Tip O'Neill with William Novak*. New York: Random House.

Pew Research Center. (2010). *Millennials: Confident. Connected. Open to change*. Washington, DC: Pew Research Center.

Scheef, D., & Thielfoldt, D. (2004, September). What you need to know about mentoring the new generations. *Learning Café*. Retrieved August 3, 2011, from http://www.thelearningcafe.net/downloads/Articles-Generations0904.pdf.

Taylor, M. (2005). Generation NeXt: Today's postmodern student: Meeting, teaching, and servicing. *Becoming a Learning Focused Organization*. Retrieved October 25, 2009, from http://www.taylorprograms.com/images/Gen_NeXt_article_HLC_05.pdf.

Tresser, T. (2007, August 2). What the world might look like when the millennials run it. *AlterNet*. Retrieved August 3, 2011, from http://www.alternet.org/story/55508.

Walker, K. L. (2009, March). Excavating the millennial teacher mine. *NASSP Bulletin, 93*(1), 73–77.

Weese, W. J. (2002). Opportunities and headaches: Dichotomous perspectives on the current and future hiring realities in the sport management academy. *Journal of Sport Management, 16*(1), 1–17.

Zemke, R., Raines, C., & Filipczak, B. (1999). *Generations at work: Managing the clash of veterans, boomers, Xers, and Nexters in your workplace*. New York: American Management Association.

index

CPSIA information can be obtained at www.ICGtesting.com
Printed in the USA
LVOW131228281111

256628LV00003B/2/P

9 781934 432266